Writing for the Business World

Writing for the Business World

Robert E. Cason, Ph.D., J.D.

Department of English
University of Texas–El Paso

Prentice Hall, Upper Saddle River, New Jersey 07458

Acquisitions Editor: Donald J. Hull
Assistant Editor: John Larkin
Editorial Assistant: Jim Campbell
Editor-in-Chief: James Boyd
Director of Development: Steve Deitmer
Marketing Manager: John Chillingworth
Production Editor: Aileen Mason
Production Coordinator: Renee Pelletier
Managing Editor: Valerie Q. Lentz
Manufacturing Buyer: Kenneth J. Clinton
Manufacturing Supervisor: Arnold Vila
Manufacturing Manager: Vincent Scelta
Senior Designer: Ann France
Design Director: Patricia Wosczyk
Cover Design: Wendy Alling Judy
Composition: University Graphics, Inc.
Cover Photo: FPG International

Copyright (c) 1997 by Prentice-Hall, Inc.
A Simon & Schuster Company
Upper Saddle River, New Jersey 07458

Library of Congress Cataloging-in-Publication Data
Cason, Robert E. (Robert Ernst)
    Writing for the business world / by Robert E. Cason.
      p.   cm.
    Includes bibliographical references and index.
    ISBN 0-13-440264-2
    1. Business writing.   I. Title.
HF5718.3.C37 1997
808'.06665—DC20   96-35424
                                   CIP

Prentice-Hall International (UK) Limited, London
Prentice-Hall of Australia Pty. Limited, Sydney
Prentice-Hall Canada, Inc., Toronto
Prentice-Hall Hispanoamericana, S.A., Mexico
Prentice-Hall of India Private Limited, New Delhi
Prentice-Hall of Japan, Inc., Tokyo
Simon & Schuster Asia Pte. Ltd., Singapore
Editora Prentice-Hall do Brasil, Ltda., Rio de Janeiro

Printed in the United States of America
10 9 8 7 6 5 4 3 2

For my parents, Ann and Bob,
and my wife, Tilly

Brief Contents

Contents

PART III: RESEARCHING AND REPORTING   71

Preface

With the publication of this book, readers may well ask whether there is any need for yet another business writing text. My answer to such a question is straightforward: this is not yet another business writing text; at least not in the sense that it is meant to compete with those already on the market. After all, many authors have produced outstanding texts that are used in colleges and universities nationwide. Many of these texts are comprehensive reference works that cover the full spectrum of business writing; my text, on the other hand, limits itself to the more common forms of business writing.

What I have produced is a "how-to" text. This is a practical guide to business writing in the sense that it provides a step-by-step approach to organizing and composing common kinds of business documents. This approach mandated selectivity; otherwise a much lengthier text would have been produced. Thus, what has been lost is the range found in many texts, but what has been gained is an in-depth and practical guide to the process of business writing.

Throughout this text I have emphasized the need for a logical structure in any kind of writing. I have provided readers with formats and guidelines, but readers should be aware that businesses often adapt formats to their own specifications, and, of course, some businesses provide formats of their own design. This book provides methods of approaching a writing task, effectively communicating ideas and formats useful in the creation of effective communication.

Formats, therefore, are not enough. In this text, readers are shown the logical ways to structure a business document from its inception, target a particular audience and purpose, and write it part by part. After reading this book the student will see how following these steps will produce a business document that is easily understood and completely fulfills the intended readers' expectations. In sum, the distinguishing feature of this text, as opposed to those already on the market, lies in its emphasis on the specific "how-to" methodology and kind of thinking that must be used in any business writing situation.

I would like to thank John Chillingworth of Prentice Hall who first suggested the idea that I write a business text. His support has been invaluable in the completion of this project. I would also like to thank my editor at Prentice Hall, Don Hull, who allowed me the freedom to explore the possibilities inherent in writing this practical guide, and who offered several suggestions rather than commands with respect to this text's contents. Of course, I cannot fail to thank the many business writing professionals whose work has so profoundly shaped my own thinking regarding the business world. Finally, but not least, I would like to thank my wife, Til. Without her support and encouragement throughout the process of preparing this text, the task would have been much, much more difficult.

Robert E. Cason
El Paso, Texas

CHAPTER 1

Communicating in the Business World

This is a how-to book. It is written so that you can write business documents using the most effective language, organization, and format. Unlike most business writing texts, this book does not dwell on theory; instead, it focuses on methods. In sum, this text provides a how-to approach: a step-by-step approach that ensures that you will do the appropriate and effective tasks required of any business writer.

Written communication is probably the most overlooked aspect of the business world—at least from the perspective of those just entering the job market or from the perspective of those with scant knowledge of the business environment. In the typical business writing class, students are often under the false impression that writing is less important than, say, accounting. They believe that someone else—a secretary or technical writer, perhaps—will do the writing for them (Locker 4). The fact is that while your accounting skills, for example, may lead to a job, your writing and speaking skills are the keys to keeping it and advancing in your career (Locker 4, 6).

Almost all businesses require their accountants, salespeople, and managers to write their own documents (Locker 5). In fact, "[t]he higher you go in management, the more time you will spend reading reports—and writing them" (Bruce, Hirst, and Keene 1). But don't think that you won't have to worry about writing because you will not be starting out as upper management. Louis Boone and David Kurtz point out that "when the National Association of Manufacturers surveyed 4,000 companies, it found that 1 out of 3 regularly turn away job candidates because of poor writing and reading skills" (27).

Some facts may help to illustrate the amount of writing going on in the business world. The average company puts out 18,000 pages of paper for each white-collar employee, and 4,000 pages are added each year (Bovee and Thill 23). Even a nonbusiness entity such as the air force generates 500 million pages annually (Locker 6). This means that each year about 30 billion documents are produced in the United States (Bovee and Thill 23). Photocopying alone costs U.S. businesses $2.6 billion a year (Bovee and Thill 23).

With so much written communication occurring, it is no wonder that corporations focus heavily on maintaining personnel with strong communication skills. Human resources personnel certainly realize that communication in the business world is a problem: "In a recent survey, 65 percent of human resources executives said that employee writing skills need improvement, 62 percent cited difficulties in interpersonal communication skills, and 59 percent cited poor customer-service skills" (Boone and Kurtz 27).

Today, corporations spend about $43 billion annually to educate their workforces, and a large percentage of these billions goes to improving their workforces' communication skills (Boone and Kurtz 27). In a recent survey of 12,000 businesses, "81 percent provide communication training" (Boone and Kurtz 27).

Communication is important to businesses because it is directly tied to success. Take, for example, Disney corporation. Why is it so successful? The answer is simple: "According to insiders, the magic ingredient is communication: communication from management to employees, from employees to management, and from the company to the public" (Bovee and Thill 2).

In the business world, communication "increases productivity, both yours and your organization's" (Bovee and Thill 4). And fundamental to any written communication is the principle of fulfilling reader expectations. Fulfilling reader expectations includes a host of principles that this book endeavors to explain and exemplify. For now, fulfilling reader expectations means giving your audience what it needs. These needs are complex and diverse, but if you concentrate on fulfilling your audience's needs, you will save time and money, and you will create goodwill (Locker 11). In so concentrating, you will also enhance your own productivity, and you will find that dealing with people inside and outside your organization will become more effective (Bovee and Thill 4).

To fulfill reader expectations you must take into account such items as how the document looks, how the document is arranged from word to paragraph, what format is effective, what vocabulary is appropriate, whether visuals should be used—in fact, the audience's needs depend upon the audience, and thus no list can be complete. Nonetheless, every audience has expectations concerning how things should look, how they should be organized, and how they should be read. Your task is to discover those needs and fulfill them. Ultimately, that is the purpose in writing this book: to detail those needs and to suggest ways you can fulfill them.

CHAPTER 2 Analyzing the Audience

Audience analysis is one of the most important aspects of business writing. Before you even begin contemplating the writing of your business document, do a thorough audience analysis. You must know your audience if you are to fulfill its needs. In targeting your audience, you must also be ethical, and, if you are dealing with a different culture, you must communicate with that culture in terms that it will understand. Let us look at audience analysis first.

Audience Analysis

Whom you are writing to will determine how you write. Therefore, it is imperative that you have some understanding of your audience. You should avoid writing in a vacuum; that is, do not write as though your letter will fit and fulfill the needs of any audience. Without an understanding of your audience, your writing will be impersonal, and it is therefore doubtful whether you can possibly anticipate and fulfill the needs of the person or persons to whom you are writing.

Although audience analysis can be lengthy and complex, do not go overboard and write a dissertation on your audience. Instead ask yourself five fundamental questions before approaching your data and organizing it:

1. Whom are you writing to?
2. What are you writing?
3. When will you write?
4. Why are you writing?
5. How will you write?

If you can answer these five questions, you will possess a good idea of your audience. And more importantly, as you will see, knowing your audience will determine the written form your data will take.

3

WHOM ARE YOU WRITING TO?

In general terms your potential audience can be divided into two groups: an external audience (i.e., the audience outside your company) and an internal audience (i.e., the audience inside your company). An external audience includes the public, clients, customers, and other companies; an internal audience consists of the people in your own company (Boone and Kurtz 6–10).

Both internal and external communication are important to the smooth operation (i.e., moneymaking operation) of the company: Effective internal communication promotes efficiency in saving time and fulfilling goals and orders in operations; effective external communication leads to keeping customers happy by creating and maintaining goodwill, promoting a good public image, maintaining good relations with suppliers, and ensuring government noninterference (Boone and Kurtz 6–10).

The importance of effective communication can be seen in the amount of time and money that many companies spend on developing internal communication. Many companies like General Electric and Hyatt Hotels realize that effective communication leads to efficiency and profits (Boone and Kurtz 6). It is when communication breaks down that companies face losses and dissolution (Boone and Kurtz 7).

The moral here is that you must know your audience if effective communication is to occur. In particular, when dealing with your own company or with other companies, you must have an understanding of the corporate culture in which you are writing. Corporate culture can be defined as "the patterns, traditions, and values that make one organization distinctly different from another" (Boone and Kurtz 18–19). In their book *Contemporary Business Communication*, Boone and Kurtz divide corporate culture into five elements:

1. Business Environment
2. Values
3. Heroes
4. Rites and Rituals
5. Cultural Network. (19)

Boone and Kurtz define each of these elements quite succinctly. First, "[t]he *business environment* refers to the marketplace in which a company sells its good or services" (19). Second, "[v]alues define both the company's philosophy for achieving success and the framework within which all employees conduct their day-to-day activities" (19). Third, heroes "represent tangible role models of the corporate culture" (20). Fourth, rites and rituals denominate "the communication styles" in the company (20). Fifth, "[t]he cultural network is the informal communication channel that transmits the messages of corporate culture" (20).

With knowledge of each of these elements, you can gain a better understanding of your audience. For example, would it help to know, hypothetically speaking, that the company to whom you will write possesses

1. a business environment of computer sales,
2. an emphasis on service and customer satisfaction,
3. a role model in Bill Gates,

4. a communication style emphasizing memos, and

5. an informal communication network that relies on e-mail?

Of course it would. With this information you know that perhaps the most effective method of communication with this company is through e-mail because it relies on computers. Computers, computer people as role models for business, the computer environment, and short messages all tell you that the most effective means of communication with this company is through the use of a computer, computer jargon and vocabulary, and logical but short messages. With this information, you can tailor your message to the form that the audience will expect. If you do so, you will find that your message will be more effective because it fulfills the needs and expectations of the messages routinely sent in the company.

Not only will the idea of corporate culture help you to understand your own company or one with whom you are dealing, but the very same ideas can and must be extended to communication with the public, clients, and other individuals. Just as you must know the five elements that make up the corporate culture when you are dealing with a company, you must also know the elements that compose the clients' or individuals' culture. To determine their culture, ask at least the following six questions:

1. What business are they in, if any?

2. What values would they most likely prize?

3. What authority figure are they likely to honor?

4. How old are they?

5. How well educated are they?

6. What is their cultural heritage?

Of course this list could be greatly expanded, and you should take into account all you know concerning the audience. Just remember that the more you know about an audience, the easier and more effectively you will be able to communicate with them. Thus, speaking hypothetically, would it be helpful to know that you are writing to a Hispanic female of twenty-six who recently graduated with an MBA from Stanford? Of course it would. When communicating with her, you would want to avoid any appearance of sexism, and, if possible, to mention qualities such as tradition, honesty, and responsibility, key ingredients in Hispanic culture. At the same time, she has an MBA, so you must communicate with her on that level; otherwise, it may appear that you are talking down to her. You must know your audience if you want to communicate effectively, and nothing does this better than demonstrating an appreciation of the person's individuality and cultural heritage.

Thus, you could say that whether you are writing to a company, to individuals in your own company, or to individuals outside of your company, you must know the culture with which you are dealing. Understanding both corporate and client culture allows you to tailor your communication to that audience. You can tailor your communication by using the appropriate formats, appeals, examples, and terminology: appropriate in the sense that they will be understood by your audience and appreciated as staunch means of communication.

WHAT ARE YOU WRITING?

Having analyzed who composes your audience, the next consideration is what to tell them. By analyzing who the audience is, you will know something about their level of education and sophistication. The more educated or business-wise your audience is, the more you can use business terminology and jargon. (See "How Will You Write?" for further discussion of this issue.)

For now, what you need to determine is how much information the audience needs. Never burden the audience with information that is tangential or unnecessary to the audience. Give the audience just what it needs to know, no more and no less. To determine what information is necessary, ask yourself a question that will come up again in a subsequent heading: Why am I writing? Give just enough information so that the purpose of the message is achieved.

WHEN WILL YOU WRITE?

In business the axiom "time is money" is an undeniable truth. You will often find that you are being rushed; therefore, you must prioritize your projects. Do the shortest ones first, and having done them, you can devote more time to the lengthier ones.

WHY ARE YOU WRITING?

To analyze your purpose in business writing, ask yourself two questions. First, are you trying to inform, persuade, analyze, or give bad news? Your answer will determine the length of your document and its format. Second, for whom are you writing this message? Are you writing it on your own behalf or for someone else? The answer to this question will affect the level of importance that you attach to the writing. Obviously, if the CEO has asked you to write a report, you will devote considerable time and energy to it.

HOW WILL YOU WRITE?

Once you have determined who, what, when, and why, consider how to write the message so that it effectively communicates with your audience. To this end, do the following:

1. Provide an appropriate level of sophistication.
2. Maintain goodwill.
3. Adopt the appropriate format.
4. Employ an effective ending.

Levels of Sophistication

Your audience's level of education or business acumen determines how sophisticated a terminology you can use. In *Technical Writing*, John Lannon points out that you can write on three levels. First, you can write on the highly technical level. This is the level for an audience that understands your jargon and terminology without the need of explanation (20–21). Second, you can write on the semitechnical level. Here, readers have some understanding of the terminology and jargon, but they require help in the form of explanation or example (21–22). Third, you can write on the nontechnical level. On this level readers require that you avoid jargon and terminology, replacing it instead with terms, concepts, and explanations that they can readily grasp (22–23).

You can adapt these levels of technical writing to the business world as well. After all, every specialized field possesses and employs its own vocabulary and jargon. Business writing is no different. If you know your audience, as you should, then you can determine what level of technicality would be the most comprehensible to it. Below are three sentences. All three are identical in meaning, but each has its own vocabulary and jargon:

1. *Highly technical:* **The judge awarded the plaintiff a summary judgment.**
2. *Semitechnical:* **Because there was no material issue concerning the facts, the judge awarded the plaintiff a summary judgment.**
3. *Nontechnical:* **Because the defendant did not dispute the accuracy of the facts, the judge awarded the plaintiff a summary judgment.**

Note that the technical message requires no explanation of terms and jargon, the semitechnical requires some explanation, and the nontechnical requires quite a bit. The level you use is determined by your audience.

Lannon goes on to point out that you are not necessarily stuck with writing on just one level. If the document is brief, you can rewrite it for different levels of your audience. If you do not wish to rewrite the same document, then write it on the level appropriate to the primary audience to which the document is addressed and simply provide abstracts, appendices, glossaries, or notes for everyone else (23–24). (For example, annual reports use this technique. Annual reports are usually written for a nontechnical audience, and the technical business material is found in the notes and appendices.)

Goodwill

Boone and Kurtz define *goodwill* as "the prestige, loyalty, and reputation that a business acquires beyond the value of its products" (8). As here defined, you might think goodwill is a rather abstract concept, and to some extent it is, but it is also a tangible business asset. When businesses are bought or sold, goodwill is a part of the sales price.

Likewise, when you write a business document, you are trying to do the same thing with your written document as you would do with a business: You must either maintain or create goodwill with your audience.

As a business writer, whether you are dealing internally or externally, you must never lose the audience's goodwill. If you do so externally, you lose not only current sales but also potential ones; and if you lose it internally, you build antagonisms between yourself and your co-workers and employer, creating inefficiencies because the message is ignored or misunderstood, or losing time because of internal personality battles.

To create and maintain goodwill, we can use seven methods, depending on the writing situation.

1. *Avoid using* **I.** When you use the pronoun *I*, you are building a wall between you and your audience. With *I*, you are either placing blame or taking credit, neither one of which leads to efficiencies.

    If your message discusses a problem, use the pronoun *we*. *We* tells the audience that both you and they share a problem. It creates a bridge of understanding between the audience and you, and placing blame is avoided.

    If your message discusses a benefit to your audience, then by all means use the pronoun *you*. *You* personalizes the good or positive news (Locker 32). If you use *I*, you may be taking credit for something that should be shared.

2. *Refer specifically to what your reader wants or can do.* You must meet reader expectations. There is nothing worse than receiving a memo that has no relevance to your situation. To make sure that the relevance is clear, keep your audience's interests before you. Emphasize the data that relates to the audience, and you will keep the audience's attention (Locker 32).

3. *Avoid mentioning how you feel or how the reader should feel.* Never assume that you know how the audience will react. For example, you might write to an audience congratulating it on its new credit line of $500. But what if the audience thinks that the credit line is too low, too miserly? Congratulations are then out of order, and you may have bred antagonism rather than joy (Locker 32).

4. *Avoid using words with negative connotations.* All words have connotations that are either positive, neutral, or negative. Use words with positive or neutral connotations to avoid antagonizing your reader or to avoid a misinterpretation of your message.

5. *Deflate the impact of the negative message.* You can lessen the impact of the negative message in four ways:
    1. Balance out the negative with positive information.
    2. Provide alternatives.
    3. Employ the passive.
    4. If possible, place the blame on something (not someone) that is beyond your control, such as government regulations, contract clauses, and warranty guidelines.

6. *Avoid sexism by employing the plural.* If you use the plural, you will avoid those situations in which you have used a word like *employee* and must subsequently pause to determine whether the employee is male or female. For example, instead of writing that *an employee should lock his or her desk before leaving the premises*, why not use the plural and avoid the *his or her* clause entirely? The sentence could just as easily read as follows: *All employees should lock **their** desks before leaving the premises.* Using the plural avoids sexism.

7. *If there is a benefit to the reader, don't hesitate in repeating it.* Good news should be emphasized because all readers welcome it.

Appropriate Format

To choose the appropriate format, consider your purpose and audience. (General formats are dealt with in chapter 3 and appendix C; for specific kinds of business formats, refer to the chapter that deals with that kind of message.)

Effective Endings

Too often, business documents end generically. In other words, the document ends with a catch phrase that is meaningless:

Looking forward to your continuing business. . . .

Hope to hear from you soon. . . .

If we can be of further assistance. . . .

The sad part about such endings is that they are often insincere, and, even worse, they are not meant to be taken seriously. When such endings are employed, the reader may well ask, "Why should I do further business with you when you haven't fulfilled my needs now?" Or, "Why do you hope to hear from me when the message asked for no response?" Or again, "How can you further assist me when you haven't assisted me now?" Such endings are meaningless. The writer is simply too lazy to think up something, so something is just stamped on the bottom and the writer is done with it.

But endings are extremely important, and you must take care in creating them. Endings are your last word to the reader, and thus they must make the reader feel good. Nevertheless, although the ending is your last word to the reader, you should formulate it first—at least the kind of ending that fits the context in which you are writing. In this way, you can lead up to the ending and provide your writing with a nice sense of balance.

Most effective endings call for an action on the reader's part. These endings are effective because they demand that the reader interact with the contents of the document.

Use one of the following seven kinds of conclusions (examples are given after each type of conclusion):

1. ***Add details with respect to people in the corporation.*** For example, refer to the excellent work of a group or individual or send personal congratulations from the CEO to a group or individual (Locker 156, 158).

2. ***Add details that demonstrate you are focusing on your corporation specifically.*** For example, give numbers demonstrating increasing profits or efficiency.

3. ***Add details that speak to the audience's needs or aspirations.*** For example, note increased profits, overtime pay, or salary bonuses (Locker 158).

4. ***Ask the reader to do something.*** For example, ask the reader to attend a meeting, fill out a questionnaire, or provide additional details.

5. ***Invite the reader to do something.*** For example, invite the reader to attend a shareholders' meeting or visit a plant.

6. ***Suggest that savings will accrue to the corporation.*** For example, point out a potential decrease in training time or decrease in employee turnover.

7. ***Suggest that the corporation will make money.*** For example, suggest increased profits or a lower debt-to-equity ratio.

Depending on the context, one of these endings should suit your purpose. Choose the one appropriate to your situation even before you begin writing. This decision will sharpen the overall focus of your paper. And by adopting one of these endings, you will avoid the generic and boring conclusion. As Kitty Locker states,

> Goodwill endings [such as the seven previously mentioned] should focus on the business relationship you share with your reader rather than on the reader's hobbies, family, or personal life. When you write to one person, a good last paragraph fits that person so specifically that it would not work if you sent the same basic message to someone else or to a person with the same title in another organization. (156)

A conclusion does not need to be long. Make your point briefly and succinctly, and it will have an impact on the audience—as long as the conclusion relates to the audience's needs.

Further, avoid the usual *in conclusion* or *in sum* ending. Because it is the last paragraph, the audience already knows that this is the conclusion—they are not blind.

One other conclusion is quite popular, but it is often used ineffectively: the summary conclusion. This conclusion summarizes the main points the document has made. Unfortunately, too many writers use this type of conclusion even when the document is not lengthy. Such writers do a disservice to their readers. If the document is not lengthy, then why bore the readers with a conclusion whose main points they can easily recall? Why miss an opportunity to leave the readers feeling good?

The only time to use a summary conclusion is when the document is lengthy or complex. Then, a summary ending is in order.

Finally, remember that any of these endings can be effective. The one you choose will depend on your corporate culture and on what you know about your audience. By knowing your audience thoroughly, you will be able to determine the most effective ending.

Boxes 2.1 and 2.2 provide checklists for analyzing an audience. Box 2.1 (page 11) deals with the corporate culture, internally or externally; box 2.2 (page 12) deals with the client or individual culture, internally or externally.

Ethical Communication

You must write ethically if you want to avoid lawsuits, antagonism, and governmental intervention and regulation (Guffey 73). Many companies try to ensure ethical conduct for these very reasons. Today, companies provide ethics training through seminars, games, software, and hot lines (Bovee and Thill 17).

ETHICS DEFINED

Mary Guffey defines ethical behavior as "that behavior which is the *right* thing to do, given the circumstances" (73). She adds that "[e]thical behavior involves four principles: honesty, integrity, fairness, and concern for others" (73). Bovee and Thill add that "*[e]thical communication* includes all relevant information, is true in every sense, and is not deceptive in any way" (17).

BOX 2.1

Determining the Corporate Culture

Identify the corporate culture of your audience:

1. What is the business environment?
2. What are the corporation's values?
3. Who are the corporation's heroes?
4. What are the corporation's rites and rituals?
5. What is the corporation's cultural network?

Identify your audience and the requisite details of your document:

1. Whom are you writing to?
2. What are you writing?
3. When will you write?
4. Why are you writing?
5. How will you write?
   a. What is the level of technicality at which you will write?
   b. How will you maintain goodwill?
   c. What is the appropriate format for writing?
   d. What type of conclusion will make an effective ending?

IMPORTANCE OF ETHICAL COMMUNICATION

Knowing the definition of ethical communication, however, is not enough. People still make unethical choices because of "the influence of competition, job pressure, ambition, financial gain (personal or corporate), or peer pressure . . ." (Bovee and Thill 17).

On occasion, people will communicate unethically because they have brainwashed themselves into believing that they could not do other than act unethically (Guffey 73). Sometimes unethical behavior is rationalized on the grounds that others are doing the same thing or worse (Guffey 73). And sometimes, people act unethically because they feel the end result outweighs the unethical conduct (Guffey 74). None of these rationalizations justifies unethical conduct. When you communicate unethically, you are endangering both yourself and your organization.

The question is how to avoid the pitfalls of unethical communication. You can communicate ethically if you follow some straightforward guidelines.

First, avoid "saying or writing something [when it is] clearly illegal" (Bovee and Thill 19).

BOX 2.2

Determining the Client or Individual Culture

Identify the corporate culture of your audience:

1. What business are they in, if any?
2. What values would they most likely prize?
3. What authority figure are they likely to honor?
4. How old are they?
5. How well educated are they?
6. What is their cultural heritage?
7. What else, if anything, do you know about your audience?

Identify your audience and the requisite details of your document:

1. Whom are you writing to?
2. What are you writing?
3. When will you write?
4. Why are you writing?
5. How will you write?
   a. What is the level of technicality at which you will write?
   b. How will you maintain goodwill?
   c. What is the appropriate format for writing?
   d. What type of conclusion will make an effective ending?

Second, don't plagiarize. Plagiarism can be easily avoided if you "give credit for ideas by (1) referring to originators' names within the text, (2) using quotation marks, and (3) documenting sources with endnotes, footnotes, or internal references" (Guffey 75).

Third, "avoid language that manipulates, discriminates, or exaggerates" (Bovee and Thill 17).

Fourth, "don't state opinions as facts, and . . . [do] portray graphic data fairly" (Bovee and Thill 17).

Fifth, use a vocabulary that the reader can understand (Guffey 75).

Sixth, give all the data objectively first before you begin interpreting it (Guffey 75).

Seventh, don't lie, understate, or exaggerate (Guffey 74).

Eighth, don't let your prejudices interfere with the content of the message (Bovee and Thill 17; Guffey 75).

Ethical communication is a necessity if your writing and speaking is to be taken seriously. Companies (as well should you) realize that "once a reputation is tainted, trust can never be regained" (Guffey 73). Because of the importance of reputation, about "95 percent of Fortune 500 corporations as well as many smaller companies have now adopted ethics statements or codes of conduct" (Guffey 73).

Intercultural Communication

In today's economy, we cannot assume that everyone shares the same culture. In the United States, one in seven people "speaks a language other than English when at home" (Bovee and Thill 57). While it may once have been the case that minorities had little impact on the economy, this is no longer the case.

Minority businesses are increasing at a fast pace, and this means that solutions may be at hand to "breaking the cycles of poverty that so deeply affect minority communities" (Nelton 19). From 1982 to 1987, minority-owned businesses grew 66 percent (Nelton 19). Box 2.3 shows the percentage increase in the number of minority-owned firms from 1982 to 1987.

Corporate America has come to realize the importance of these minority-owned businesses. In fact, corporations are increasingly purchasing from them: "[c]orporations that are members of the National Minority Supplier Development Council now purchase more than $23 billion in goods and services annually from minority firms compared with $86 million in 1972, when the council was chartered" (Nelton 19–20).

What this all means, for you, the business writer, is that because business opportunities have expanded because of the growing strength of minority-owned businesses, you must pay closer attention to cultural differences.

INTERCULTURAL COMMUNICATION DEFINED

As Courtland Bovee and John Thill define it, *intercultural communication* is "the process of sending and receiving messages between people of different cultures. You will be most effective when you learn to identify the differences between sender and receiver and to accommodate those differences without expecting either culture to give up its own identity" (59).

Each of us is a member of a particular culture that holds "a shared system of symbols, beliefs, attitudes, values, expectations, and norms for behavior" (Bovee and Thill 58). Because of our cultural identity, when you communicate with members of

---

BOX 2.3

Minority Businesses Increasing

Minority Group	% Increase	Number of Minority-Owned Businesses
Asian American/Pacific Islander	89.3	355,300
Hispanic	80.5	422,400
African American	—	424,200
Native American	—	21,400

Source: Nelton, Sharon. "Minority Business: The New Wave." *Nation's Business* Oct. 1995: 19.

another culture, the chances for miscommunication are high if you have not paid enough attention to the needs of the audience to whom the message is directed. After all, each culture "assign[s] meaning to a message according to its cultural context, the pattern of physical cues and implicit understanding that convey meaning between two members of the same culture" (Bovee and Thill 62). In some cultures, for instance the United States and Germany, "people rely more on verbal communication and less on circumstances and implied meaning to convey meaning" (Bovee and Thill 62). In other cultures, for instance South Korea and Taiwan, "people rely less on verbal communication and more on the context of non-verbal actions and environmental setting to convey meaning" (Bovee and Thill 62). If you fail to pay attention to cultural differences, you may begin to stereotype people (Guffey 46). You may even fall into the trap of ethnocentrism: a "belief in the superiority of one's own race" (Guffey 46) or "the tendency to judge all other groups according to our own group's standards, behaviors, and customs" (Bovee and Thill 67).

Remember that cultural differences are not only found in minority cultures in the United States; cultural differences are found the world over. Awareness of cultural differences is especially important because we are now competing in a global economy.

IMPORTANCE OF INTERCULTURAL COMMUNICATION

When communicating with those of a different culture from your own, you must be alert to cultural differences if miscommunication is to be avoided (Bovee and Thill 58). As Bovee and Thill state,

> Cultural differences can affect your ability to send and to receive messages. When you write to or speak with someone in another culture, you encode your message using the assumptions of your own culture. However, the receiver decodes it according to the assumptions of the other culture, so your meaning may be misunderstood. The greater the difference between the sender's culture and the receiver's culture, the greater the chance for misunderstanding. (59–60)

One of the major obstacles to adequate communication facing many Americans is the assumption that other cultures prize the same values as they do (Bovee and Thill 61). Many examples of such misplaced or misassigned values leading to misunderstanding can be found, but awareness can lead to understanding, as the following examples show.

Americans are goal oriented. They believe that employing fewer people to accomplish a task is a good thing. In India and Pakistan, however, the opposite is true because unemployment is astronomical (Bovee and Thill 61).

Americans address superiors with a *Mr.* or a *Mrs.*, but in China these forms of address are replaced by business titles such as *President* or *Manager* (Bovee and Thill 61). You could easily offend a person if you choose the wrong form of address.

Americans display their business importance with expensively furnished offices, but in the Middle East, businesspeople prefer modest arrangements, keeping their valued items at home. To assume that a person's modest office means that you are dealing with a less-than-important person could lead to a grave mistake on your part (Bovee and Thill 61).

Americans want to make agreements quickly, determining the smaller details later. A Greek businessperson would find such an approach sneaky and underhanded because a discussion of the fine details displays "good faith" (Bovee and Thill 61). Latin Americans likewise choose a slow and deliberate approach in reaching an agreement (Bovee and Thill 61).

American businesses usually have one person who has a strong influence in deciding whether to make an agreement. Other cultures depend on several people to make such a decision (Bovee and Thill 61).

Americans see time as of the essence: It is important to reach an understanding and an agreement as quickly as possible. Germans believe this as well (Bovee and Thill 62). However, Asians and Latin Americans want to establish a relationship first and then discuss business (Bovee and Thill 62).

Americans usually speak to one another with a distance of about five feet separating them. Germans and Japanese believe this to be too short a distance, while Arabs and Latin Americans think it is too far. Thus, Americans who do not know these differences may appear arrogant to a Latin American simply because of distance, or they may offend an Arab by moving backwards when the Arab closes the intervening distance during a conversation (Bovee and Thill 62).

Americans shake their heads from side to side to say *no*, but Bulgarians move their heads up and down to indicate the same thing. Japanese indicate *no* with their right hands, while Sicilians move their chins up (Bovee and Thill 63).

Americans don't visit someone's home unless specifically invited to do so. In India, people issue general invitations and expect them to be acted upon. As a result, if Americans were invited to come by someone's house at some unspecified time, they might not do so since the invitation was so generally expressed. However, in India should they not make the visit, they will have insulted the person who made the invitation (Bovee and Thill 63).

As you can see, culture makes an enormous difference in your business dealings. You must know the culture with which you are dealing if communication is to be effective.

EFFECTIVE INTERCULTURAL COMMUNICATION

When communicating with a different culture, you can take certain steps to ensure effective communication.

First, know something about the culture with which you are communicating (Bovee and Thill 68).

Second, learn the language, or at least a few words and phrases, of that culture to demonstrate your respect (Bovee and Thill 68–69; Guffey 48).

Third, do some research and find out something about that culture's history and customs (Bovee and Thill 69).

Fourth, speak to other people who deal or have dealt with that culture (Bovee and Thill 69).

Fifth, place the burden of communication on yourself, not on the person from that other culture (Bovee and Thill 69).

Sixth, don't be judgmental with respect to a person's culture (Bovee and Thill 69).

Seventh, display respect for a different culture (Bovee and Thill 70).

Eighth, be empathetic (Bovee and Thill 70), that is, attempt "to see the world through another's eyes" (Guffey 47).

Ninth, avoid stereotyping based on culture, speech, or behavior (Guffey 48).

Tenth, make sure to "check frequently for comprehension" (Guffey 49).

Eleventh, listen carefully and politely without interrupting the other person's flow of speech (Guffey 49).

Twelfth, use a simple vocabulary (Guffey 49).

These rules focus primarily on oral communication, but you can use similar guidelines to ensure effective written intercultural communication.

First, use the business formats used in that culture (Guffey 50).

Second, use a translator when "(1) your document is important, (2) your document will be distributed to many readers, or (3) you must be persuasive" (Guffey 50).

Third, avoid lengthy or complex sentences and paragraphs (Guffey 50).

Fourth, avoid contractions (Guffey 50).

Fifth, use relative pronouns such as *that, which,* or *who* to introduce relative clauses (Guffey 50).

Sixth, use a simple vocabulary (Guffey 50).

Seventh, don't use slang or jargon (Guffey 50).

Eighth, don't use acronyms or abbreviations (Guffey 50).

Ninth, use numbers because everyone understands them, but use the actual number (such as *165*) rather than writing it out (*one hundred sixty-five*) (Guffey 50).

Tenth, use the local currency to express dollar amounts (Guffey 50).

Eleventh, identify the date as that culture identifies it (Guffey 50).

When you can effectively communicate interculturally, you will have an edge over the competition. To cite just one example of intercultural communication providing such an edge, look at Pacific Bell. It "invites customers to discuss service problems in English, Spanish, Chinese, Korean, or Vietnamese" (Bovee and Thill 66). This company has expanded its customer base and encouraged more business by focusing on intercultural communication (Bovee and Thill 66).

CHAPTER 3

Designing the Document

When you create a business document, it is not enough that you are organized and logical. How a document looks is as important as what it says. You are immediately judged by the appearance of the business document. If it looks good at first glance, people will pay you more heed; if it looks bad, the immediate impression people have will be that you probably don't know what you are talking about. The same rule applies to business documents as it does to giving a speech: You must have a positive ethos; you must be credible. Shoddy or sloppy work will not give you or your writing credibility. In sum, you want to fulfill reader expectations, that is, you want to come across as a professional who knows what readers want and expect. To fulfill those expectations, you must properly design all of your business documents.

To achieve the proper ethos, to reach your reader most effectively, design your documents carefully and follow the appropriate formats. Both are crucial parts of document design.

Tools for Designing the Document

To design a document effectively, use the following nine tools appropriately:

1. Spacing
2. Headings
3. Capitalization and italics
4. Typefaces
5. Margins
6. Z-pattern
7. Decorative devices
8. Signposting
9. Lists

SPACING

Provide enough spacing so that items on the page are easy to read (Locker 128). For the page as a whole, make the bottom margin slightly larger than the top. This will give a certain balance to the page, and the text itself will not appear to have been crowded together. In addition, make sure that adequate spacing surrounds lists as well as visuals. Never crowd items on a page. If you lack adequate room on the page, then just add the items to the next page.

In addition to spacing the general layout of the page, single-space your paragraphs and double-space between. (Do not indent the first line.) Also space headings adequately: skip a line between the major heading and its following text; do this with subheadings as well.

In sum, documents should invite readers; they should not frighten them.

HEADINGS

Proper headings make the document accessible to the reader. Readers expect headings that tell them exactly what each section of a document contains. You must strive to fulfill their expectations. Headings must be informative; they must also allow for easy skimming of a document should the reader choose to do so. If you fail to meet their expectations because your headings are imprecise, vague, or too general, you will both frustrate your reader and hurt your credibility.

Headings are designed to logically organize information not only so readers can understand the information and its organization, but also so they can read those sections relevant to themselves or those sections that are only immediately relevant. Good headings save readers time; bad headings waste time and lead to inefficient communication, often resulting in loss of productivity from misunderstanding.

Headings come in three varieties:

1. Questions
2. Phrases
3. Statements

No matter what kind of heading you choose, they should all tell the reader at a glance what that part of the document details.

Questions are particularly useful when dealing with complicated material and a general audience. For example, for a heading about insurance or financial data, a question may be more effective for an unsophisticated audience because such a heading can express the very question that this audience would have asked:

What Does the Health Insurance Plan Cover?

Phrases are designed to impart specific topics in a logical sequence that the reader will recognize and understand. The question heading could easily be turned into a phrase by turning the question into an assertion:

Health Insurance Plan Coverage of Out-of-Town Emergencies

Statements impart the same information as phrases, but they are longer, and they are complete sentences. The phrase heading could readily be turned into a statement by turning the noun phrase into a clause:

Health Insurance Plan Covers Out-of-Town Emergencies

The choice of heading form will depend on your intended audience. Keep its needs before you by asking yourself what kind of heading will be most accessible to your audience. Whatever heading you choose, be precise. Do not create headings that are so general they provide no information. The three previous headings for example, could have been written as poorly as follows:

1. The Plan?

2. The Plan

3. The Plan Covers Emergencies

These headings are poorly constructed. Heading 1 is inexact because it barely qualifies as a question, and it doesn't suggest an answer to the question. Heading 2 is so broad that the entire message could be placed under this one heading. Heading 3 is inexact because it does not specify what emergencies are covered.

When you write headings for a document, make sure that they are of the same kind: that is, they are all questions, phrases, or statements. Do not mix them together because this will cause confusion for readers. Readers may begin to wonder why the headings have changed, rather than focusing on the information those headings and sections contain. In essence, mixing headings leads to reader distraction. However, this is not a rule set in stone. It all depends on the length of the document. If you are writing a memo, letter, brochure, or short report, then stick to one kind of heading. If, on the other hand, you are writing an annual report, research document, or book, then different headings may be appropriate because these longer documents will contain divisions by section, part, or chapter. Readers will recognize these major divisions, and they will not expect identical headings throughout such a document.

Headings should also be no more than one line in length. Do not provide headings that are overly long because, after all, the purpose of headings is precision, not verbosity. You want to make sure that headings save reading time, and you cannot do this with lengthy headings.

CAPITALIZATION AND ITALICS

Other than in major headings, be very careful in your use of capitalization. Capitalization slows readers down (Locker 130). Of course, if your purpose is to slow readers down and attract attention to specific information, then use capitalization. Many legal documents use capitalization for just this very purpose.

Likewise, italicizing should be limited to those items that you want to emphasize or draw attention to. You must remember that when you italicize, the reader automatically assumes there is a reason for it. If you italicize for no apparent reason, the reader will become confused and distracted, wondering why the italics are there, instead of focusing on the information disseminated.

TYPEFACES

The computer that was used to typeset this book must have about a hundred type-faces. One could easily go berserk in the use of them. The shorter the document, the fewer the typefaces that you should use. For example, a memo should probably use no more than two different typefaces. In fact "[m]ost business documents use just one typeface—usually Times Roman or Helvetica" (Locker 132–33). It all depends on the length of the document and how likely it is that the number of fonts used may distract the reader from the meaning of the text.

MARGINS

Margins help readers understand the text through accessibility. If a document appears too crowded or squished together, the reader will be intimidated by it. Herein lies the importance of spacing as well as margins. The following guidelines for margins will help make the document attractive and inviting.

Make the bottom margin larger than the top. To the reader, the document will appear shorter, less time-consuming to read, and thus more inviting.

Use one-inch margins on the sides. This will ensure that the document does not appear overcrowded.

Use justified or unjustified margins depending on your audience. Justified margins are aligned on both left and right-hand margins. Unjustified margins are aligned only on the left and are "ragged" on the right. Unjustified margins are easier to read, though they may lack the professional look that you want. By contrast, justified margins are more difficult to read, but they do give a document a professional look. Therefore, if your audience is sophisticated with respect to reading business documents, then use justified margins (Locker 133); on the other hand, if your audience, such as a client, is unsophisticated with business documents, then use unjustified margins to make the document easier to read (Locker 134).

Z-PATTERN

When reading, the eye moves in a Z-pattern. As a result, readers first notice items in the upper left or bottom right sections of the page. Therefore, attempt to place important items, such as visuals, phone numbers, and addresses, in the upper left or bottom right sections of the page. In this way, the very placement of the items assures that the reader will spot them immediately (Locker 134).

DECORATIVE DEVICES

Today, most computers carry standard graphic and icon systems that allow you to import decorative devices and place them anywhere on a page. Although these decorative devices look cute and tempting to use, beware. Decorative devices should be used, if at all, with great moderation. Do not simply place trophies or globes because they look nice. Decorative devices, just like visuals, are an integral part of the text. If they are not integral to the text in that they further meaning, then they are useless and should be avoided (Locker 135).

SIGNPOSTING

Signposting is one of the most useful tools that a writer can employ to ensure that the document is organized and easy to read. A signposting statement tells the reader exactly how many parts there are to a given piece of writing and the order in which you will address them.

Take for example the following signposting statement:

A good thesis statement for an informative abstract has four parts.

If the four parts will be briefly explained immediately following the signposting sentence, then you need not specify those parts. In this case, the sentences that follow the signposting statement could read as follows:

First, you must state the author's name. Second, you must state the title of the article. Third, you must provide a verb that denotes what the author of the article is doing: is the author *illustrating, arguing, stating, detailing?* Fourth, you must provide an accurate paraphrase of the author's thesis.

The writer in this example has briefly detailed the four parts of a thesis statement for an abstract, and each part is designated with the words *first, second, third,* and *fourth*. These words provide the reader with an easy to understand organizational pattern.

If, on the other hand, the four parts are lengthy, each part requiring a separate paragraph, place a colon after the word *parts* in the signposting statement and list the four parts, as follows:

A good thesis statement for an informative abstract has four parts: the author's name, the title of the article, a descriptive verb, and a paraphrase of the author's thesis.

To follow through, discuss each of the four parts in the order in which they were presented. Each item is treated in a separate paragraph, and each paragraph begins with a topic sentence, which the rest of the paragraph elaborates on:

Topic Sentence for Paragraph 1: **First, you must state the author's name.**

Topic Sentence for Paragraph 2: **Second, you must state the title of the article.**

Topic Sentence for Paragraph 3: **Third, you must provide a verb that denotes what the author of the article is doing.**

Topic Sentence for Paragraph 4: **Fourth, you must provide an accurate paraphrase of the author's thesis.**

LISTS

Lists are some of the most effective devices that you can use both to organize your information and to make it highly understandable to the reader. If you can list items, especially when they detail complicated matters (such as financial data), then use a list. Lists come in two essential forms.

In one form, the introduction to the list is a complete sentence followed by a colon, and then the list follows:

A good thesis statement for an informative abstract provides four pieces of information:

1. Name of author
2. Title of article
3. Descriptive verb
4. Paraphrase of thesis

In this type of list, a complete sentence must precede the colon, or the sentence is ungrammatical.

In the other kind of list, the list grammatically completes the introductory sentence, as follows:

A good thesis statement for an informative abstract provides the

1. name of the author,
2. title of the article,
3. descriptive verb, and
4. paraphrase of the thesis.

Note that here the list is part of the introductory sentence; therefore, no colon appears. Furthermore, because each item in the list is a phrase, each item must be set off with commas and the word *and* should precede the last item, with a period ending the list and the sentence. (If the list consisted of clauses, then each listed item— other than the last—would end with a semicolon and the word *and* would precede the last item, with a period ending the list and the series of clauses.)

By their very nature, lists are abbreviated. They provide information in a simplified yet informative fashion. Do not provide lists wherein each listed item goes on for several lines. In such a case, use a signposting statement followed by sentences or paragraphs.

A good list is centered on the page, set off with spacing around it, and contains items of similar length and parallel form. *Parallel form* means that if the first item is a noun, all following items must be nouns; if the first item is a verb ending in *-ing*, all following items must be verbs ending in *-ing*, and so on.

Conclusion

When you design a document, take care. You are often judged immediately by appearances, and thus proper document design is crucial to you and your business.

Memos and letters must follow specific guidelines so that you can fulfill reader expectations and enhance your own credibility. Appendix C provides guidelines for formatting business memos and letters.

Box 3.1 provides a further perspective on document design in an article concerning the problems advertisers are facing with respect to document design: the very problems that this chapter has addressed.

Joshua Levine's Article "Gutenberg's Revenge"

Funky type has become the marketer's latest tool to grab audiences as they flip briskly through magazine pages and surf the TV channels. Letters are leaping around ads and commercials like dogs off the leash. Words get squeezed and stretched. Sentences career wildly, suddenly plunging off in new directions. Headlines jumble several different typefaces together, as if the art director had run out of the one he started with. Type is running riot.

One of advertising guru David Ogilvy's cardinal rules was an injunction against using reverse type—white lettering on a black background. Keep the lettering clear, clean and simple, he advised. But the mind-set of today's agencies is that type is art—who said anything about reading?

Take the Maybelline ad where the words "full, lavish, through it all" are pumped up in different typefaces, making the message hard to read and even hard to look at.

Roper Starch Worldwide, which measures the attention paid to magazine ads, reports that while 47% of readers noticed the ad—slightly below the average score for other cosmetic ads—only 11% bothered to read most of the copy, even though there's not much of it to read. That's a dismaying 19% below the average for the cosmetic category. Most readership scores cluster closely around the norm.

The Nike ad is a good deal more stylish, but it, too, looks like it's flunking the readership test: Only 12% read most of the ad, a full 43% below the category average, although Roper Starch cautions that these are preliminary results.

Type is running amok on television, too. Ad agency Wieden & Kennedy, which also does Nike's ads, is widely credited with having started the trend with commercials for Subaru in 1992. The spots featured type scrolling down the screen in a layered pattern. By now, the technique has become something of a cliché, particularly with car companies. "Type is more important than ever on television," says Kent Hunter, executive design director of Frankfurt Balkind Partners. "Print is influencing TV, and TV is influencing print."

continued

Are there any guidelines these days? Graham Clifford, who stands guard over type at ad agency Chiat/Day, has a few general admonitions for wayward art directors: Don't squash letters together, keep them at their original scale. Stick to standard point sizes, measures for how big or small letters can be. Never use the slash mark instead of an apostrophe, and for heaven's sake, keep the number of different typefaces to a minimum—almost never more than five, and that's pushing it.

Sounds simple enough. So why do art directors seem hell-bent on promoting eyestrain and myopia? To some degree because they can. Computers are revolutionizing type design. In the old days—the good old days to purists—letters were arranged by hand on a tray in a set number of type styles, many of which had been created years earlier by classic type designers like Giambattista Bodoni and Claude Garamond. Later, type was set by pouring molten lead into molds on a Linotype machine.

In the 1970s the use of cameras to photograph type ended the era of so-called hot type. Now, with a desktop computer, an art director can squeeze or stretch a letter at will, ignoring the original designer's scale entirely, and making the current inventory of some 3,000 standard typefaces almost irrelevant. "Anyone with a computer can create his own typeface," says Frankfurt Balkind's Hunter, whose firm did just that for Comcast's 1992 annual report.

Not everyone is impressed. "I call it the 'ransom note' approach to advertising, except the people who get ransom notes are compelled to read them. No one has to read an ad," says Philip Sawyer of Roper Starch.

Now many advertising agencies are employing type directors to oversee trigger-happy art directors—a job that British agencies, with their greater attentiveness to type, have had for years. The reign of terror phase of the type revolution may almost be over.

Source: Levine, Joshua. "Gutenberg's Revenge." *Forbes* 9 May 1994: 166–67.
Reprinted by Permission of FORBES Magazine © Forbes Inc., 1994.

Exercises

3.1: Locate a document that requires revision. Look in computer manuals, business journals, business magazines or newspapers, or business textbooks. Look at the announcements on your company or school bulletin board. Complete the following steps:

1. Locate the poorly designed document, and make a copy of it.
2. Change the design and appearance of the document to make it attractive. Do not worry about changing the content of the document; for now, just focus on proper document design.
3. Turn in the document, using one of the following options:

   Option 1: Fax the original document, and e-mail the revised document.
   Option 2: Submit both documents to your instructor in class.

PART II: DEVELOPING THE MESSAGE

CHAPTER 4

Writing the Informative Message

The kind of messages discussed in this chapter are informative, not persuasive, and they are primarily positive. (Chapter 5 discusses the appropriate format for messages that are primarily negative, and chapter 6 for those that are persuasive.) Informative messages cover a host of possible writing scenarios: policy announcements, thank yous, and instructions on how to do something.

The easiest way to decide whether the message is an informative one is to ask three questions:

1. Is the message's primary purpose to inform rather than to persuade?
2. Is the message a positive or neutral one?
3. Is the message brief?

If the answers to these questions are yes, then use the informative message format detailed in this chapter. The informative message must be brief, for if it is long—that is, more than three or four pages—it is a report or some other kind of business document. In sum, the informative message has two objectives: "(1) to answer all the questions honestly and completely and (2) to leave a favorable impression that prepares the way for future business or smooths working relationships" (Bovee and Thill 235).

Informative Messages: Basic Guidelines

When you have decided that the informative message is the appropriate format for your purpose, then make a few brief notes on these basic elements: style, audience, length, format, originality, and organization.

By considering these elements before you begin writing, you will give your message a power and effect beyond the usual routine and boring messages too often found in business.

STYLE

Because informative messages are brief and positive, style is not as important as in many other writing situations. Simply focus on providing the information in a clear and organized fashion.

AUDIENCE

Know your audience. If you know to whom you are writing, then you can determine what will most interest readers and what requires further development and clarification.

LENGTH

Informative messages must be short. Readers appreciate informative news that is positive or neutral; therefore, it is most important to be brief, to be clear, to categorize information, and to list information whenever possible.

FORMAT

Because informative messages are short, the memo format is usually most appropriate and effective. The following are the essential elements of an effective informative memo:

- a precise subject line that immediately tells the reader the subject of the memo
- an opening sentence that gives the positive news and reminds the reader of the memo's purpose
- a forecasting sentence that states what the memo will discuss
- precise headings that organize the information

ORIGINALITY

Make informative messages as original as possible. No one in a business organization likes to read dry, boring messages; no one becomes enthused over a memo that follows the same old format and is dull to boot. Strive for originality, even in routine messages; otherwise, the reader may become lackadaisical and pay little heed to the information. You can achieve originality in a number of ways:

- Provide precise, informative headings.
- Use lists whenever possible, and don't hesitate to signpost important information.
- Pay close attention to document design: that is, make the memo aesthetically pleasing to the eye.
- Provide concise details.
- Add details with respect to people in the corporation, or add details that demonstrate you are focusing on your corporation specifically.

ORGANIZATION

Provide your reader with an organization that is easy to follow:

- Make the subject line the title of the document. The reader should know at a glance what the memo is about.
- Use both a reminder statement and a forecasting sentence to begin the document.
- Employ the first heading to discuss background information that sets up the subsequent headings by providing necessary details or clarifications.
- Organize the headings in a logical manner.
- Use a goodwill ending that speaks to the readers' or corporation's needs or aspirations. (Locker 150–51)

Writing the Informative Message

The simplest way to understand what is involved in writing an informative memo is to write one. Therefore, this chapter takes you step by step through writing an informative memo. Box 4.1 presents a scenario to use to practice constructing the memo.

Box 4.2 (page 31) provides a situation requiring the informative memo format.

BOX 4.1

An Informative Message Scenario

At Eaton Corporation, the morning quiz is underway.

Ten employees sit around a boardroom table. A supervisor asks, "What were our sales yesterday?"

A worker scans a computer printout and replies, "$625,275."

"And in the month?" asks the manager.

"$6,172,666," says another worker.

The quiz continues: What was the cost of materials and supplies used the day before? What was the cost of labor, shipping, and utilities?

Meanwhile, out on the shop floor another employee demonstrates to the plant manager a new technique for making welding electrodes that could save the plant $5,126 annually. This marks the 193rd time this year that employees have come up with ideas for improving the plant's operations. Clearly, workers at Eaton aren't just taking tests; they're also doing their homework.

Eaton's business—making gears, engine valves, truck axles, and circuit breakers—may not be glamorous, but its progress is breathtaking. Last year, Eaton lost $12 million; in its first quarter this year, it netted $33 million. The company's productivity (output per hour

continued

---

worked) has risen 3 percent every year during the past decade—compared to 1.9 percent for all U.S. manufacturers. Employees' suggestions have helped the firm save $1.4 million—and earned workers $44,000 in credits toward purchases at the factory store.

How does Eaton do it? Managers attribute much of the company's success to its improved communication with workers. Show employees how the firm's success benefits them, say supervisors, and they'll find creative ways to help. Hence the daily morning quizzes in which managers and workers assess the plant's progress on a continuing basis. In the company cafeteria, a TV monitor compares the daily performance of each shift and department to its cost and performance goals. Attention to the common cause, says metal fabricator Ricky Rigg, "gives you a sense of direction, and makes you appreciate what you do more." Adds machinist Rodney Romine: "If the company can't make money, you can't expect to have a job very long."

Eaton has also found that communication improves when employees work in teams. Boasting such names as "The Hoods" and "The Worms," worker-led groups constantly look for production bottlenecks and areas where costs can be cut. Sometimes, the search pays off in ways that nobody expected. For example, "Scrap Attack," a team of eight forge-press operators, had long been trying to reduce the plant's scrap-metal waste by 50 percent. Along the way, team members noticed that the dies used to forge gears on one press consistently lasted 25 percent longer than any of the other dies employed to perform the same task. Why? "Nobody knew," recalls team leader Anthony Ourada, "but we got to thinking about it." Eventually, the group discovered that one press operator preheated the dies before using them—a practice that extended their life. Now—at a cost savings of $50,000 a year—every press operator in the plant preheats dies.

Another worker team responsible for maintaining plant machinery decided that machines broke down too much. The workers approached their boss with an offer: "You're buying all this on the outside. We can do it for you better." At costs of $80,000 and $250,000 respectively, the team proceeded to build two new machines to replace equipment for which outside vendors had charged Eaton $350,000 and $250,000. The new machines have taken over the most boring tasks in the department and have freed workers to handle more challenging jobs. Moreover, the department's output doubled in one year, and the team plans to double it again in another year. "It's nice to start out with a concept and see it through," says Romine, "especially when it gets rid of monotonous work. We're more or less our own bosses."

Office clerk Luci Donaldson sums up the Eaton attitude: "Our opinions matter here. What we say counts—and it's not just to appease us."

Source: O'Boyle, Thomas. "Working Together." *The Wall Street Journal* 5 June 1992: A1+.
Reprinted by Permission of *The Wall Street Journal* © 1992 Dow Jones & Company, Inc. All Rights Reserved Worldwide.

BOX 4.2

Writing the Informative Message

Your boss at Eaton asks you to prepare an informative report to describe for the company's board of directors the plant's new system and its benefits. Write this report, keeping your audience in mind and addressing its needs and concerns.

Source: Boone, Louis E., and David L. Kurtz. *Contemporary Business Communication.* Englewood Cliffs, NJ: Prentice Hall, 1994. 232. Courtesy of Prentice Hall.

ESTABLISHING THE FOCUS

To write an effective memo, prepare well beforehand. First, decide on the focus of the memo. In other words, what is the primary information that your memo will disseminate? This will be the subject of discussion, and it will provide you with a subject line. According to the scenario in box 4.1, the new system improves communication. Therefore, the subject for the informative memo is communication.

Second, consider to whom you are writing. This intended audience will determine how you can immediately gain its attention. According to the situation in box 4.2, your intended audience is the Eaton Board of Directors. You must ask yourself, "What would interest not just this board of directors, but any board of directors?" The answer is simple: money and profits. The article has already pointed out that the communication system at Eaton has led to cost savings. Therefore, your subject line must state this point to establish the focus of the memo and also to interest the intended audience.

Third, be concise and precise so that the reader will know what the memo is about. Using the memo format detailed earlier in this book, your memo heading, including the subject line, will read as follows:

Date: 29 Nov. 1994

To: Eaton Board of Directors

From: J. Smith

Re: Eaton's New Communication System Creates Profits

This subject line is crucial to both you and your intended audience. For you, a precise subject line will determine the content and focus of the memo; for the audience, the subject line states the subject under discussion. It is imperative that you do not mislead your audience. For example, if you use the subject line just mentioned, the memo should not detail the good feelings and camaraderie that the communication system fosters. If you do this, you are not fulfilling reader expectations, and the audience will be irritated because you did not fulfill the promise established in the subject line.

Think of the subject line as the thesis statement for your memo. Once you have a solid subject line, then your headings will be more precise statements that prove or explain it.

CATEGORIZING THE INFORMATION

Once you have determined the focus of the informative memo, categorize the available information. At the outset of this process, just make a list of all the information you have relating to the subject line. Do not worry about editing or categorizing the information yet; just get it on paper first. For example, based on the Eaton article in box 4.1, the following information can be listed:

1. Eaton workers have morning discussions with their supervisors with respect to the cost of doing business to see how the plant is doing.

2. Employees have saved the company money 193 times this year.

3. Last year Eaton lost $12 million; this year it made $33 million.

4. Eaton's productivity has risen 3 percent a year for the decade, compared to the industry average of 1.9 percent.

5. Employees have made suggestions that have saved Eaton $1.4 million.

6. Supervisors say that if employees know how the company's success benefits them, then they will be more interested in helping to save on costs.

7. Employees' suggestions have netted employees $44,000 in credits at the company store.

8. Morning quizzes compare costs of doing business, and TV monitors in the cafeteria display comparisons between shifts and between costs and performance goals.

9. Employees work in teams to improve communication.

10. Groups look for opportunities to cut costs and to improve plant efficiency.

11. One group discovered a new way to make dies last longer; this saves Eaton $50,000 a year.

12. Another group built machines at the costs of $80,000 and $250,000; outside vendors would have charged $350,000 and $250,000.

13. These machines caused an increase in departmental output of 100%.

Once you have made your list, begin to categorize it. Ask yourself under what headings these items can be logically grouped. Our subject line already provides two categories: communication and profits. Indeed, if you look over your list, you will see that all thirteen items in the list can be categorized under these two headings. Thus, next to each item on the list, write either communication (com) or profits (prof):

com   1. Eaton workers have morning discussions with their supervisors with respect to the cost of doing business to see how the plant is doing.

prof   2. Employees have saved the company money 193 times this year.

prof   3. Last year Eaton lost $12 million; this year it made $33 million.

prof   4. Eaton's productivity has risen 3 percent a year for the decade, compared to the industry average of 1.9 percent.

prof   5. Employees have made suggestions that have saved Eaton $1.4 million.

com   6. Supervisors say that if employees know how the company's success benefits them, then they will be more interested in helping to save on costs.

com   7. Employees' suggestions have netted employees $44,000 in credits at the company store.

com   **8. Morning quizzes compare costs of doing business, and TV monitors in the cafeteria display comparisons between shifts and between costs and performance goals.**

com   **9. Employees work in teams to improve communication.**

com   **10. Groups look for opportunities to cut costs and to improve plant efficiency.**

prof   **11. One group discovered a new way to make dies last longer; this saves Eaton $50,000 a year.**

prof   **12. Another group built machines at the costs of $80,000 and $250,000; outside vendors would have charged $350,000 and $250,000.**

prof   **13. These machines caused an increase in departmental output of 100%.**

After you have categorized your information, decide the order in which the headings will appear in the memo, and come up with headings that tell the reader what each section of the memo contains. Determining the order is relatively simple if you approach the issue logically: The board of directors must know the communication system first in order to understand how the profits and savings came about. If you do it the other way around, the discussion of the system will be lost beneath the impressive profits and savings. Hence, the discussion of the communication system comes first, followed by an analysis of profits and savings.

Next, write headings that are not only informative but also attractive to your audience, the board of directors. Headings for these two sections of the memo can read as follows:

What Is the New Communication System?

What Are the Financial Rewards of the New Communication System?

You may use questions, statements, or phrases in your headings. The choice is yours, but if you are explaining a system, is not a question more appropriate than a statement or phrase? Further, are not questions in and of themselves intriguing to the reader? Also note that the headings relate to the subject line of the memo, and they are designed to create reader interest.

With these headings to guide you, arrange the list into two parts—com and prof—beneath each heading:

What Is the New Communication System?

com   **1. Eaton workers have morning discussions with their supervisors with respect to the cost of doing business to see how the plant is doing.**

com   **6. Supervisors say that if employees know how the company's success benefits them, then they will be more interested in helping to save on costs.**

com   **7. Employees' suggestions have netted employees $44,000 in credits at the company store.**

com   **8. Morning quizzes compare costs of doing business, and TV monitors in the cafeteria display comparisons between shifts and between costs and performance goals.**

com   **9. Employees work in teams to improve communication.**

com   **10. Groups look for opportunities to cut costs and to improve plant efficiency.**

What Are the Financial Rewards of the New Communication System?

prof 2. Employees have saved the company money 193 times this year.

prof 3. Last year Eaton lost $12 million; this year it made $33 million.

prof 4. Eaton's productivity has risen 3 percent a year for the decade, compared to the industry average of 1.9 percent.

prof 5. Employees have made suggestions that have saved Eaton $1.4 million.

prof 11. One group discovered a new way to make dies last longer; this saves Eaton $50,000 a year.

prof 12. Another group built machines at the costs of $80,000 and $250,000; outside vendors would have charged $350,000 and $250,000.

prof 13. These machines caused an increase in departmental output of 100%.

Before proceeding to the actual writing of each section, write your reminder and forecasting statements. The reminder statement tells the reader why the memo has been written and states in general terms what the memo is about. In our scenario, the reminder statement could read as follows:

This memo provides information with respect to Eaton Corporation's profitable new communication system.

Note that the reminder statement is not all that different from the subject line. It shouldn't be. Otherwise the reader will already feel misled. Once you have written the reminder statement, forecast the memo's organization in one sentence. All you need do is recapitulate your headings:

The following memo discusses how the new communication system works and how profitable it has become.

You can now see why waiting to write these statements after categorizing the information makes things easier. (If you write these statements first, you may find that they will not fit the established categories.)

Now it is time to work on the information beneath your headings. Let us look at the items listed beneath your first heading:

What Is the New Communication System?

com 1. Eaton workers have morning discussions with their supervisors with respect to the cost of doing business to see how the plant is doing.

com 6. Supervisors say that if employees know how the company's success benefits them, then they will be more interested in helping to save on costs.

com 7. Employees' suggestions have netted employees $44,000 in credits at the company store.

com 8. Morning quizzes compare costs of doing business, and TV monitors in the cafeteria display comparisons between shifts and between costs and performance goals.

com 9. Employees work in teams to improve communication.

com 10. Groups look for opportunities to cut costs and to improve plant efficiency.

Write the first section by doing the following: (1) Establish a topic sentence; (2) arrange the listed items in a logical order; (3) use transitions. Establishing a topic sentence is little different from writing a subject line: Simply ask yourself, "What is the main point that this section of the memo discusses?" The six items listed show that group effort is Eaton's key to effective communication. Your topic sentence can state this point as follows:

Eaton Corporation has established an effective communication system based on the concept of group work.

Now provide the details that explain the topic sentence. First, arrange the items from your list in a logical order. An effective order to use here is one that moves from the individual employee to groups to general cost benefits. (It is best to be general with respect to costs here because financial rewards or profits will be discussed under the next heading.) In any event, whichever order you choose, make sure that you use transitions to keep the items together. This section of the memo can read as follows:

Eaton Corporation has established an effective communication system based on the concept of group work. Every morning Eaton workers meet with supervisors who give quizzes concerning the plant's productivity. In addition, monitors in the cafeteria display comparisons between shifts and between cost and performance goals. Supervisors say that if employees know how the company's success benefits them, then they will be more interested in helping to save on costs. To this end, employees work in groups to improve communication. These groups look for opportunities to cut costs and improve plant efficiency. The plant has benefited from these groups, but so have the employees: To date, employees' suggestions have netted employees $44,000 in credits at the company store.

Note that all of the items in the list have been used, that they are arranged in a logical order, and that transitions have been effectively employed. To show how the paragraph was written, we can divide it up by giving items from the list their numbers, by italicizing transitions, and by providing the order of the paragraph in the margin as follows:

topic sentence	**Eaton Corporation has established an effective communication system based on the**
employees	**concept of group work** [topic sentence]. **Every morning** *Eaton* **workers meet with supervisors who give quizzes concerning the plant's productivity** [1]. *In addition,* **monitors in the cafeteria display comparisons between shifts and between costs and performance goals** [8]. *Supervisors* **say that if employees know how the company's success benefits them, then they will be more interested in helping to save on costs**
groups	[6]. *To this end,* **employees work in groups to improve communication** [9]. **These** *groups* **look for opportunities to cut costs and improve plant efficiency** [10]. **The**
general cost benefits	*plant* **has benefited from these groups, but so have the employees: To date, employees' suggestions have netted employees $44,000 in credits at the company store** [7].

Now that you have finished the first section of the memo, you are ready to turn to the second. Follow the same guidelines as you did with the first section: (1) Establish a topic sentence; (2) provide a logical order for the items on your list; (3) use adequate transitions to tie the items from the list together. Look at the items listed beneath your second heading:

What Are the Financial Rewards of the New Communication System?

prof **2. Employees have saved the company money 193 times this year.**

prof **3. Last year Eaton lost $12 million; this year it made $33 million.**

prof **4. Eaton's productivity has risen 3 percent a year for the decade, compared to the industry average of 1.9 percent.**

prof **5. Employees have made suggestions that have saved Eaton $1.4 million.**

prof **11. One group discovered a new way to make dies last longer; this saves Eaton $50,000 a year.**

prof **12. Another group built machines at the costs of $80,000 and $250,000; outside vendors would have charged $350,000 and $250,000.**

prof **13. These machines caused an increase in departmental output of 100%.**

This is the most important section of the memo because it contains information that will be most interesting to the board of directors, your intended audience: profits. Cost savings and profitability are the main elements of this list. Thus, they should be used to construct a topic sentence as follows:

Eaton's new communication system has led to cost savings and profits through improved worker efficiency.

This topic sentence accomplishes three objectives: (1) The focus is still on communication as the memo's subject line indicates; (2) the focus has been narrowed to cost savings and profits; (3) the last part of the topic sentence—"improved worker efficiency"—provides a good transition from the information under the first heading.

The next step is to provide a logical order for the items on the list. There are three different general ideas expressed: (1) Eaton's improved profitability over the last year; (2) Eaton's improved productivity over the last decade when compared to the rest of the industry; and (3) Eaton employees' improved communication via groups leading to greater plant efficiency.

The task is now to order these three elements. A general to specific approach would probably be the easiest to use because the paragraph would build up to those facts of primary interest to Eaton's Board of Directors. Using this order, begin with Eaton's overall improved productivity (item 2), move to Eaton's profitability over the last year (item 1), and then focus the majority of this section's information on demonstrating how Eaton's improved communication system has led to cost savings and profitability.

Also, use a list. A list is extremely effective in that it presents highly important information from the audience's point of view, and it presents it in a manner that makes it stand out from the surrounding text.

Using this logical order, the section can be written as follows:

Eaton's new communication system has led to cost savings through improved worker efficiency. Although Eaton Corporation has achieved a rise in productivity of 3 percent a year for the last decade, compared to the industry average of 1.9

percent, this has not helped Eaton's profitability. Last year, Eaton lost $12 million. However, with the new communication system, Eaton Corporation has made $33 million this year.

This new communication system has encouraged employees to make 193 suggestions this year alone. These suggestions have saved Eaton $1.4 million. To illustrate the effectiveness of these suggestions, two examples spring immediately to mind:

1. Employees discovered a new way to make dies last longer. Savings to Eaton Corporation: $50,000 a year.

2. Employees built machines for $80,000 and $250,000; vendors would have charged Eaton $350,000 and $250,000 for identical machines. Savings to Eaton Corporation: Employees are released from routine tasks to concentrate on more challenging work, and department output has increased 100%.

This section of the memo has been split into three parts to make it more rhetorically effective. The first paragraph introduces the Board of Directors to the idea that although Eaton had been doing well, it had not done well enough to avoid a loss. This then logically leads to the reintroduction of the communication system and its profitability. To the Board of Directors, this comparison between the past and the present makes the numbers for the present that much more telling. The second paragraph once again uses the subject line's thesis that communication has led to improved profits. The list then highlights how profitable the new system has been. Sentence fragments are employed in each paragraph to further highlight the profit and cost-saving aspects of the new system. Because everything in this memo relates to the communication system, the paragraph is well integrated; it has only one main idea but several parts that are fully and effectively developed.

To show how the section was written, we can divide it up by giving items from the list their numbers, by italicizing transitions, and by providing the order of the paragraph in the margin as follows:

topic sentence	**Eaton's new communication system has led to cost savings through improved**
Eaton's overall productivity	**worker efficiency** [topic sentence]. *Although* **Eaton Corporation has achieved a rise in productivity of 3 percent a year for the last decade, compared to the industry average of 1.9 percent** [4], **this has not helped Eaton's profitability** [3]. *Last year,* **Eaton lost $12 million** [3]. *However,* **with the new communication system, Eaton Corporation has**
Eaton's improved profits	**made $33 million this year** [3].
	This *new communication system* **has encouraged employees to make 193 suggestions this year alone** [2]. **These** *suggestions* **have saved Eaton $1.4 million**
Cost savings and profitability	[5]. **To illustrate the effectiveness of these** *suggestions,* **two examples spring immediately to mind:**
	1. **Employees discovered a new way to make dies last longer. Savings to Eaton Corporation: $50,000 a year** [11].

>   **2. Employees built machines for $80,000 and $250,000; vendors would have charged Eaton $350,000 and $250,000 for identical machines [12]. Savings to Eaton Corporation: Employees are released from routine tasks to concentrate on more challenging work, and department output has increased 100% [13].**

To finish this memo, one more thing needs to be done: Establish a goodwill ending. Most people when faced with ending a memo achieve only a generic ending. Too often, memos such as the one illustrated in this chapter end with one of the following types of statements:

>   *Looking forward:* **Eaton Corporation looks forward to heightened profitability.**
>
>   *Restatement:* **Eaton Corporation has a new communication system that helps both the employees and the corporation.**

You can readily see how ineffective such endings are. In the first one, the "looking forward" phrase has become so overused in so many business documents that it means little. Furthermore, is it not logical that a corporation would look forward to profits? What corporation looks forward to losses? This is merely false enthusiasm that attempts to hide the generic ending. The second ending is little better. Obviously, the communication system helps Eaton, so why restate the obvious? Again, the writer has little to say, so the writer restates what has been said.

When you write your ending, do not be generic. Say something about something to real people. To create an effective ending, do one of the following:

1. Add details with respect to people in the corporation.
2. Add details that demonstrate you are focusing on your corporation specifically.
3. Add details that speak to the audience's needs or aspirations.
4. Ask the reader to do something.
5. Invite the reader to do something.

To illustrate the effectiveness of these suggested endings, an example of each follows:

>   **1. All three of our departmental groups—Hoods, Worms, and Scrap Attack—assure Eaton's Board of Directors that ever-increasing efficiency is their raison d'être.**

Here, the writer has made the message personal and used a phrase—"raison d'être"— to appeal to a sophisticated audience. These are real people portraying their working philosophy.

>   **2. Eaton Corporation has achieved a communication system that other corporations will undoubtedly emulate.**

By referring to the communication system, the writer here ties the memo together while at the same time lauding the system's benefits.

>   **3. With the new communication system working so effectively, the Board of Directors has an efficient system that can be used throughout the corporation.**

The writer has made a suggestion to the board, and one the board would want to employ because it would fulfill the board's need and aspirations for increasing profits.

4. The plant managers here at Eaton ask the Board of Directors for any suggestions with respect to other plant areas that could be improved.

A question can often be a compliment; this is the case with number 4. By asking the board for input, you would be acknowledging its expertise.

5. All of the employees at the plant invite Eaton's Board of Directors on a tour of the plant to see how the new communication system works. Please contact John Dereck at 555-5483 to arrange for a tour.

This ending makes an offer that displays the writer's pride in Eaton and a willingness and enthusiasm to share it.

Any of these endings can be effective. The one you choose will depend on your corporate culture and on what you know about your audience. For example, number 1 may be too pretentious, because of "raison d'être", for some corporations, while number 3, suggesting that the new communication system should be used throughout the corporation, may be seen as too forward in others. You must know your audience. This will determine the appropriate ending for you.

Box 4.3 provides the completed informative memo that this chapter has developed. Box 4.4 (page 40) provides a review sheet for your own informative memo.

BOX 4.3

The Completed Informative Memo

Date: 29 Nov. 1994
To: Eaton Board of Directors
From: J. Smith
Re: Eaton's New Communication System Creates Profits

This memo provides information with respect to Eaton Corporation's profitable new communication system. The following memo discusses how the new communication system works and how profitable it has become.

WHAT IS THE NEW COMMUNICATION SYSTEM?

Eaton Corporation has established an effective communication system based on the concept of group work. Every morning Eaton workers meet with supervisors who give quizzes concerning the plant's productivity. In addition, monitors in the cafeteria display comparisons between shifts and between cost and performance goals. Supervisors say that if employees know how the company's success benefits them, then they will be more interested in helping to save on costs. To this end, employees work in groups to improve communication. These groups look for opportunities to cut costs and improve plant efficiency. The plant has benefited from these groups, but so have the employees: To date, employees' suggestions have netted employees $44,000 in credits at the company store.

continued

WHAT ARE THE FINANCIAL REWARDS OF THE NEW COMMUNICATION SYSTEM?

Eaton's new communication system has led to cost savings through improved worker efficiency. Although Eaton Corporation has achieved a rise in productivity of 3 percent a year for the last decade, compared to the industry average of 1.9 percent, this has not helped Eaton's profitability. Last year, Eaton lost $12 million. However, with the new communication system, Eaton Corporation has made $33 million this year.

This new communication system has encouraged employees to make 193 suggestions this year alone. These suggestions have saved Eaton $1.4 million. To illustrate the effectiveness of these suggestions, two examples spring immediately to mind:

1. Employees discovered a new way to make dies last longer. Savings to Eaton Corporation: $50,000 a year.

2. Employees built machines for $80,000 and $250,000; vendors would have charged Eaton $350,000 and $250,000 for identical machines. Savings to Eaton Corporation: Employees are released from routine tasks to concentrate on more challenging work, and department output has increased 100%.

All of the employees at the plant invite Eaton's Board of Directors on a tour of the plant to see how the new communication system works. Please contact John Dereck at 555-5483 to arrange a tour.

BOX 4.4

Informative Message Review Sheet

1. Is the subject line specific enough? Does it provide a concise statement of focus for the entire memo?

2. Does a reminder statement begin the memo? Does it state the purpose of the message combined with a general statement of the subject?

3. Does a forecasting statement follow the reminder statement? Does it precisely forecast the headings?

4. Are the headings specific and informative? Are they all of one form?

5. Does each sentence begin with an adequate topic sentence?

6. Do the paragraphs maintain a logical and coherent order? Are the transitions adequate?

7. Is the most important section of the memo the longest?

8. Does the most important section contain a list to effectively highlight information?

9. Is there an effective goodwill ending? Or is it generic?

Conclusion

As you can see, writing an informative memo is not difficult if you prepare well. This format can fit all kinds of situations—and it can be effective in all of them. Brevity is the crux of this effectiveness, so you must be sure to provide your reader with concise yet precise details.

One of the primary considerations is your audience. Remember whom you are writing to and tailor your memo to fill their informational needs. If your audience is diverse and has different information needs, then do one of two things: (1) You can write in such a way that everyone's needs are filled because you are ensuring that there is something in the memo for each segment of your audience, or (2) you can rewrite the memo for each segment of your audience. (Because the informative memo is brief, the latter can be accomplished without too much writing hardship.)

Although this chapter has used the memo as the model format, the informative message need not be a memo. In some situations a letter, for example, may be more appropriate—it all depends on your audience and your purpose. The most effective format could even be e-mail. With today's computerized communication network, e-mail has, in certain business cultures, replaced the informative memo. In fact, e-mail is not much different from the informative message. The only difference lies in the intended audience: with e-mail, the message is usually sent to one person or a small group, and therefore the message can be made personal as well as abbreviated. As box 4.5 illustrates, e-mail is best approached as a shortened informative message.

BOX 4.5

Gil Schwartz's Article "E-ffective Mail"

I got an electronic message the other day from a guy whom I thought was my friend. "It has come to our attention you haven't yet RSVP'd to yr invitation vis a vis the november 9 security analyst's meeting in petaluma at which you are scheduled to participate in a panel on out-year restructuring," read the missive. "Pls inform Donna on extension #4568 about your intentions/needs for transportation and hotel accommodations immediately. Bert." Man, was that terse.

I called him up. "Hey, Bert," I said. "You mad at me about something?"

"No, man!" he yelped. Bert always speaks like a man at one end of a wind tunnel. "I ain't mad! I just wanted to snap you a quick e-mail on it! Don't you just love your e-mail? Ain't it a real time-saver!"

"Sure, Bert," I said. "Here you've only spent time writing the message, I've spent time reading it, and we've had a nice phone call about it, too. That's what I call a real time-saver."

So it goes. To the time we spend on everything else in this life, we now must add the time we are forced to spend clarifying e-mails.

continued

The people who communicate the worst love e-mails the most. "Did you get my e-mail?!" they chortle. And you must answer, "Yeah, Chuck, I got your e-mail. Now, what was it supposed to be about? And can we talk about whatever it is . . . right now? On the phone? Like we used to?"

The tragic thing is, it doesn't have to be this way. E-mails don't have to stink as a communications vehicle. There are really only three elements to excellent e-mail: clarity, brevity, and extreme courtesy. It's a stone-cold medium, *so put a smile in your voice when you write that puppy, will you, Bud?*

Thanks. Let's move on. Here are six essential templates to help the novice e-mailer craft e-messages while remaining somewhat human, if you believe that is indeed a virtue.

1. **The "Please get back to me about something" message.** Sure, you need a response. But don't be nugatory—be nice! *Viz: Dear _____, I can't believe it's been so long since we traded e-mails! Let's ameliorate that situation real soon! Like now! And while you're at it, what's your response on the Forbisher proposal? I await your reply . . . like today! Time's a-wasting! Your associate, Larry.* See? Friendly! Demonstrative! Affable! That's the ticket!

2. **The "I will be attending the meeting on the 18th" message.** Getting to someone with timely data on upcoming plans is important. But why make it perfunctory just because it's short? Do better. As in: *Dear _____, Until this morning I had no reason to live. Yes! I will attend your seminar on the tax implications of limited partnerships in leveraged development scenarios! Wouldn't miss it! Yours till the prime rate falls, Barry.* For one second, the person receiving this may doubt your seriousness as a person. That's good, especially if you are an essentially serious person.

3. **The "Here are my ideas on the Flabushnik situation" message.** The purpose of any such communication is to make your recipient want to know more. To wit: *Dear _____, The Flabushnik thing will work if we 1) pay him enough money, 2) make him go away by next Thursday. Send up a smoke signal if you agree. Thnx. Harry.* Pithy? Yep! Cybernetic? No way!

4. **The "Here's what I think of your idea on the marketing issue" message.** Sometimes you need to communicate something equivocal. All the more reason to be tender, warm, and loving. *Dear _____, A free poached salmon with guacamole is waiting for you next Tuesday at 12:30 p.m. at Cafe Fauteuil. At that time, you may also hear the six things I think are wrong with your proposal of October 3rd. See ya there! Best, Gary.* Who could resent that?

5. **The "Here's what I plan to do in regard to Ms. Cromagnon" message.** Most sensitive are human resource issues that pertain to individuals who need schooling of some sort. Beware! A whisper of an indication with a soupçon of deniability is all that's required: *My dear _____, Ms. Cromagnon's obvious strengths as an employee must have become obvious to someone at some point in her illustrious career. Please forward such evidence to me, as I must confess that her existing file is bulging with conflicting impressions. Looking forward to your reply, I remain yours very truly, Maury.*

6. The "Here's what I really think about the chairman's plan to acquire Romania" message. Finally, various and sundry people will be stupid enough to call for dangerous opinions to be expressed in this forum. Resist. *Call me, _____, There are some things that don't belong on e-mail and this here is one of them. Ten-four. Jerry.*

And when you sit down to write your 23rd cryptic minimessage of the day—how about a really bright idea, Sparky?
Pick up a phone!

Source: Schwartz, Gil. "E-ffective Mail." *PC Computing* Oct. 1994: 49.
Reprinted from PC Computing October 1994 Copyright © 1994 Ziff-Davis Publishing Company.

Exercises

4.1: Take the same document that you revised for its design elements in exercise 3.1 in chapter 3. This time, complete the following steps:

1. Rework the contents of the document by providing proper topic sentences, lists, appropriate paragraph sequencing, headings if appropriate, margins, etc.

   Option 1: Fax the original document, and e-mail the revised document.
   Option 2: Submit both documents to your instructor in class.

4.2: Reread box 4.1. Based on its information, write a memo to other plant managers who are not using your communication system.

4.3: Reread box 4.1. Based on its information, write a memo to prospective employees (Boone and Kurtz 232).

4.4: Locate an informative memo that was sent to you by your employer, your financial aid office, or a school official. Provide a copy of the original document for the instructor. Rewrite it according to the guidelines given in this chapter.

CHAPTER 5

Writing the Negative Message

There come times in every business when you must give bad news to the client, customer, employee, or job applicant. These negative situations, for example, may involve refusing credit; denying an attempted refund, setoff, or rebate; firing an employee; or turning down a job applicant. Although these situations are the most common ones, they are not the only ones. Negative situations come in a variety of forms. Nonetheless, you have a format available. You can use this format for almost any negative message. But as with most business messages, maintaining goodwill is a primary goal.

Purpose of a Negative Message

Businesses write negative messages because clients, customers, or employees cannot always be given what they desire. Yet, though you cannot always give them what they want, you must maintain their goodwill, for if goodwill is not maintained then you have lost potential sales. As you can imagine, the task of refusing someone and yet maintaining goodwill is not an easy one. In the business world, it is simply not enough to politely refuse a request; you must develop methods that will ensure that the very customer whom you have denied will want to continue doing business with you.

This chapter will show you a step-by-step method by which you can refuse yet satisfy the customer or client.

Format

The most effective format for a negative message to a customer, client, or employee is a short letter, no longer than one page. No client or customer will appreciate a long, drawn-out refusal. The letter should follow the guidelines set forth in appendix C.

THE NEGATIVE LETTER

For the purpose of illustration, let us examine a typical business scenario:

> **You run Smith's appliance store. On 5 June 1994, you sold a gas stove to David Sanders, a longtime friend and customer, for $862.76. Two days before delivery, David Sanders sends you a letter stating that he would like to offset the cost of his new stove by turning his old stove over to you. He believes that his old stove has a value of $200, and he would like to apply this to the purchase price of his new stove. In the course of the letter, David tells you that his stove is seven years old, and it runs on electricity. Because you are in the appliance business, you are quite familiar with David's stove. It is an HPC model 300, and it is no longer being manufactured. You also know that parts for it are no longer available.**

What do you do? You want to make the sale and maintain your profit margin. At the same time, you don't want to lose David's goodwill over a mere $200. He has, after all, purchased many items from you over the course of the last 5 years.

Your friends in the appliance business tell you that you have a sales contract, and that's that. But you are not going to sue for that amount. It would take you five years to get to court, and, assuming that you win the suit, you would only receive the difference between David's sale price and what you actually sold the stove for. You have a problem, but there is a way out: Use the negative message formula.

The Negative Message Formula

You are going to write a fine negative letter to David Sanders. It will be a letter that denies his offset request yet maintains his goodwill. To accomplish this, you will follow a formula that can be applied to most negative situations.

The letter will consist of four parts: buffer statement, explanation, alternatives, and goodwill ending (Bovee and Thill 269; Guffey 196; Locker 182–83). Each part will be a paragraph in length.

Buffer Statements   The first sentence or two of your negative message to David Sanders is the buffer statement. The purpose of the buffer statement is to avoid alienating or angering the reader. Say something positive, and relate this positive statement to the explanation and alternative paragraphs that follow (Guffey 198). From the buffer statement, the reader should not be able to determine whether what follows is good or bad news. However, a note of warning: Do not mislead the reader. For example, if you are turning down a credit application, avoid saying something like, "Good customers like you are always appreciated." This implies an acceptance. Similarly, avoid writing, "In tough economic times, credit is hard to come by." This implies a refusal.

Writing a good buffer statement depends on the context of the negative situation. Some buffer statements simply work better than others because they are more appropriate to the negative situation or to the reader's circumstances.

In addition, in some circumstances you may not wish to use a buffer statement at all. Sometimes the negative message is not all that bad, or you know that the reader already knows bad news is coming (Locker 186). Sometimes people or businesses prefer bluntness to indirection. If you know this to be the case, then omit the buffer.

Finally, sometimes people will become hostile when confronted with bad news. It is then best simply to be direct (Locker 186).

Bearing these qualifications in mind, you must find the buffer statement most appropriate and effective for David's situation. In their book *Contemporary Business Communication*, Boone and Kurtz point out that there are five kinds of buffer statements:

1. *Appreciation*: Thanks the reader for his or her contribution, thoughts, claim, credit application, job application, or inquiry.

2. *Agreement*: Refers to an area of common ground shared by the reader and the writer.

3. *General principle*: Starts with a statement that defines company business practices.

4. *Chronology of past communication*: Retraces what has happened to reach this point.

5. *Compliment*: Praises the reader's actions or contributions. (238)

In our hypothetical situation, then, we have five possible buffers to choose from:

1. *Appreciation:* **Thank you for your order of a new stove.**

2. *Agreement:* **In purchasing a new gas stove, we both agree that its cost savings far exceed those of an electric stove.**

3. *General principle:* **It is the policy of Smith's Appliance to ensure customer satisfaction.**

4. *Chronology of past communication:* **When you purchased your new stove, we discussed the possibility of a trade-in if we could see a market for selling your old stove.**

5. *Compliment:* **By purchasing your new gas stove, you have demonstrated that you are a discerning consumer.**

So, which of the above buffer statements do you choose? The answer is to choose the one that is related to the refusal that follows in the second paragraph. Although not all buffers are equally easy to use and there are degrees of difficulty involved in using them, you should be able to use any buffer. Therefore, to ease your decision concerning the choice of buffer, choose the buffer that is related to your reason for refusal.

Explanation   Once you have selected your buffer statement, then explain why you cannot do that which is being requested of you. This second paragraph will lead up to the actual refusal.

When constructing the second paragraph, bear in mind three general but crucial principles. First, make this paragraph about six to eight sentences long. If it is any longer, you may upset and alienate the reader. Remember, you are trying to speed the reader through this paragraph so that you can help the reader with the information you will provide in the next paragraph (Bovee and Thill 272; Guffey 199).

Second, provide logical reasons for your refusal. These reasons for refusal should be given *before* the actual refusal itself. As Bovee and Thill state "[S]omeone who realizes you are saying no before he or she understands why may either quit paying attention altogether or be set to rebut the reasons when they are finally given" (270). Do not attempt to exaggerate or underplay the reasons for your refusal. Be straight with your reader. Finally, be selective with your reasons for refusal. You may have a host of reasons for refusal, but choose the two or three best reasons. Avoid providing weak reasons. If you do include both strong and weak reasons, rest assured that the reader will focus on the weak ones. The reader will then believe your refusal to be inadequate or unreasonable (Locker 189). Also avoid using even strong reasons for refusal if they reflect badly on the personnel or operations of the business (Locker 189). If possible, you might place the blame for the refusal on a law or government agency. You have no control over either one of these, so any bad feelings that the reader may have concerning your refusal will be transferred to either or both of them. But do not blame a person or a company policy. The former is in bad taste, while the latter will lead readers to believe that "the policy is designed to benefit you at their expense" (Locker 188).

Third, make sure that your refusal comes across loud and clear (Locker 188). You want to avoid further discussion or debate on this topic. If the refusal is unclear, the reader will be confused and will once again demand what you thought you had refused. At the same time, you don't want to anger or alienate the reader by making the refusal personal. You have three options available. Option one is to write the refusal sentence in the passive voice. As Guffey puts it, "Passive voice verbs enable you to depersonalize an action" (201). Option two is to place the refusal at the end of the paragraph. The reasons for refusal, then, will logically lead up to the actual refusal, and the refusal will be that much more effective. As Bovee and Thill sum it up, "It is important to explain *why* you have reached your decision before you explain *what* that decision is. If you present your reasons effectively, they will help convince the audience that your decision is justified, fair, and logical" (270). Option three is both to write the refusal in the passive voice and to place it at the end of this paragraph.

Fourth, avoid the pronoun *you* throughout this paragraph—except in the first sentence, as you will see in the discussion of the paragraph's opening sentence. If you use *you* in relation to your reasons for refusal, then you will make the refusal personal and you will only create antagonism.

Now, let us construct our second paragraph to David Sanders. The first thing to do, whatever the buffer, is to create a transitional sentence that leads into the discussion of the reasons for refusal in the second paragraph. Avoid beginning the sentence with words such as *although* or *despite* because these words already imply the upcoming refusal. Instead, construct this sentence by referring to a prior communication. This should be relatively simple. You must have communicated with David Sanders in some way, either during the sale or after it, verbally or in writing. Therefore, begin this second paragraph with a sentence that refers to this prior communication. A useful beginning might be *when last we spoke* or *in your letter of.* Here, the pronoun *you* can be employed since it suggests nothing negative. But if there is a *you* in this paragraph, make sure that it only occurs here, in the first sentence.

In addition to making a transition in the opening sentence, remember to mention what the customer has requested. In our scenario, David has requested that you accept a trade-in to offset the cost of the new stove.

The first sentence to David, then, can read as follows:

In your letter of 10 June 1994, you requested a trade-in of your old stove to offset the cost of the new one.

Now it is time to provide David with the logical reasons his stove cannot be accepted as a trade-in. To downplay both the reasons for refusal and the refusal itself, state that you have analyzed or researched the possibility of a trade-in. Once you have suggested the possibility of a trade-in, then you can give the reasons for refusal. Signpost these reasons as if they were merely facts to be considered. But before writing this paragraph, get the facts in order.

In David's situation, you know that his stove

1. is 7 years old,
2. is no longer being manufactured,
3. lacks replacement parts, and
4. runs on electricity—a costly source of energy that most consumers would wish to avoid.

Once you have listed the relevant facts, categorize them. You can do this in two ways. First, give the reasons for refusal in the order of least to most important. Place the most important last because it will precede the refusal sentence and thus will enhance the logic of the refusal itself. Second, consider whether any of your reasons for refusal can be combined. If they can be combined, then do so. In this way, you will reduce the length of the explanation paragraph. Here, the first three reasons can be combined as one category, and the fourth can stand alone as another category. But which of the two categories is the most important? It is axiomatic that people are motivated and influenced by economics. Hence, number 4 is probably the reason that David will be most influenced by in the sense that it will forcefully and logically connect with the refusal that will follow it.

Now you are ready to write this section of this paragraph. Following the guidelines, the paragraph can continue as follows:

> **I have analyzed the situation, and I have discovered two important facts. First, because the HPC model stove is seven years old, it will undoubtedly require replacement parts in the near future. I contacted the manufacturer who said that this stove is no longer being manufactured. Anyone who purchased your stove would therefore have a difficult time finding replacement parts. Second, your stove runs on electricity—a costly source of energy that most consumers would wish to avoid.**

Note that this paragraph contains the pronoun *I* throughout. This is a good choice. By using this pronoun you are demonstrating your personal involvement, your concern for the needs of the customer. Furthermore, you have placed the blame on the stove rather than on the reader, David. It is the stove's fault, not David's. This is a good technique to employ. Always strive, if possible, to place the blame or the cause of the problem onto something else. You will often encounter federal or state guidelines—such as OSHA rules—that can be blamed. Or you can place the blame on the product itself. However, never blame a person. This simply makes you look like one who is passing the buck.

You are now ready to write the last sentence of this paragraph. The refusal sentence consists of two parts: a reference to the reasons for refusal and the refusal itself. To refer to the reasons for refusal, begin by saying something like *for these reasons*, or *based on the foregoing observations*. The rest of the sentence will state the refusal in the passive voice. Use the passive voice to avoid the pronoun *you*, which would only antagonize your reader. Thus, the last sentence can read as follows:

> **Based on the foregoing observations, a trade-in or offset cannot be given.**

Note that you did not refer directly to the reader, yet the reader knows exactly what is refused and who is doing the refusing. This paragraph is also only seven sentences long.

Alternatives The alternatives paragraph is probably the most important one you will write, yet it is also the easiest. In this paragraph you want to demonstrate your concern for your customer. After all, you may have refused the request, yet you do want to maintain goodwill and thus ensure future business with the customer. As Locker points out, you should provide an alternative for a number of reasons.

1. It offers the reader another way to get what he or she wants.
2. It suggests that you really care about the reader and about helping to meet his or her needs.
3. It enables the reader to reestablish the psychological freedom you limited when you said *no*.
4. It allows you to end on a positive note and to present yourself and your organization as positive, friendly, and helpful. (190)

It would be a good idea, however, to provide more than one alternative. If you provide at least two alternatives, you are giving the reader a choice. As Locker states, this is crucial so that the reader regains the "psychological freedom you limited when you said *no*" (190).

If you fulfill the requirements of this paragraph, you will probably ensure future business with your customer. If you fail here, the customer may lose confidence in you or your business. With a little care, you can ensure future success with the customer.

Because your reader has swiftly gone through the second paragraph, it is important that you begin the third with a word that will ensure continued reading. After all, the reader has just been turned down; why continue reading the letter? The word that ensures continued reading is *however*. With this one word, you dilute the power of the refusal sentence, which immediately preceded this word. When the reader sees *however*, the reader knows that the opposite—or near opposite—of what has just been said is forthcoming. And you will provide this opposite.

After this *however*, the rest of the sentence states that you are providing the reader with alternatives that can meet the request. In this letter to David the sentence can read as follows:

However, I can provide you with two other dealers who may be willing to buy your HPC model stove.

In this paragraph, follow these guidelines:

• Employ the pronoun *you*.
• Provide at least two alternatives and explain them.
• Provide complete addresses and telephone numbers.
• Make this paragraph longer than the explanation paragraph. Use a list if you need to lengthen this paragraph to make it appear longer than the second paragraph.

You are giving good news, and using the pronoun *you* will bring you and your reader closer together. Provide names, addresses, and phone numbers because you then

heighten your appeal for future business with this customer. You will have demonstrated that you have made a real effort on the reader's behalf. You want to make this
the longest paragraph because you want to appear more helpful than negative. If this
paragraph does not contain more sentences than the second, then use a list to make
it appear longer.

Thus, when you write to David, the sentences following your opening sentence
of the third paragraph can read as follows:

> **Dave's Discount Warehouse buys used stoves. I have done business with Dave in
> the past, and we still keep in touch, so I know he can be of use to you. The other
> alternative is Elking Machinery. The employees there told me that they buy used
> appliances. Let me give you their addresses:**

> **Dave's Discount Warehouse**
> **David Stephens, Owner**
> **1875 W. Ridge**
> **Bayeaux, TX 79912**
> **(912) 858-3675**

> **Elking Machinery**
> **Robert Barron, Manager**
> **9567 Industrial**
> **Bayeaux, TX 79912**
> **(915) 858-3969**

Although this paragraph contains only five sentences, by providing a list of
names and addresses it actually appears longer than the second paragraph. Thus, at a
glance, the reader focuses on the positive aspects of helping David rather than on refusing him.

Also note that this paragraph adds a personal touch. By indicating that you have
personally dealt with these people before, you are implying that you are sending David
to real alternatives, rather than having just picked the alternatives out of a phone book.

There are those, however, and my business writing students are often among
them, who argue that by providing alternatives you are sending business away rather
than keeping it. To some degree, this is true. But note what has been done in the alternatives paragraph. David has been sent to second-hand dealers not to other appliance retailers who directly compete with you. This is important. You might lose business by sending David to your competitors, but you have not done this. Even assuming
that you did send David to a competitor, though, it should not matter all that much.
David will remember who helped him, and that person is you. In the future, when
David requires a service or a product, you will be foremost in his mind. Looked at
in this way, have you really lost any business? You may have lost a current sale, but
you have probably saved future sales. This thinking is illustrated in the movie *Mira-
cle on 34th Street*. In this film, a Macy's Santa Claus sends customers to other stores
when Macy's does not have the item they want to buy. The result is that Macy's does
more business than ever before because customers know that if Macy's doesn't have
the item they want, Macy's will help them find the item at another store. Thus, they
shop at Macy's first, thereby increasing Macy's sales potential.

Of course, you may find yourself in a situation where you may be able to provide the required service yourself. If this situation arises, then promote your own services first. In other words, if you can fix the situation, emphasize that in the alternative paragraph. You should also provide another alternative, but this alternative can be downplayed. Devote most of the paragraph to what you can do for the customer. Then in the last lines of the paragraph provide an additional alternative. Following this format will increase your chances of gaining additional revenue. If the reader chooses the other alternative, you still maintain goodwill.

Goodwill Ending   The close of this letter should be brief. It should reiterate the fact that you have actually helped David solve his problem.

The simplest way to accomplish this and thereby maintain David's goodwill is (1) to refer to the alternatives and (2) to suggest that in choosing one of them the customer will receive satisfaction.

In David's case, we can easily accomplish this task by writing a sentence as follows:

By choosing either of the dealerships above, you will be able to receive fair market value for your HPC model stove.

If you look at the buffer statements that you could have chosen, you will note that they are all related to the idea of stoves, customer satisfaction, or maintaining goodwill. This closing statement carries all three of these ideas in one sentence.

Once David has read this letter, he should be satisfied with the response. Although you refused his request, you gave him alternatives that he can pursue to get what he wants. You have been helpful. And David will remember this the next time he requires an appliance. In sum, you have kept his business, which is the primary purpose of the negative letter.

Also note that the ending is not generic. It is not one of those thank-you-for-your-business endings that may as well be rubber-stamped at the end of a letter (Locker 190). Further, it avoids the other typical if-you-have-questions-call-me-at-000-0000 endings that only invite the reader to call and reargue the issue that you have already resolved with your negative letter (Bovee and Thill 272–73).

Write an ending that is not a cliché, that does not refer to the refusal, that does not apologize for the refusal, and that does not use words such as *hope, try*, or *attempt*—all words that suggest your letter has not fulfilled its purpose in refusing the request. Instead, end on a positive and sincere note (Locker 190).

Box 5.1 (pages 52–53) provides the completed negative letter to David Sanders.

Conclusion

In writing the negative letter, keep in mind the following five considerations:

1. Length
2. Tone
3. When to apologize
4. Negative words
5. Legal issues

BOX 5.1

The Completed Negative Letter

Bob's Appliance
6800 N. Smith St.
Bayeaux, TX 79912

12 June 1994

David Sanders
456 Elk St.
Bayeaux, TX 79908

Dear Mr. Sanders:

In purchasing a new gas stove, we both agree that its cost savings far exceed those of an electric stove.

In your letter of 10 June 1994, you requested a trade-in of your old stove to offset the cost of the new one. I have analyzed the situation, and I have discovered two important facts. First, because the HPC model stove is seven years old, it will undoubtedly require replacement parts in the near future. I contacted the manufacturer who said that this stove is no longer being manufactured. Anyone who purchased your stove would therefore have a difficult time finding replacement parts. Second, your stove runs on electricity—a costly source of energy that most consumers would wish to avoid. Based on the foregoing observations, a trade-in or offset cannot be given.

However, I can provide you with two other dealers who may be willing to buy your HPC model stove. Dave's Discount Warehouse buys used stoves. I have done business with Dave in the past, and we still keep in touch, so I know that he can be of use to you. The other alternative is Elking Machinery. The employees there told me that they buy used appliances. Let me give you their addresses:

Dave's Discount Warehouse
David Stephens, Owner
1875 W. Ridge
Bayeaux, TX 79912
(912) 858-3675

Elking Machinery
Robert Barron, Manager
9567 Industrial
Bayeaux, TX 79912
(915) 858-3969

By choosing either of the dealerships above, you will be able to receive fair market value for your HPC model stove.

Sincerely,

Bob Johnson
Owner

LENGTH

Keep your letter to about one page. No reader wants to receive a long-winded explanation. Besides, if the letter even appears lengthy, many readers will avoid reading it all.

TONE

Your tone will determine how effective your negative message is. Strive to be tactful yet informative. As Bovee and Thill explain, the appropriate tone helps in achieving three important objectives:

- Helping your audience understand that your bad-news message represents a firm decision
- Helping your audience understand that under the circumstances, your decision was fair and reasonable
- Helping your audience remain well disposed toward your business and possibly toward you (268)

WHEN TO APOLOGIZE

Apologizing to your reader that something has gone amiss and that it is your fault is not necessarily a bad thing to do. Marcia Mascolini has pointed out in a recent issue of *The Bulletin of the Association for Business Communication* that many "real" negative letters from businesses to customers do contain an apology (45). This, she points out, goes against much of current opinion with respect to negative messages: Many textbook writers argue against apologizing (45). Mascolini adds that more research is needed on this question and many others with respect to negative messages before any clear-cut or definitive answers can be given (47).

Perhaps a rule of thumb with respect to this issue can be formulated. If you have done something wrong, then feel free to apologize. But do it early and do it once. If you apologize more than once, you may appear to be both groveling and vulnerable:

two characteristics that the reader may see as an advantage to be exploited to your detriment. Further, do not apologize when the fault lies with the customer or when there is no fault at all (Bovee and Thill 271). Too many people apologize for nothing. It is as if the apology is made simply to make the customer feel good. But does the customer really benefit? After all, the refusal is still there. Isn't it more likely that the business that sent the negative letter will appear groveling or vulnerable?

For example, what if you told David that you are sorry that you can't accept his old stove as a trade-in? Doesn't this look like you are at fault? Don't you think that David might see this possibility as well and therefore try to exploit it? Would this not lead to the destruction of the effectiveness of your negative letter? Could it be possible that David would sever his business with you after he ultimately discovers that you were serious about your refusal? Any benefit in apologizing merely to make the reader feel good is certainly outweighed by the hazards.

NEGATIVE WORDS

Strive to avoid words such as *unfortunately*, and never blame the reader.

LEGAL ISSUES

You must weigh certain legal considerations before you send your negative letter. If, for example, you are an employee of a company, remember that you are acting as the company's agent when you send the letter. But whether you are acting as an agent or acting on your own behalf, do not

1. make promises when you don't know that they will or can be fulfilled;
2. admit fault for something that led to damage to a person or a person's property;
3. use offensive language against the reader: don't call the reader such things as "liar," "cheat," or "embezzler";
4. provide information that the reader does not need. (Guffey 197–98)

All such actions can lead to legal actions. A court may construe the first as a breach of contract, the second as an admission of liability, the third as defamation, and the fourth as any number of legal grounds for action, depending on the kind of information volunteered (Guffey 197–98).

Box 5.2 provides a review sheet for the negative letter.

Exercises

5.1: Write buffer statements for the following scenarios.

1. **Scenario:** Your company, Visa Gold, has sent out credit card applications offering 6.9% APR. One person who responded has an income of $1500 a year; he's a student. You must turn him down gently; he might apply later when he has an income.

   Appreciation:

   Agreement:

BOX 5.2

Negative Letter Review Sheet

1. Does this letter follow the proper letter format?
2. Does the letter begin with a buffer statement? How good is it?
3. Is there an adequate transition to the refusal paragraph?
4. Does the writer give precise and logical reasons for the refusal?
5. Does the writer place the blame for the refusal onto some inanimate entity?
6. Is the refusal written in the passive voice?
7. Is the alternatives paragraph longer than the refusal one? Does it begin with *however*?
8. Does the writer provide at least two alternatives?
9. Are the alternatives specific enough?
10. Does the letter end with a goodwill ending? Does it refer to the alternatives?

General principle:

Chronology:

Compliment:

2. **Scenario:** Your customer purchased a new jeep four years ago. The purchase price was $25,000 because it was a special model with all the newest features: antilock brakes, tinted windows, CD player, leather seats, fuel injected V-6. Last week, the customer rolled onto the lot, and you didn't recognize the jeep. It looked twenty rather than four years old: One headlight was smashed, dings and long scrapes scarred the paint, and the interior was discolored and trashed. The customer tells you that he drove the jeep all through the jungle mountains of Costa Rica. He also states that a jeep should be able to take the punishment a customer dishes out. He has asked you for a new paint job. You know that the paint warranty has expired, and, judging by the body damage, the customer will need a new jeep in the near future. You must turn down his request, but, at the same time, you want to preserve the possibility of a future sale.

Appreciation:

Agreement:

General principle:

Chronology:

Compliment:

3. Scenario: You are a salesperson at a large department store. One of the hottest selling items this season has been the Ultimate Food Processor. Today, you received a letter from a woman, a chemist, who purchased the food processor. She states that the item is defective, and she demands a replacement. She says that she mixed several chemical ingredients in the processor, and now the processor no longer works. She has obviously tried to use the food processor as some kind of centrifuge, and that was certainly not the processor's intended use.

Appreciation:

Agreement:

General principle:

Chronology:

Compliment:

4. Scenario: You have a job opening for a salesperson at your department store, and the position must be filled soon. You have had numerous applications for the job, but one person, Bob Simons, has particularly impressed you. After making his application, Bob has come by your store on several occasions to discuss the position and his enthusiasm for it. You would like to hire Bob, but he has little experience in sales. Two other people who applied have more experience as well as training. You have to turn Bob down, but you would like him to reapply at some later date when he has the requisite training and experience.

Appreciation:

Agreement:

General principle:

Chronology:

Compliment:

5.2: Rewrite the following sentences to downplay their negativity:

1. Your credit card application cannot be granted.
2. You will not receive a new stove as you requested.
3. You are hereby terminated for the above reasons.
4. Simply put, your failure to follow the warranty guidelines means that a new saw will not be sent.
5. Due to improper maintenance, you have violated the warranty contract.
6. Failure to follow the above guidelines must result in your immediate dismissal from this employment.
7. How can you request a new stove when yours is two years old?

8. Company policy states that an employee, such as you, who has shouted at a customer must be fired. Therefore, you are hereby officially fired.

9. Because you lied on your application form, there is just no way that we would hire you.

10. Your request is absurd. Please think of something else, and let us know what it is.

11. We cannot offer you a job at this time.

5.3: Choose one of the scenarios in exercise 5.1, and write a negative letter in response to the request.

5.4: You are the manager of Westside Automotive and Repair. For the last six years, Irwin Engles has brought his car in once a year for a tuneup. He did so this year on 6 November. Your mechanics provided his car with its usual tuneup, and the car ran fine. Two weeks later, you receive a letter from Irwin Engles demanding his money back since his engine had to be repaired. According to Irwin, everything was going smoothly until 13 November. On that day he went shopping in Juarez, Mexico. While there, he purchased gas for his car. From then on, his car began stalling and dying. He took it to Quicker Automotive Service Center. The mechanics there told him that his engine required massive servicing because of clogged fuel injector lines, a filthy fuel pump, and corroded spark plugs. Irwin did not tell the mechanics that he had purchased gas in Juarez. You know that the gas in Mexico has a lower octane level than that in the United States, and sometimes the gas contains impurities. You don't want to lose Irwin as a customer.

Write him a negative letter.

CHAPTER 6

Writing the Persuasive Message

To some degree, all writing is persuasive. Even when you want to merely inform, you are selecting and arranging the information that you think is relevant and that the reader will appreciate. For this reason, many people argue over even simple matters.

Think, for example, of a traffic ticket for speeding. You were caught on radar, and the police officer will testify to that fact. This appears to be a rather straightforward case that you could not possibly win. But people do win all the time even when they were speeding according to the radar device and the officer. How could you win? You could possibly avoid the legal penalty if you could demonstrate that the radar device was operating ineffectively, that it had not been checked for some time, that the officer may have inaccurately read his radar, that the machine may have picked up someone else doing the speeding. It is the selection of material and its arrangement that may help you to avoid the speeding ticket and its consequent fine. In effect, you are trying to persuade the court that the facts are not as they seem, that your interpretation and arrangement of those facts most accurately describes what took place when the officer caught you.

This example exemplifies what Aristotle said in his *Rhetoric*: "Even if our speaker had the most accurate scientific information, still there are persons whom he could not readily persuade with scientific arguments" (page 6). It is not enough to believe that your viewpoint or position is the correct one: You must prove it to the reader. In this scenario, both you and the officer have the task of proving that your version and interpretation of the events is the correct one. Thus, a persuasive message selects the information that supports your view to the maximum effect. You want the reader to accept your view. Therefore, you must find the most effective manner in which to arrange the material that will persuade the reader that your view is not just better than other viewpoints but the best one given the circumstances. By using certain methods and principles, you can effectively demonstrate why your position or viewpoint is the best one.

This chapter shows you how to persuade people that your position is the best one available. To this end, the chapter discusses the general categories of persuasive appeals and the format for persuasive messages, and it provides you with a hypothetical scenario and a step-by-step resolution of the scenario.

General Categories of Persuasive Appeals

More than two thousand years have passed since Aristotle developed the principles of persuasion in his *Rhetoric*. Since that time, the names of some of these principles have changed, but the principles remain the same. Aristotle divided persuasion into three general categories of appeals (that is, ways by which the audience can be persuaded): ethos, pathos, and logos.

ETHOS

An ethical appeal is one that is based on credibility. In other words, you can persuade people based on who you are and how you are perceived by the audience. Commercial advertising provides many examples of ethical appeals. Just think of all those beer commercials that employ famous athletes who say nothing more than that they drink a particular beer. The advertiser is trying to persuade you to buy the beer because the famous athlete buys and drinks it. This is a form of identification: The audience desires to emulate the athlete and is thereby persuaded to buy the beer.

But you are not a famous athlete, so you may ask how you can use this appeal. You must remember that ethos also includes the idea that you must bring a certain level of credibility to your message. This is why ethos is so crucial to your ability to persuade the audience: The audience must believe that you know what you are talking about because you have the requisite expertise. If you do not establish your ethos from the very outset of the persuasive message, then all is lost. No audience will believe in what you say if it cannot believe in your ethos. No matter the power of your logic, if ethos is lacking, the message becomes ineffective.

To achieve this ethos or credibility in your writing, you must know your audience and fulfill its expectations with respect to employing the correct format, the appropriate level of technicality, the right vocabulary, a neatly designed document, and a logical arrangement of the material. If you fulfill these audience expectations, then your ethos is good; if you cannot, then your message loses power and effectiveness.

PATHOS

A pathetic appeal is one that plays to the audience's emotions. You try to persuade by making the audience sad because something is not being done that should be done or because something is occurring that should not be occurring. Take, for example, those commercials that show starving children to persuade us to donate to the cause to help them.

Be very careful in using pathetic appeals. Audiences are quick to realize when you are trying to persuade with emotion. This appeal cannot be overused, or the audience may get the idea that what you lack in real substantive logic you are trying to make up with emotion. Therefore, pathetic appeals must be used sparingly. Furthermore, pathetic appeals do not fit all persuasive situations. They are effective only in situations that lend themselves to emotion. You may, for example, use an emotional appeal when dealing with abortion or the death penalty, but you would not use a pathetic appeal to demonstrate why one car should be purchased rather than another.

In most business writing scenarios, pathetic appeals should be avoided unless the context is an emotional one—a rare circumstance indeed. (The only real exceptions in business writing to the use of the pathetic appeal occur in the fields of advertising and marketing. These kinds of business writing are, however, not within the scope of this book. In fact, they are a different kind of business writing because their purposes are not to fulfill reader expectations but to change or create them.)

LOGOS

A logical appeal is the most effective form of persuasion in business writing for two reasons. First, it relies on fact and inference. These two categories, if adequately demonstrated, appeal to readers because all people like to think of themselves as logical, though they are usually not. Thus, if you can show connections that make sense, readers can be persuaded. Second, logical appeals can be tailored to the situation and context in which you find yourself writing.

When you write a persuasive message, you must ensure that you differentiate between facts, inferences, and opinions. If you do not do so, you leave yourself open to scintillating counterarguments. Aristotle defines facts as the real; in other words, one could say that a fact is that which is not disputed, or better still, a fact is that which the majority of people believe to be true or indisputable. An inference, according to Aristotle, is the probable; in other words, based on the available data, an inference can be drawn that is probably correct. Finally, Aristotle calls an opinion the possible. An opinion may or may not be true, but its accuracy cannot be determined because it lacks supporting data.

Making sure to distinguish between fact, inference, and opinion, you have twenty-eight logical methods that can be used to persuade an audience. (Aristotle, who came up with this number, says that there are more, but that torture, murder, and kidnapping are ineffective means of persuasion since their effectiveness ends when the means used to persuade are no longer used.) But rather than detailing the twenty-eight means of logical persuasion, some of which are difficult to grasp and all of which would be an achievement to remember, you can reduce and categorize them into nine effective logically persuasive tools:

1. History
2. Analogy
3. Example
4. Comparison and contrast
5. Consequences
6. Definition
7. Authority
8. Statistics
9. Maxims

History

You can persuade by using history. You can argue that because something happened in the past with good or bad consequences, the same will happen now with the same consequences. For example, if you are arguing that your corporation should settle a lawsuit immediately, you could argue that Y Corporation did something like this two years ago with good result.

Analogy

Analogy and metaphor can be used to persuade. Here, you are persuading by comparing two items that are different, so that one item helps the reader understand the other. For example, if you are arguing that the deficit is not such a bad thing, then you might point out that the deficit is like a credit card: It is not a bad thing unless you do not possess the ability to pay it off.

Example

Example is an effective way to persuade, especially if your examples are on point. With an example, you are persuading through exemplification and illustration. For example, to argue that your neighbor is a bad person, you could provide the reader with examples demonstrating how bad the neighbor is.

Comparison and Contrast

Comparison and contrast can be used to persuade as long as the items of comparison are of the same class. In other words, do not compare two items that are too different. Comparison and contrast, for example, can be used to argue about the current crisis in the former Yugoslavia. If you are against the idea of U.S. military intervention, then you could argue that involvement in Yugoslavia would be similar to involvement in Vietnam. On the other hand, if you were for U.S. intervention, you could argue that U.S. involvement would be like that in Kuwait.

Consequences

When you persuade from consequences, you are attempting to demonstrate what will happen if something does or does not occur. For example, if you are arguing that abortion should remain a constitutional right, you can show that if the right were denied, women would suffer in back alleys with unsavory abortion doctors; or that women would be economically burdened with the care of a child, resulting in poverty for both; or that children would suffer, lacking love and adequate care. On the other hand, if you were arguing that the right to an abortion should be prohibited, you could argue that the unborn child's rights were being denied; that abortion leads to the psychological impairment of the mother; or that abortion could lead to a further erosion of our basic humanity.

Definition

You can sometimes effectively persuade when the meaning of a word requires definition. For example, let us say that you are an attorney defending a client who is on trial for carrying a knife on his person while attempting to board a plane. The applicable statute states that a person who carries a *hidden* weapon has violated federal law and may serve up to five years in prison. As the attorney, you could argue the meaning of the word *hidden*. *Hidden* connotes an intention to conceal; however, your client carried the knife in a sheath on a belt in view of all persons who might observe him. Therefore, the statute does not apply because your client did not meet the requisite state of mind connoted by the word *hidden*.

Authority

You can demonstrate the validity of your position by citing an authority who agrees with you. An authority is one who carries great expertise in a particular area: one whose expertise is hard to counter. Thus, if you are trying to persuade someone that your concept with respect to quantum physics is valid, you could cite, to great effect, Albert Einstein.

Statistics

Numbers are powerful persuasive tools. People are often persuaded by numbers and statistics. That is why in many debates everyone has statistics on hand to bolster their position. In business, if you can demonstrate that your idea will either make money or save it, you have an effective tool that you can employ.

Maxims

A maxim is a time-honored cliché that most people believe to be true. Thus, "early to bed and early to rise makes a man healthy, wealthy, and wise" is a maxim. Most people accept the inherent truth of it. You, too, can use maxims, but just make sure that they fit the context. And when employing a maxim, be careful. Like pathetic appeals, audiences know a maxim when they see or hear one, so don't overdo it. Maxims are often good ways to introduce a topic or to conclude one, but if used too often, you will lessen their effectiveness.

As you can see from the foregoing examples, logical appeals can be used for or against a position. Decide which ones suit your discussion by deciding what is both relevant to the topic at hand and appropriate to your audience. Because the audience is particularly important in persuasive messages, make a thorough audience analysis before writing the persuasive message.

A Format for Persuasive Messages

Persuasive messages can take many forms, but an easy one to employ is the IRAC method. IRAC is a persuasive method taught in many law schools throughout the country. As such, when employed correctly, you can be sure that it will be effective. IRAC is an acronym that stands for the four parts of the persuasive message: (1) issue, (2) reasoning, (3) analysis, and (4) conclusion.

ISSUE

When using the IRAC method, first determine the issue under discussion. Address the real issue; false issues simply obfuscate and irritate the audience.

Whether this persuasive message is a letter or a memo, begin with a reminder statement that displays empathy with the audience's concerns. Follow this statement with a concise formulation of the issue that you must resolve. (You could even add a buffer statement if you believe that this will lessen the negative impact, if there is one, of your message.)

REASONING

The second section of your persuasive message provides background information on the issue: that is, how it came about. In this section, briefly relate the points that have raised the issue. In many cases, especially those involving customer complaints, you are merely repeating what both you and your audience already know. But repetition ensures that you are addressing the audience's concerns. This will lend credibility to your writing because you are demonstrating that you want to resolve the issue.

ANALYSIS

The third section of your persuasive message must be the longest part of the message. Here, you resolve the issue by employing the logical appeals that make your case and are effective with the audience. (You can use paragraphs or sentences depending on the length of the message.) Order the reasons that you believe resolve the issue in an emphatic order: from least to most important. In addition, provide your answer or resolution right at the outset of this section of the message. Your audience will then know your response. What follows is the support for that response. Do not, however, attempt to give every possible reason that resolves the issue. Limit yourself to two or three. In this way you avoid unduly taxing the audience's attention.

Also take into consideration other options or alternatives that may run counter to your own. Challenge these other options by showing that they are not as good as your own.

Finally, because this is the longest part of the message, organization must be exact. If there is more than one paragraph, make sure that it follows a logical pattern. If signposting is possible, then signpost.

CONCLUSION

For the conclusion to the persuasive message, choose one of the kinds of conclusions specified in appendix B of this book.

RESOLVING A SCENARIO USING IRAC

The following scenario will be used to construct a persuasive message using the IRAC method:

> You are a manager at a restaurant known for its business clientele. This morning you received a letter from a Ms. Nicole Jones who describes herself as an African-American businesswoman. In her letter, she tells you that your restaurant is discriminatory. One week ago, she relates, she entered your restaurant with a white male, one of her employees. The hostess sat them far at the back of the restaurant next to the kitchen even though many other tables throughout the restaurant were empty. When the waiter,

a white male whose name tag read *Jim*, finally appeared after a wait of more than fifteen minutes, Ms. Jones states that he was unenthusiastic with respect to serving them. She states that the waiter did not greet them, but instead immediately asked for their order. He appeared "edgy" in that he was constantly looking around the room. Ms. Jones believes he was "edgy" because he probably thought that she and her employee were an interracial couple. As the final insult, Jim gave the check to Ms. Jones' employee, thus demonstrating sexism as well. She has asked for an apology, that disciplinary action be taken against Jim, and she is even contemplating legal action.

What do you do? You must persuade Ms. Jones that you are not a discriminatory restaurant.

When using the IRAC method, first determine the issue that is under discussion. As mentioned before, address the real issue; false issues simply obfuscate and irritate the audience. The issue with respect to Nicole Jones is straightforward: She feels discriminated against, and you must persuade her that your restaurant does not discriminate on the basis of race or sex—her two primary allegations.

You can begin this letter to her with a reminder statement that states that you have received her letter:

> **Upon opening my mail this morning, I received your letter detailing your visit to my restaurant last week.**

After this, you must establish some empathy with your audience. Show Ms. Jones that you are distressed by what you read, that you understand her concerns, and that something must be done. In other words, state the issue with the right amount of feeling and concern:

> **I am deeply concerned that you feel that my restaurant discriminates against people because of their race or gender.**

You have now established the issue. Next, briefly summarize those points that gave rise to the issue in the first place. In this scenario there are four points Ms. Jones raises with respect to the discrimination issue. Arrange these points in an emphatic order:

1. Poor seating arrangements
2. Excessive wait for the waiter
3. Jim's edginess and lack of proper decorum
4. Jim's sexism in giving the check to the man instead of Ms. Jones

Note these four points in your second paragraph because they are the foundation of the issue. Note them briefly and succinctly: succinctly, so that Ms. Jones knows that you are not avoiding the issue, and briefly, so that you do not use an inordinate amount of time relating what both of you already know. This paragraph can read as follows:

> **Your letter pointed out that you felt discriminated against for four reasons. First, you stated that the seating arrangements were terrible. Second, you felt that the wait to be served was excessively long. Third, you believe that the waiter displayed edginess because you were an interracial couple, and that is why he lacked the proper decorum. Fourth, you feel that the waiter was sexist in giving the check to your dining companion rather than to you.**

Now that you have determined the foundations that gave rise to the issue, let us assume that you investigated Ms. Jones' allegations. You discovered that Ms. Jones was seated next to the kitchen because though the other tables were empty, none of them had been cleaned or prepared for the next customer. Jim took a long time getting to Ms. Jones' table because he was in the back running an errand for the cook. He was nervous and "edgy," but according to him he was working another employee's shift; in other words, he was in his twelfth hour of work when he waited on Ms. Jones. He does not remember that he did not greet the customers, nor does he remember that he gave the check to the man instead of Ms. Jones.

With this information, you can provide answers to Ms. Jones' allegations. You must also address her call for an apology and for disciplinary action against Jim, and you must alleviate her concerns so that she does not sue you.

Begin this section of the letter with a transitional sentence that is placating; state your general answer to the allegation; and then discuss the first point raised.

The above four items are very serious. Our restaurant prides itself on treating everyone equally, and thus your comments deserve investigation and resolution. Let me begin by apologizing for the seating arrangements. At the time that you arrived, the dinner hour was ending. Thus, while many tables were empty, they had not yet been cleaned or prepared for the next customers.

Note that the paragraph establishes a placating mood, and it begins with a statement that the restaurant does not discriminate. An apology and explanation are then given with respect to the first point raised.

Each paragraph can do the same thing in the same order. Thus, paragraph two could read as follows:

I also spoke with our hostess about your long wait. She told me that Jim, the only waiter left on duty at the time, had been sent on an errand by the cook. Though this is no excuse for the long wait, it was not done intentionally.

Note that here again, there is both explanation and apology. Paragraph three does the same thing:

When I spoke with Jim, your waiter, I discovered that he had been working for twelve hours. This would explain his edginess, but it certainly does not explain his lack of decorum. I have given Jim a reprimand, and he will no longer be allowed to take someone else's shift.

Paragraph four continues in the same vein:

Finally, I also asked Jim why he gave the check to your dining companion rather than to you. He could give no answer. I can only assume that he requires a reeducation with respect to sexism, and that is why he will be attending business seminars on gender and racial discrimination—seminars offered by the local university to alleviate these kinds of biases.

You have now addressed all of Ms. Jones' concerns. But you must have a good ending. You want her to be satisfied with your explanation and response, but, as a business person, you want to ensure her future business. Thus, you could reiterate your concerns with respect to the issue, and you might offer her and a dining companion a free meal so that she can appreciate the kind of business you really are, thus creating the possibility and probability of her future patronage of your restaurant:

Let me end by thanking you for bringing this important issue to my attention. In today's world, there is no place for the kind of treatment you received. I would like to extend an invitation to you to visit my restaurant again, at my expense, and see for yourself the improvement that has occurred.

This letter employs the IRAC method to great effect. Ms. Jones should be satisfied with your response, and there is a good chance that she will take you up on your offer. By answering the issue completely, thoroughly, and by using the right apologetic vocabulary, you may have gained a good customer rather than creating bad will.

Box 6.1 displays the completed letter.

BOX 6.1

The Completed Persuasive Letter

1810 Jackson
Dallas, TX 88941

18 Nov. 1994

Dear Ms. Jones:

Upon opening my mail this morning, I received your letter detailing your visit to my restaurant last week. I am deeply concerned that you feel that my restaurant discriminates against people because of their race or gender.

Your letter pointed out that you felt discriminated against for four reasons. First, you stated that the seating arrangements were terrible. Second, you felt that the wait to be served was excessively long. Third, you believe that the waiter displayed edginess because you were an interracial couple, and that is why he lacked the proper decorum. Fourth, you feel that the waiter was sexist in giving the check to your dining companion rather than to you.

The above four items are very serious. Our restaurant prides itself on treating everyone equally, and thus your comments deserve investigation and resolution. Let me begin by apologizing for the seating arrangements. At the time that you arrived, the dinner hour was ending. Thus, while many tables were empty, they had not yet been cleaned or prepared for the next customers.

I also spoke with our hostess about your long wait. She told me that Jim, the only waiter left on duty at the time, had been sent on an errand by the cook. Though this is no excuse for the long wait, it was not done intentionally.

When I spoke with Jim, your waiter, I discovered that he had been working for twelve hours. This would explain his edginess, but it certainly does not explain his lack of decorum. I have given Jim a reprimand, and he will no longer be allowed to take someone else's shift.

Finally, I also asked Jim why he gave the check to your dining companion rather than to you. He could give no answer. I can only assume that he requires a reeducation with respect to sexism, and that is why he will be attending business seminars on gender and racial discrimination—seminars offered by the local university to alleviate these kinds of biases.

Let me end by thanking you for bringing this important issue to my attention. In today's world, there is no place for the kind of treatment you received. I would like to extend an invitation to you to visit my restaurant again, at my expense, and see for yourself the improvement that has occurred.

Sincerely,

Jay Gordon, Manager

The Place
6805 Norton
Dallas, TX 88942

Conclusion

In reading Ms. Jones' letter, some people would argue that she is being overly sensitive. But whether her grounds for alleging discrimination are solid or weak is irrelevant. She is a customer, and her concerns must be taken seriously. If you don't adequately address customer concerns, or if you simply ignore them, you will create a climate that forebodes disaster. Any time a customer or client has a complaint or wishes that something be done, you must address it immediately. That is how one breeds goodwill.

In the letter to Ms. Jones, you should note that the writer's ethos is high. The correct format has been used: Ms. Jones is a businessperson, and thus justified margins and the letter format are appropriate. The logos is good even though the only appeals used are explanation.

As stated previously, ethos, logos, and pathos are used according to the circumstances in which you find yourself writing, but if the message is a persuasive one, the IRAC method can always be employed.

Box 6.2 (page 68) provides a review sheet for your persuasive letter.

BOX 6.2

Persuasive Letter Review Sheet

1. Does the letter follow the appropriate format and design for its intended audience?

2. Does the letter begin with a reminder statement?

3. Does the letter state the issue in a tactful manner?

4. Does the letter provide background information that gave rise to or is directly related to the issue? Does the second section give a general answer to the issue? Is signposting employed? Should it be employed?

5. Is the analysis section the longest part of the letter? Is it well organized? Does it follow an emphatic order?

6. Does the analysis section provide solid information with respect to the issue? Does it take into account alternatives and counterarguments?

7. Is there an effective goodwill ending?

8. What is the strongest part of the letter?

9. What is the weakest part of the letter?

Exercises

6.1: You are the manager of the automotive section of your department store. Last month, John Jones came in and purchased four new tires. Yesterday, he sent you a letter. In it, he states that one day after his purchase, one of his tires went flat. He came to your store on the same day and demanded a new tire. According to him, your salesclerk would not give him a tire because it had been slashed on the sidewall. (The tire warranty covers "ordinary use," not vandalism.) He also states that the salesclerk laughed at him when he suggested a refund and that she "smiled hilariously" when he left the store. After ten years of buying from your store, John Jones promises never to shop there again.

Write him a persuasive letter in which you persuade him to continue doing business with you.

6.2: You own Bob's CD Palace. Last week, Eric Andrews bought five CDs which were on sale. Prominently displayed over the cash register was a sign reading "No Refunds or Exchanges on Sale Items." Your manager, George, had put it there. Two days ago, Eric came into your store and showed an employee, Sam, a CD which was chipped along the edges. Sam pointed the sign out to Eric, thus refusing to refund or exchange. Eric then spoke with George. He, too, pointed out the sign. Eric argued that because the CD was defective, he should at least be able to exchange it for another one. George disagreed, and, in a moment of anger, told Eric to go to hell. He also shoved Eric in the direction of the exit. This incident took place in front of Sam and four other customers.

Today, you receive a letter from Eric detailing the events just mentioned. He states that according to the Uniform Commercial Code, you cannot refuse to exchange an item or refund the price of such an item when the item is defective. He also tells you that he is contemplating legal action based on fraud and George's assault and battery.

You don't want a lawsuit. Write him a persuasive letter.

6.3: You are a production manager at Macro Computers. Recently, you have been receiving memos from some of your computer programmers. These memos follow no particular format, and they are extremely disorganized. Most of the memos lack adequate subject lines, omit forecasting and reminder statements, lack headings, and consist only of lists. You speak to other managers, and they laugh, saying it's no big deal. You think it is a big deal since each memo takes you ten minutes to figure out what it is trying to communicate. You believe this situation should be rectified, so you decide to write a letter emphasizing the importance of written communication and proper formats to your plant manager.

6.4: As the manager at X-Mart, a large department store, you have six assistant managers working for you. One of these, Evan Antoine, is consistently late and rude to customers (as well as to you). Last week you decided that you had finally had enough. You had discovered that Evan helped himself to petty cash in the office—without returning it—and he gave all of his friends his own 12% discount on purchases. When you confronted Evan with these facts, he told you that you had no "real" proof and that he would sue for wrongful discharge and harassment should you fire him. (He doesn't know that you have kept the receipts involving sales to his friends and that you have even found a security videotape that shows these transactions occurring. Furthermore, you have a stack of customer complaint letters on your desk that illustrate Evan's rudeness.)

You decide to fire him, but you want to avoid any lawsuit. Write Evan a letter.

CHAPTER

7

Abstracting Information

The ability to summarize information is the foundation of all research. Throughout your professional career you will be asked to provide information that comes to you from others or that is based on research. Sometimes this information will be part of a larger piece of writing, such as a report. In these instances, you can quote or paraphrase information and easily incorporate it into the body of the text. However, you will sometimes be asked to provide information based on one single source. For example, you may be asked to provide a summary of an article or a book. On these occasions, you write an abstract. Simply put, "[a]n abstract summarizes and highlights the major points of a longer piece of writing" (Brusaw, Alred, and Oliu 8). When we provide this information to others, we have to put it in a form that will be readily accessible to the reader.

Abstracts come in two forms: (1) informative and (2) descriptive. To write both forms, we must understand how to paraphrase information.

Paraphrasing

The ability to paraphrase is the first qualification necessary to write a good abstract. A paraphrase takes an original text and translates it into our own words. A good paraphrase should accomplish three goals. First, make the paraphrase shorter than the original text. If the paraphrase is longer than the original text, then you have defeated the primary purpose of paraphrasing: to condense information. If the paraphrase is longer than the original text, then you might just as well have quoted the text. Second, use synonyms to properly paraphrase a word, a phrase, or a clause. Remember that you are trying to translate the original material into your own words. Third, make sure that your paraphrase means *exactly* the same thing as the original text. A good paraphrase never distorts meaning; instead, it should be identical in meaning to the original.

To accomplish these three goals, adhere to the following three restrictions. First, avoid all quotations. If you quote words or phrases in your paraphrase, then you are being lazy. A good paraphrase should present information to the reader in a fresh and condensed fashion. Moreover, the ability to properly paraphrase information demonstrates to your reader that you fully understand the material that you are presenting. Second, do not paraphrase all words. Proper nouns cannot be paraphrased, nor should you attempt to paraphrase certain words and concepts, such as *equity* or *bankruptcy*. Such words do not have a single-word synonym. Thus, if you attempt to paraphrase them, your paraphrase will be much longer than the original text. Third, use language appropriate to your audience. How sophisticated and knowledgeable is the audience to whom you are writing? Your answer will determine the level of sophistication at which you will write. By doing a preliminary audience analysis before you begin paraphrasing, you will know how much business language and jargon is appropriate.

Keeping these goals and restrictions in mind will help you begin the process of paraphrasing information. To properly paraphrase a sentence, go word by word, phrase by phrase, clause by clause. Then go back over the sentence to make it grammatically correct. As an illustrative example, let us look at the opening sentences from Gale Eisenstodt's article "Breaking Up" (the complete article is given in box 7.1):

> **To comprehend fully the secret of Japan's success in manufacturing, bypass the shiny, capital-intensive plants of Toyota or Hitachi. Instead, stop by Osaki Kinzoku Co.'s dingy little factory in Tokyo's Ohta district.**

A proper paraphrase of this sentence can read as follows:

> **To completely understand Japan's industrial prosperity, you should avoid Toyota and Hitachi and look at subcontractors like Osaki Kinzoku Company.**

Note that the paraphrased sentence includes the essential message of the original. Examine what has been paraphrased by comparing it with the original:

Original	*Paraphrase*
To comprehend fully	**To completely understand**
Japan's success in manufacturing	**Japan's industrial prosperity**
bypass	**avoid**
stop by	**look at**
dingy little factory	**subcontractors like**

Compare the paraphrase and original again. Note that not all the words have been paraphrased. Obviously, the proper nouns *Hitachi* and *Toyota* have not been paraphrased, nor have the words *new* and *capital-intensive*. Because Toyota and Hitachi are already associated in the public mind with modern, high-tech, capital-intensive industries, the repetition of these adjectives is unnecessary. Remember that you are interested in the essential message, not merely the duplication of every word in a synonymous form. Thus, adjectives like *shiny* and *dingy* have also been omitted because they merely provide color for the primary message.

Read the article in box 7.1, and determine the main points of the article. Then read the discussion that follows about how to write an informative abstract and a descriptive abstract.

BOX 7.1

Gale Eisenstodt's Article "Breaking Up"

To comprehend fully the secret of Japan's success in manufacturing, bypass the shiny, capital-intensive plants of Toyota or Hitachi. Instead, stop by Osaki Kinzoku Co.'s dingy little factory in Tokyo's Ohta district.

There you'll find 65 workers diligently electroplating parts for most of Japan's big electronic makers. "Our customers are always squeezing us on pricing," says President Hiroji Yoshikawa, apologizing for Osaki Kinzoku's spartan reception room. "We don't have a lot of money left to decorate."

Yoshikawa is part of Japan's all-pervasive subcontracting system. Some 70% or so of parts production is farmed out by the major automakers, and maybe around 50% in such industries as consumer electronics. More than 70% of Japan's manufacturing work force is employed at companies with fewer than 300 workers. Compare this with 33% of U.S. manufacturing workers employed by companies with under 500 people.

Although feudalistic in many ways, the subcontractors are a major factor behind Japanese manufacturer's ability to produce goods that are so competitive in world markets. In return for the promise of steady orders, the subcontractors commit their own capital, and do the most belt-tightening when times get lean.

The clearest examples come from the automotive sector. U.S. carmakers may call in over 1,000 hopeful subcontractors to bid on work when a new car is designed. In Japan carmakers typically deal directly with only 200 to 300 fairly large suppliers that in turn subcontract part of their work to thousands of smaller companies. Thus around 50,000 suppliers serve Japan's 11 automotive makers in a kind of multitiered pyramid, with wages generally falling the further down the pyramid the company is. Wages at firms with fewer than 30 workers are typically 40% lower than at large firms, and there is no lifetime employment at the smaller firms.

As well as keeping labor costs low, the subcontracting system also means that new car models can be turned out fast with less risk, since the investment burden for new production machinery is distributed down the chain.

Example: When Nissan raced to gain market share in the 1980s by offering ever more models and extras, the company could count on the loyal support of Tsuyoshi Tabata, president of a tiny, second-tier producer of bolts for test models. To keep up with the swelling orders, Tabata sank 10% of annual revenues into new machinery. His then eight-man staff typically worked 13-hour days in the noisy machine shop beneath his house.

continued

Costs rose, too, at $47 million (sales) Yokohama-based Kyowa Metal Works, as Nissan stepped up its demands for more types of manual transmission parts. "If Nissan said to make it, we made it," says President Kunio Sawada matter-of-factly.

In another Yokohama factory, working conditions are spartan where 240 workers make parts for automatic window motors. Yet, to get the right part to Nissan even faster, three years ago the company invested in a point-of-sale inventory control system and a computerized ordering system.

Such give-and-take relationships were easy to maintain when Japan's economy was booming. But the honeymoon is ending. Japan's growth is slowing secularly, big companies are stuck with too many white-collar workers and are busy downsizing. Some big companies, computer giant NEC Corp. among them, are keeping their own employees busy by pulling in-house work they previously gave to small outside suppliers.

As the yen strengthens, more big companies will be going abroad. A lot of small firms can't afford to follow. Declares Osaki Kinzoku's Yoshikawa: "Something has got to change."

Change is in the air, and it does not bode well for many of the subcontractors. Consider the marketing pressure until recently to launch ever more models. Nissan cars, for example, currently use 110 different radiators and over 300 types of ashtrays. As these small suppliers tooled up to produce tinier lots, their break-even points rose. Today they are suffering huge diseconomies of scale, with no growth in sight to bail them out.

Now that car sales have fallen, Japan's carmakers, desperate to cut costs, are reversing the process. The Japanese are paring part variations by 30% to 40%. This strategy shift is helping stronger subcontractors but is pushing others to the wall.

In the old days, the pain would have been shared. "Until new carmakers felt obliged to continue to give orders to less competitive suppliers," says Hiroyuki Sato, an auto parts analyst at the Nikko Research Center in Tokyo. But to remain competitive in the face of the rising yen and Detroit's resurgence, Japan's carmakers must give loyalty a lower priority. Declares Yasuo Tsuchiya, research director at Mitsubishi Research Institute: "To improve productivity now it is necessary to have more flexible ties."

To survive, many of the small subcontractors must become more independent, too. They are flogging their wares to firms they never would have considered doing business with previously. One winner: Until recently Kyowa Metal Works made parts almost exclusively for Nissan. Now the company's president, Kunio Sawada, says he is increasing sales to Mitsubishi Motors, among others, and is trying to diversify even further. "In a ketretsu you have to be a yes-man," says

Sawada with a grin. "That isn't very interesting."

Change is not limited to Japan's automotive sector. Nikuni Machinery Industry Co. ($45 million sales) is a subcontractor for camera maker Nikon. But Nikuni is unusual in that it also makes and markets its own product—industrial pumps—and these days it is putting more effort into pushing pump sales. "Our dependence on Nikon (50%) is still too high," says Executive Director Noboru Hayashi, who is worried that Nikon may move even more if its business overseas than it already has.

Japan's subcontracting system faces another strain that began to appear even before the present economic downturn. The system depends on a large labor force willing to work long hours for measly pay and no job security. In this sense the subcontracting system is a relic of the Fifties and Sixties. Today's young Japanese do not want these jobs, and they have options. So the subcontractors must turn—shudder!—to foreign workers. Osaki Kinzoku employs seven Nigerian and Brazilian workers because it can't get local staff.

Running short of skilled labor and constantly being squeezed on pricing, some subcontractors have been forced to stop investing in new technology. Japanese government statistics show that since 1980 the productivity gap between large and small firms has been widening.

Hiroki Kamata, president of Soken Planning, a computer consulting firm, reckons that the current crisis among subcontractors highlights a much deeper problem facing Japan: a shortage of true entrepreneurs. Says Kamata: "In the past the Japanese economy did well with feudal, pre-capitalist, nonmarket relationships. But in new industries this mechanism doesn't work."

Kamata points to Japan's weakness in computer software as an example. Most Japanese software companies act as subcontractors to larger firms, writing programs for proprietary systems instead of producing products for a broader market.

A sign that Kamata's fears are well grounded: Unlike in the U.S., in Japan the rate of new business starts is declining. This is not a reassuring sign at a time when Japan, like the U.S., needs the job-creating powers of new companies if the economy is to redeploy its work force productively.

Source: Eisenstodt, Gale. "Breaking Up." *Forbes* 24 May 1993: 88–89.
Reprinted by Permission of FORBES Magazine © Forbes Inc., 1993.

Informative Abstract

Using the principles of accurate paraphrasing, we can learn how to write an informative abstract. An informative abstract is longer than a descriptive abstract: It provides a complete summary of all relevant information.

The basic guidelines of the informative abstract are that it should (1) be no longer than one fourth the length of the original text, (2) contain sentences that do not exceed the number of paragraphs in the original, (3) paraphrase all relevant information, and (4) be completely objective. In brief, "[t]he informative abstract retains the tone and essential scope of the original work while omitting its details" (Brusaw, Alred, and Oliu 9).

BEGINNING THE ABSTRACT

Look back at Eisenstodt's article. Note that there are twenty-one paragraphs. The sentences in our abstract will not exceed the number of paragraphs in the article. (This is one easy way to ensure that your abstract will be one fourth the length of the original text.) On a sheet of paper, list numbers from 1 to 21. Now follow these steps to begin your rough draft of the abstract:

1. If you have not already done so, read through the article one time to get a sense of its meaning and point.
2. Read through again, and this time underline the thesis statement (that is, the one sentence that encapsulates the entire meaning of the article).
3. Underline all topic sentences *and* anything else in the paragraph that will be relevant and useful in explaining the topic sentence. (In business articles, the topic sentence is usually the first sentence of each paragraph.)

WRITING THE THESIS STATEMENT

The thesis statement is the first sentence of the informative abstract. This is a crucial part of your abstract because it will help you in writing and organizing the relevant information.

A good thesis statement provides a focus for both you and your reader. Everything in the abstract should be related to the thesis statement; in other words, all of the sentences in the abstract must explain or prove the thesis statement. Sentences that do not explain or prove the thesis statement should be deleted because they are irrelevant to furthering the primary message of the abstract, which is inherent in the thesis statement.

Your thesis statement must be well defined. Do not provide a thesis statement that is too broad or too narrow. For example, the following thesis statement is too broad:

Gale Eisenstodt discusses Japanese subcontractors.

While this thesis statement is true, it does not include the point of the entire article. At the other extreme is a much too narrow thesis statement:

Gale Eisenstodt states that Japanese subcontractors are the backbone of Japanese industry.

Again, this thesis statement is accurate, but it fails to incorporate the point of the whole article. The thesis statement must restate the author's main point or assertion: the one that the author's *entire* text proves or validates.

A useful way to write a thesis statement is to follow an equation:

In [author's name]'s + article [title of article], + he or she + [verb] + that + [paraphrase of the author's thesis statement].

For example, you can use this formula to create an accurate thesis statement about Eisenstodt's article:

> **In Gale Eisenstodt's article "Breaking Up," she states that Japan's subcontractors have been the backbone of its economic success, but they are now in trouble and so is Japanese business.**

IMPLEMENTING THE STEPS

After you have written your thesis statement, on your numbered sheet of paper, paraphrase in single sentences the topic sentences. Make sure to include all other relevant details of each paragraph in your paraphrase. This latter point is extremely important! By their nature topic sentences are general statements concerning the contents of the paragraph that follows. As a result topic sentences may be vague. Therefore include in your highlighting and paraphrasing any additional details in the paragraph that will make the topic sentence as specific and precise as possible.

Next are the twenty-one paraphrased sentences, each of which includes the topic sentence and any other relevant information from the paragraph:

1. **To completely understand Japan's industrial prosperity, you should avoid Toyota and Hitachi and instead look at subcontractors like Osaki Kinzoku Company.**

2. **At Kinzoku Co., workers produce items for Japanese electronic companies, and, because the company is highly cost conscious, the workers toil in surroundings that lack the amenities of the large corporations.**

3. **In Japan 70% of laborers work for companies that have less than 300 workers, as compared to 33% of U.S. laborers who work for companies that have less than 500 workers.**

4. **Subcontractors are the primary factor in Japan's ability to be globally competitive.**

5. **In Japan thousands of subcontractors serve the few giant corporations, and as a result, wages are kept low.**

6. **Subcontractors allow car manufacturers to produce new models quickly because the investment risk is shared by subcontractors and the major corporations they serve.**

7. **For example, when Nissan wanted to increase sales, it relied on a subcontractor who was willing to reinvest some of the profits into new technology, and who pushed workers to put in thirteen-hour days.**

8. **To meet Nissan's demands one subcontractor willingly incurred costs in order to make different types of transmission parts.**

9. **To meet Nissan's demands another subcontractor invested in state-of-the-art computer complexes that controlled inventory and ordering.**

10. **Today, however, because of the decline in economic growth, Japanese corporations are working to rightsize, and one way to accomplish this is to do more of the subcontracting work themselves.**

11. **Some Japanese corporations will move operations abroad because of the stalwart yen, and this can only hurt subcontractors that are unable to do likewise.**

12. Small subcontractors that went along with the major corporations' demands to diversify their production models, and thus produce smaller lots of goods, now face enormous economic pressure because of smaller profit margins in an economy that is already slowing.

13. Japanese auto sales are down, and the major automakers are diminishing the diversity demands by up to 40%, thereby decreasing the need for so many subcontractors.

14. At one time Japanese automakers were loyal to their subcontractors, and they would have apportioned the risk among themselves and their suppliers, but this is no longer the case.

15. In order to remain in business, subcontractors are beginning to produce more goods than those required by the major corporations.

16. This need to diversify production is not found only among auto subcontractors; it is an industry-wide phenomenon.

17. Subcontractors are facing labor problems because the pay is poor, the work hours are long, and there is little job stability; therefore, Japanese subcontractors are beginning to hire foreign workers.

18. With all of these problems, subcontractors can no longer afford to install up-to-date technology.

19. One of the major obstacles to economic growth lies with the lack of new businesses.

20. For example, Japanese software companies are really subcontractors for bigger corporations, instead of being businesses that work for their own growth and profit.

21. If Japan is to awaken from its economic doldrums, it must encourage new business growth that effectively restructures its labor power.

REVISING FOR UNITY AND CONCISENESS

You are now ready to revise: to clean up and make precise your paraphrased sentences. To revise, look down the list of your paraphrases and

> omit example paragraphs unless they add necessary specificity,
>
> omit transitional paragraphs and redundancies, and
>
> be specific and precise in your word choice.

Note the following revisions made to the previous twenty-one sentences. Remember that if one paragraph provides the essential message, then paragraphs that follow and merely provide examples of that essential message are irrelevant. Therefore, paragraphs 1, 2, 7, 8, 9, and 20 have been omitted. These paragraphs merely give examples of ideas that other paragraphs have already detailed.

3. In Japan 70% of laborers work for companies that have less than 300 workers, as compared to 33% of U.S. laborers who work for companies that have less than 500 workers.

4. Subcontractors are the primary factor in Japan's ability to be globally competitive.

5. In Japan thousands of subcontractors serve the few giant corporations, and as a result, wages are kept low.

6. Subcontractors allow car manufacturers to produce new models quickly because the investment risk is shared by subcontractors and the major corporations they serve.

10. Today, however, because of the decline in economic growth, Japanese corporations are working to rightsize, and one way to accomplish this is to do more of the subcontracting work themselves.

11. Some Japanese corporations will move operations abroad because of the stalwart yen, and this can only hurt subcontractors that are unable to do likewise.

12. Small subcontractors that went along with the major corporations' demands to diversify their production models, and thus produce smaller lots of goods, now face enormous economic pressure because of smaller profit margins in an economy that is already slowing.

13. Japanese auto sales are down, and the major automakers are diminishing the diversity demands by up to 40%, thereby decreasing the need for so many subcontractors.

14. At one time Japanese automakers were loyal to their subcontractors, and they would have apportioned the risk among themselves and their suppliers, but this is no longer the case.

15. In order to remain in business, subcontractors are beginning to produce more goods than those required by the major corporations.

16. This need to diversify production is not found only among auto subcontractors; it is an industry-wide phenomenon.

17. Subcontractors are facing labor problems because the pay is poor, the work hours are long, and there is little job stability; therefore, Japanese subcontractors are beginning to hire foreign workers.

18. With all of these problems, subcontractors can no longer afford to install up-to-date technology.

19. One of the major obstacles to economic growth lies with the lack of new business.

21. If Japan is to awaken from its economic doldrums, it must encourage new business growth that effectively restructures its labor power.

REVISING FOR COHERENCE

Our next task is to revise for coherence: We must make sure that our abstract contains adequate transitions, and that sentences have been combined whenever possible to create conciseness and brevity. The numbers of our paraphrased paragraphs have been omitted, and the relevant changes have been italicized so that you can see them easily. (We will leave out sentence number 21 here and save it for the construction of our conclusion.) In addition, the sentences will now appear in paragraph form, as they will when your abstract is complete:

In Japan 70% of laborers work for companies that have less than 300 workers, as compared to 33% of U.S. laborers who work for companies that have less than 500 workers. *One result of this labor discrepancy* has been that subcontractors are the primary factor in Japan's ability to be globally competitive. *This competitiveness results* from thousands of subcontractors *serving* the few giant corporations, *thereby keeping* wages low. *For example,* subcontractors allow car manufacturers to produce new models quickly because they share the investment risk with the large corporations that they serve. Today, however, because of the decline in economic growth, *some* Japanese corporations are working to rightsize, and one way to ac-

> complish this is to do more of the subcontracting work themselves. *Other* **Japanese corporations will move operations abroad because of the stalwart yen, and this can only hurt subcontractors that are unable to do likewise.** *All this now leaves* **small subcontractors that went along with the major corporations' demands to diversify their production models, and thus produce smaller lots of goods,** *facing* **enormous economic pressure because of smaller profit margins in an economy that is already slowing.** *With* **Japanese auto sales down, and the major automakers diminishing the diversity demands by up to 40%,** *there is a* **decreasing need for so many subcontractors. At one time Japanese automakers were loyal to their subcontractors, and they would have apportioned the risk among themselves and their suppliers, but this is no longer the case. In order to remain in business, subcontractors are beginning to produce more goods than those required by the major corporations. This need to diversify production is not found only among auto subcontractors; it is an industry-wide phenomenon.** *But this need to diversify production is not the only problem:* **Subcontractors are facing labor problems because the pay is poor, the work hours are long, and there is little job stability; therefore, Japanese subcontractors are beginning to hire foreign workers. With all of these problems, subcontractors can no longer afford to install up-to-date technology.** *And without this investment capital,* **one of the major obstacles to economic growth lies with the lack of new businesses.**

Note that this paragraph uses four types of transitions: synonym, repetition, idea, and transitional expression.

In addition if the article uses signposting, then use it in your abstract. For example, if Eisenstodt had said (or if you could easily infer it) that subcontractors suffer eight major problems, then signposting would have been simple to include in our abstract. If you signpost in the informative abstract and you must also write a descriptive one, then signposting will ease your task when writing the descriptive abstract.

COMPLETING THE INFORMATIVE ABSTRACT

Your informative abstract is almost complete. You simply must add a conclusion and a bibliographic citation.

Look at the end (or at paraphrase number 21) of the original text. Paraphrase it, and indicate to the reader that this is the author's conclusion by stating something like *the author concludes, she ends*, or *she finishes*. The conclusion to your abstract could read as follows:

> **Eisenstodt concludes on this bleak note, and she goes on to say that if Japan is to reawaken from its economic doldrums, it must encourage new business growth that effectively restructures its labor power.**

At the bottom of the abstract, write *Source* followed by a colon, both in bold print, and then give a correct bibliographic citation for the paraphrased text:

> **Source:** Eisenstodt, Gale. "Breaking Up." *Forbes* 24 May 1993: 88–89.

Because this article is brief and concise, one paragraph should do. However, if the original material to be paraphrased is lengthy or complex, use more paragraphs in your abstract if necessary to more clearly separate ideas or points for the reader.

The completed informative abstract is in box 7.2.

The Completed Informative Abstract

In Gale Eisenstodt's article "Breaking Up," she states that Japan's sub-contractors have been the backbone of its economic success, but they are now in trouble and so is Japanese business. In Japan 70% of laborers work for companies that have less than 300 workers, as compared to 33% of U.S. laborers who work for companies that have less than 500 workers. One result of this labor discrepancy has been that subcontractors are the primary factor in Japan's ability to be globally competitive. This competitiveness results from thousands of subcontractors serving the few giant corporations, thereby keeping wages low. For example, subcontractors allow car manufacturers to produce new models quickly because they share the investment risk with the large corporations that they serve. Today, however, because of the decline in economic growth, some Japanese corporations are working to rightsize, and one way to accomplish this is to do more of the subcontracting work themselves. Other Japanese corporations will move operations abroad because of the stalwart yen, and this can only hurt subcontractors that are unable to do likewise. All this now leaves small subcontractors that went along with the major corporations' demands to diversify their production models, and thus produce smaller lots of goods, facing enormous economic pressure because of smaller profit margins in an economy that is already slowing. With Japanese auto sales down, and the major automakers diminishing the diversity demands by up to 40%, there is a decreasing need for so many subcontractors. At one time Japanese automakers were loyal to their subcontractors, and they would have apportioned the risk among themselves and their suppliers, but this is no longer the case. In order to remain in business, subcontractors are beginning to produce more goods than those required by the major corporations. This need to diversify production is not found only among auto subcontractors, it is an industry-wide phenomenon. But this need to diversify production is not the only problem: Subcontractors are facing labor problems because the pay is poor, the work hours are long, and there is little job stability; therefore, Japanese subcontractors are beginning to hire foreign workers. With all of these problems, subcontractors can no longer afford to install up-to-date technology. And without this investment capital, one of the major obstacles to economic growth lies with the lack of new businesses. Eisenstodt concludes on this bleak note, and she goes on to say that if Japan is to reawaken from its economic doldrums, it must encourage new business growth that effectively restructures its labor power.

Source: Eisenstodt, Gale. "Breaking Up." *Forbes* 24 May 1993: 88–89.
Reprinted by Permission of FORBES Magazine © Forbes Inc., 1993.

Descriptive Abstract

A descriptive abstract is a summary of a summary; in other words, the descriptive abstract condenses the informative abstract. If you have made an informative abstract already, then you work from that; if you did not do so because it was not required, then make a rough draft of an informative abstract first.

The descriptive abstract is only a few sentences long (Brusaw, Alred, and Oliu 8). In fact, you can create a fine descriptive abstract in three sentences or less. The first sentence uses the same thesis statement used in the informative abstract. The second sentence states the major points that the author makes. Look at your list of paraphrased sentences, and put checks next to those sentences that contain information supporting the author's conclusion. (If you have signposted in the informative abstract, then simply take those signposted sentences and use them here.) The third sentence is optional. If the original article includes a conclusion that does more than merely summarize what has been said, then include the ending; if the original merely summarizes what has already been said, then the descriptive abstract will not have a third sentence. The second sentence is the heart of the descriptive abstract, but each sentence counts in such a short abstract.

The following provides a step-by-step analysis of how to write a descriptive abstract, using Gale Eisenstodt's "Breaking Up," once again, as the text to be summarized.

SENTENCE ONE OF THE DESCRIPTIVE ABSTRACT

The first sentence is the easy part. For a descriptive abstract, use the same thesis sentence as in the informative abstract:

> **In Gale Eisenstodt's article "Breaking Up," she states that Japan's subcontractors have been the backbone of its economic success, but they are now in trouble and so is Japanese business.**

SENTENCE TWO OF THE DESCRIPTIVE ABSTRACT

The second sentence of the descriptive abstract is much more difficult because it is the only sentence of the abstract that requires a reworking of the informative abstract. In this second sentence, use a list to highlight and specify the article's major points that support the thesis statement. Go through the list of paraphrased sentences, and highlight those passages that illustrate the article's thesis statement. (Of course, if you signposted in your informative abstract, this step will be greatly simplified.) Below is the list of the revised paraphrased sentences from Eisenstodt's article, with the highlighted points italicized:

3. **In Japan 70% of laborers work for companies that have less than 300 workers, as compared to 33% of U.S. laborers who work for companies that have less than 500 workers.**

4. **Subcontractors are the primary factor in Japan's ability to be globally competitive.**

5. **In Japan thousands of subcontractors serve the few giant corporations, and as a result,** *wages are kept low.*

6. **Subcontractors allow car manufacturers to produce new models quickly because the investment risk is shared by subcontractors and the major corporations they serve.**

10. **Today, however, because of the decline in economic growth, Japanese corporations are working to rightsize, and one way to accomplish** *this is to do more of the subcontracting work themselves.*

11. **Some Japanese corporations will** *move operations abroad* **because of the stalwart yen, and this can only hurt subcontractors that are unable to do likewise.**

12. **Small subcontractors that went along with the major corporations' demands to diversify their production models, and thus produce smaller lots of goods, now face enormous economic pressure because of** *smaller profit margins in an economy that is already slowing.*

13. **Japanese auto sales are down, and the major automakers are** *diminishing the diversity demands* **by up to 40%, thereby decreasing the need for so many subcontractors.**

14. **At one time Japanese automakers were** *loyal to their subcontractors,* **and they would have apportioned the risk among themselves and their suppliers,** *but this is no longer the case.*

15. **In order to remain in business, subcontractors are beginning to produce more goods than those required by the major corporations.**

16. *This need to diversify production* **is not found only among auto subcontractors; it is an industry-wide phenomenon.**

17. **Subcontractors are** *facing labor problems* **because** *the pay is poor, the work hours are long, and there is little job stability;* **therefore, Japanese subcontractors are** *beginning to hire foreign workers.*

18. **With all of these problems, subcontractors can** *no longer afford to install up-to-date technology.*

19. **One of the major obstacles to economic growth lies with the lack of new businesses.**

20. **If Japan is to reawaken from its economic doldrums,** *it must encourage new business growth that effectively restructures its labor power.*

Based on our italicized portions of this list, let us now construct our list of the author's major points:

1. Low wages
2. Corporations doing more of the subcontracting work themselves
3. Corporations moving abroad
4. Subcontractors facing smaller profit margins
5. Subcontractors forced to diversify their production
6. Corporations no longer loyal to their subcontractors
7. Subcontractors demanding long work hours and offering little job stability
8. Subcontractors faced with a labor shortage and using foreign workers
9. Subcontractors no longer affording up-to-date technology

You now have nine major points to include in the second sentence if the descriptive abstract is to be precise and specific. The best way to accomplish this feat is to make a list that will be part of the second sentence. In this list, combine and condense major points whenever possible, making sure that the list is parallel in structure.

Because the thesis statement begins with a reference to subcontractors, let us begin with a similar reference in order to provide a transition between the two sentences:

Japanese subcontractors have difficult times ahead because they

1. **offer low wages, long hours, and little job stability;**
2. **possess smaller profit margins than ever before;**
3. **must diversify their production to remain competitive;**
4. **have a labor shortage, resulting in the hiring of foreign workers;**
5. **can no longer afford up-to-date technology;**
6. **lack corporate loyalty in that corporations are no longer willing to share the investment risk;**
7. **face business losses because many corporations are doing the subcontracting work themselves; and**
8. **cannot follow corporations abroad in the quest for a cheaper labor pool.**

SENTENCE THREE OF THE DESCRIPTIVE ABSTRACT

In a descriptive abstract, only write a third sentence if the author's conclusion does more than merely summarize the article. In the *Forbes* article, Eisenstodt makes a prediction in her conclusion; therefore, we will include it as the third sentence of the descriptive abstract. It will be the same sentence as was used in the informative abstract:

> **Eisenstodt concludes on this bleak note, and she goes on to say that if Japan is to reawaken from its economic doldrums, it must encourage new business growth that effectively restructures its labor power.**

All that is left is to cite the source at the bottom of the descriptive abstract. Write *Source,* follow it with a colon, both in bold print, and end with a complete bibliographic citation:

> **Source:** Eisenstodt, Gale. "Breaking Up." *Forbes* 24 May 1993: 88–89.

The completed descriptive abstract is in box 7.3.

Conclusion

In this chapter, you have seen how to construct informative abstracts and descriptive abstracts. Although the chapter has focused on writing abstracts based on articles, abstracts can be written for any type of writing.

To write an abstract of a book, for example, follow the same guidelines as those found in this chapter. The only difference may be that each paragraph of the abstract will be based on each chapter of the book. And, of course, you will have to come up

---

BOX 7.3

The Completed Descriptive Abstract

In Gale Eisenstodt's article "Breaking Up," she states that Japan's subcontractors have been the backbone of its economic success, but they are now in trouble and so is Japanese business. Japanese subcontractors have difficult times ahead because they

1. offer low wages, long hours, and little job stability;

2. possess smaller profit margins than ever before;

3. must diversify their production to remain competitive;

4. have a labor shortage, resulting in the hiring of foreign workers;

5. can no longer afford up-to-date technology;

6. lack corporate loyalty in that corporations are no longer willing to share the investment risk;

7. face business losses because many corporations are doing the subcontracting work themselves; and

8. cannot follow corporations abroad in the quest for a cheaper labor pool.

Eisenstodt concludes on this bleak note, and she goes on to say that if Japan is to reawaken from its economic doldrums, it must encourage new business growth that effectively restructures its labor power.

Source: Eisenstodt, Gale. "Breaking Up." *Forbes* 24 May 1993: 88–89.
Reprinted by Permission of FORBES Magazine © Forbes Inc., 1993.

---

with a thesis statement that includes all the chapters of the text. But the idea is the same. All abstracts should be written as you have seen them constructed in this chapter.

One question remains: What kind of abstract should you write when the choice is left up to you? In other words, what if you are asked to write an abstract of an article, but it isn't specified whether the abstract is to be informative or descriptive? Which do you choose?

The answer depends on your audience and purpose. If the intended audience includes those who must have a complete understanding of the original text as well as those who only require a cursory understanding, then write an informative abstract. On the other hand, if your audience requires only an overview of the text, then write a descriptive abstract. Your purpose is a major factor here. Descriptive abstracts are especially useful tools in lengthy reports, progress reports, proceedings of meetings, and other kinds of writing that must describe a great deal of information in a condensed but readable form (Brusaw, Alred, and Oliu 10).

Box 7.4 (page 86) provides a review sheet to use in evaluating your abstracts.

BOX 7.4

Abstract Review Sheet

Use the following sheet to evaluate your abstracts.

1. Does the first sentence of the abstract follow the assigned thesis statement format?
2. Is the abstract objective?
3. Does the thesis statement provide an accurate and inclusive overview of the original text?

Informative Abstract

4. Does the informative abstract provide a clear pattern of organization? Does it employ signposting? If not, should it? Where is signposting necessary?
5. Are there adequate transitions throughout the abstract?
6. Are the words and sentences precise and clear? Is the information clearly given, or is more explanation necessary?
7. Does the informative abstract end with the author's conclusion?
8. Is everything paraphrased that should be paraphrased?

Descriptive Abstract

9. Does the first sentence follow the thesis statement as given in the informative abstract?
10. Does the second sentence provide a list of reasons in support of the author's thesis? Are they specific enough? Is the list parallel?
11. Should a third sentence be included? Does it add new information, or does it merely summarize what has been said?

Exercises

7.1: Paraphrase the following sentences. Omit the parenthetical references:

1. "When family businesses become successful, they often look for ways to return to their community some of the support the community has afforded them" (Estess 78).
2. "Whether used to nab criminals or boost a business's bottom line, computers, cellular phones, modems and microchips are being woven by companies into the workplace with increasing frequency" (Simons and Fischer 45).
3. "Write protection is a simple procedure, surprisingly enough, requiring no government registration" (Rathbone 27).
4. "You can start MS-DOS Help in two ways: you can display the table of contents and choose a topic from it; or you can bypass the table of contents and display information about a specific command" (Concise User's Guide 16).

5. "Sometimes the File Manager snoozes and doesn't keep track of what's *really* on the disk" (Rathbone 219).

6. "To familiarize ourselves with the MBO system, let's look at a case history, Columbus' discovery of the New World, though how I tell the story takes considerable liberties with the grammar-school version of the event" (Grove 112).

7. "Shenzhen's rebound is an indicator of the changes afoot as China attempts to clean up its troubled capital markets" (Einhorn and Roberts 106).

8. "At Bank of Montreal, Barrett and his team decided that a turnaround strategy had to include a new approach to performance management" (Birchard 47).

9. "Chipmakers are following a prudent guideline: Those who plow the most into new production facilities win" (Port and Parks 134).

10. "Labor problems between ethnic Chinese workers and indigenous people are commonplace, regional uprisings dot the outlying areas, and the country [Indonesia] is deep in debt" (Byrne 72).

11. "Clearly, if executives talk about empowering employees, decentralizing decision-making authority, and putting everyone on teams to respond quickly to customers, measurement systems have to change, too" (Birchard 51).

12. "With a large number of local companies eager to float stock, the Shanghai market has made it difficult for companies from outside the city to gain listings" (Einhorn and Roberts 106).

13. "The company increased its capital budget steadily over the last 10 years, and in 1994 climbed to the No. 1 spot, eclipsing such DRAM heavyweights as NEC Corp. and Toshiba Corp." (Port and Parks 134).

14. "The mix of pleasure and pain might well be applied to the Japanese stock market, which is experiencing painful losses after spectacular gains in the fairly recent past" (Curtis 78).

15. "Unnerved by several credit-union collapses and Japan's first postwar bank failure, investors now are demanding that big banks pay a premium to borrow in global money markets" (Bremner and Glasgall 60).

16. "The future of derivatives is an uncertain matter, depending partly on whether the subject is leveraged derivatives or all others" (Loomis 68).

17. "Nothing, not even a faster processor, will do as much to improve performance as an extra 4 or 8 MB of RAM" (Wildstrom 22).

18. "The thread running through last year's disasters was the misuse of derivatives, now standard equipment in the financial quarters of many companies" (Loomis 50).

19. "Windows 95 has a voracious appetite for memory" (Wildstrom 22).

20. "In the first quarter of 1995, the Nikkei index of Japanese stocks lost nearly one-fifth of its value, becoming the worst performing region in the world after hapless Latin America" (Curtis 78).

21. "Eventually, programmers will find ways to improve Win95 memory use" (Wildstrom 22).

22. "But 23 years' experience writing and producing advertising jingles left Mark with precious little exposure to the world of high finance" (Evanson 48).

23. "If the manager has a group of people reporting to him or a circle of people influenced by him, the manager's output must be measured by the output created by his subordi-

nates and associates" (Grove 40).

24. "Because quality levels vary over time, it is only common sense to vary how often we inspect" (Grove 31).

25. Entrepreneurs are independent by nature, and many are impervious to the influence of outside advice—which leads to the first great divide in the concept of raising money by affiliation: advisory boards vs. 'real' boards, or boards of directors" (Evanson 51).

7.2: You are a stock consultant in Salmon Brothers, a growing investment corporation. Last week, one of your longtime clients, George Meaney, an economics professor, called your CEO, Ms. Roberta Jackson, to ask whether he should purchase Windows 95. Because he is a valued client, this is no trivial request. Ms. Roberta Jackson has laid this problem on your desk. She tells you to handle the situation and let her know what you did.

You remember reading an article in *Fortune* magazine a few months ago that discussed Windows 95. You find the article in the September 19, 1995 issue. The article begins on page 193 and concludes on page 196. You decide to write an informative abstract to George Meaney and a descriptive abstract to Roberta Jackson. You also decide to send the informative abstract in letter form to George Meaney and the descriptive abstract in memo form to Roberta Jackson. In addition, in the same memo, you decide to tell Roberta Jackson how you handled the situation with George Meaney. (Go to the library to look this article up.)

7.3: Read Emily Thornton's article in box 7.5.

BOX 7.5

Emily Thornton's Article "Japan's Struggle to Restructure"

The wave of restructuring that remade corporate America in the 1980s is washing ashore in Japan. It's called *risutora*, and it has become a mantra for managers of companies large and small. Two years of growth so slow it feels like recession, coupled with sluggish markets overseas and a soaring yen, have magnified a new and nagging problem: Corporate Japan, long the international paragon of efficiency and competitiveness, is losing its edge.

Japanese productivity now ranks in the bottom half of industrialized nations, far below that of the U.S. and many EC countries. Saturated world markets and growing competition elsewhere in Asia have dimmed prospects that the Japanese juggernaut can return to the galloping growth of previous decades. Suddenly marquee corporations are weighed down by bloated and unprofitable businesses, too much manufacturing capacity, and too many employees. Says Kenichi Ohmae, the prolific author and chairman of McKinsey & Co.'s Tokyo office: "Almost any Japanese industry you look at, product by product, has about 30% too much capacity. What's different now is that waiting for another year or two won't relieve the problem. It is a fact of life."

Consequently much of Japan Inc. is scrambling to revamp itself. This being Japan, however, *risutora* is a somewhat hazy concept. For most companies it merely means cost cutting—curtailing overtime, reducing hiring, asking employees to limit travel and to use the subway rather than a taxi, and entertaining clients less lavishly. In a few extreme cases companies are actually closing plants and reassigning workers.

Many tactics seem almost silly: At carmaker Nissan security guards sweep through offices on Thursdays to enforce the new rule that employees must leave by 6 P.M. to save on overtime. Cosmetics giant Shiseido requires office workers to ignore ringing telephones between 1 P.M. and 3 P.M. each day so they can put out more paperwork. Some managers at Nippon Telephone & Telegraph are trying to limit business presentations to one sheet of paper. In fact real restructuring is so foreign to corporate Japan that the government's Ministry of International Trade and Industry (MITI) has convened a secret committee of more than a dozen prominent CEOs to come up with definitions and guidelines.

There is complete unanimity about what *risutora* most definitely does not mean, and No. 1 on that list is layoffs. At least for now. Since the end of World War II, large, paternalistic Japanese companies have granted lifetime employment in return for loyal service. It is a tradition as sacred and ingrained as keeping foreigners out of the rice business. Even early retirement programs have been frowned upon. Says Jiro Ushio, chairman of Ushio Inc., a maker of halogen lamps, and head of MITI's special committee: "From the viewpoint of top management, we should make bold moves now. But it is very hard to do. We have lived for a long time with the so-called Japanese system of no layoffs, no losers. This kind of atmosphere is very hard to break."

Nevertheless, Japanese companies, which are nothing if not pragmatic, know they need to act now to remain world leaders. Some CEOs, like Shiseido's Yoshiharu Fukuhara, think vigorous belt-tightening could forestall more distasteful cutbacks later. Says he: "This will be the last chance for Japanese companies to do restructuring within the bounds of traditional lifetime employment." Other managers are beginning to describe their problems in more dire terms. Says Masashi Suzuki, executive vice president in charge of restructuring at Nomura Securities: "Russia once lost a war with Japan because it used large, slow-moving ships. Ours were smaller and could maneuver more quickly. Now it's as if we are the huge aircraft carrier. Basically everything about the way we are doing business has to change."

Some of the most common moves:

Improving productivity. The Japanese have finally been forced

continued

to face the fact that their productivity levels are no longer globally competitive. In fact they rank seventh of 12 industrialized countries. That's especially bad news for a country facing a labor shortage later in the decade. The U.S., which ranks fourth behind Belgium, France, and Canada, has a GDP per employed person 26% higher than Japan's. One Japanese consultant, who asks not to be named, calculated how many employees would have to be laid off for Japan to reach the U.S. level of productivity. Answer: 20 million, or nearly a third of Japan's work force.

The worst performers are those wearing white collars. Says Doug Shinsato at Tohmatsu Touche Ross Consulting: "During the bubble years the Japanese focused investment on the factory floor but nowhere else. The headquarters of any manufacturing company looks like state-of-the-art 1940s or 1950s. Most workers don't have PCs, and they don't add a lot of value. They just shuffle a lot of paper."

Nissan hopes to raise white-collar productivity by 30% in the next three years. One tactic is to cut down on meetings. Says Toshiaki Yasuda, who is assistant to the president: "Before, we used to have meetings just to inform each other what we were doing. Now we are having meetings to actually make decisions."

Honda Motor has taken the first step toward a pay system based on merit, not seniority. Last year marked the first time bonuses, which account for approximately 40% of salaries, were based on how well managers met self-defined goals rather than on how long they've been with the company. Honda hasn't yet implemented the proposed second part of that policy: penalizing employees for poor performance. Fujitsu, the electronics giant, has begun its own pay-for-performance system. Starting now, 10,000 managers will be setting their own performance goals.

Redrawing the organization chart. For years, Mitsukoshi Department Store, Japan's oldest, had five levels of management in every store. Providing enough titles to meet the rising expectations of baby-boomers was at least one reason for the cumbersome structure. Then last year, facing its first loss since 1985, the company decided it needed only two levels. No one got fired, of course, and nearly everyone has the same duties. Has productivity improved? Mitsukoshi says it can't yet tell.

At Nomura Securities, top management used to tell branches which stocks to push. Now, facing a deeply depressed market plus impending deregulation of fees, Japan's biggest securities house is trying to cozy up to customers by encouraging branch managers to listen to clients and tailor stock picks. Says Suzuki: "We have to change our selling style 180 degrees."

Closing plants. This isn't actually taboo in Japan. The aluminum and textile industries shut plants in the 1970s when they could no longer compete with foreign rivals. But now, companies in industries the Japanese dominate globally are being forced by slower growth and overcapacity to do it. The announcement by Alps Electric, an electronic parts manufacturer, that it would close three plants raised eyebrows. The real shocker came when Nissan Motor said in February that it would close one main factory in Zama, on the outskirts of Tokyo, in 1995. After all, Japanese automakers are supposed to be the most competitive in the world. Right?

Nissan plans to transfer 2,500 of the 4,000 workers from Zama to another plant on Kyushu, 250 miles away. The remainder will stay at Nissan's machine tool plant in Zama, which will stay open. Employees of the plant's suppliers won't be so lucky. Prospects are especially poor for the 40 or so companies that have repaired and cleaned machinery solely at the plant.

Non-layoff layoffs. The Japanese are still disdainful of American methods of slashing head counts. Listen to Chikara Ohkubo, director of policy planning at the influential Federation of Employers' Associations: "In some American companies it seems as if layoffs have become a narcotic. After the first time, the company just keeps doing it again and again. You don't have to be that intelligent to figure out that if you cut the most expensive cost—personnel—your corporate performance will improve in the short term. Still, there are many steps that can be taken before that. As long as we can, we must avoid the American way."

What are some of those many steps? One is "voluntary early retirement." Says Keijiro Shoji, executive vice president at Mitsubishi Electric: "Everyone is laying off people these days. What do you think voluntary early retirement is? That's a layoff, Japanese style." Japan Airlines, which lost $409 million in the year ended in March, is offering early retirement—very early retirement—to employees as young as 35. All administrative workers over 50 have been offered a yearlong holiday at 80% of salary. The idea is that they should use the time to look for another job. Those who can't find one can return to the company.

TDK, the world's largest manufacturer of magnetic tapes, even considered for a while keeping 50 managers over age 50 on "standby" at home at 90% of pay for a decade until they reached the retirement age of 60. Meanwhile, Minolta Camera, after offering early retirement packages to 1,700 employees in February (only 115 accepted), announced in April that it would put 6,700 employees on "release from work" with pay for 12 days during the April-to-September period. The savings would come from not running factories during those times.

Kunio Shirotani, 50, a former employee of Clarion, Japan's largest maker of car stereos, can speak from experience about Japan's benevolent non-layoff layoffs. After getting memos for four years that

continued

he was an early retirement target, he finally left in March after 25 years. He got $187,000 in severance pay. If he had worked for ten more years at his present salary, he would have earned $841,000, so he figures the company is saving more than $600,000. Says he: "It's not exactly the same as a layoff, but it's very close. If you don't want to leave, you don't have to. But then the company might ask you to do strange work or transfer you to somewhere you don't want to go. So it feels very much the same."

Other popular techniques to get employees to leave include taking away titles or even their work. The Fuji Research Institute estimates that a million Japanese are what it classifies as working unemployed. In Japanese parlance they are called "window gazers" who are paid to do nothing.

Employees are reluctant to take early retirement because the rigid, seniority-based structure of major companies makes it nearly impossible for them to join another one in mid-career. Shirotani says only about half those who left Clarion with him have found work, and most settled for jobs at less prestigious medium-size companies. Shirotani's own plan is to open a woodcraft store across from his younger daughter's junior high school. He's also trying to turn his passion for buses into a business. He is an officer of the 850-member Japanese Bus Fan Club, which owns ten vintage Japanese buses. Shirotani wants to build a museum for them. For now the buses are moldering in the countryside on a small plot between a landfill and a farm.

Pruning product lines. One reason some American companies emerged stronger from restructuring is that they focused on their best products. Intel Corp. may be the best example. In the 1980s the company dropped out of a business it invented—semiconductor memory chips—and concentrated instead on microprocessor chips, a market it dominates. Intel is now the world's largest maker of chips, period.

The same strategy is beginning to look appealing in Japan. Says Hirotaka Takeuchi, a professor of commerce at Hitotsubashi University: "In the late 1980s, Japanese companies moved in droves to similar industries and produced 'me too' products. Now consumers are telling them they don't all need to offer a full line."

Streamlining product lines proceeds at a snail's pace, however, mainly because companies won't just lay off workers when items are discontinued. Still, there are notable exceptions. Matsushita Electric since 1988 has slashed the number of its audio products from 5,000 to 1,200 and aims to knock off another 200 this year. Isuzu Motors is abandoning the passenger car market in favor of trucks. Honda has gotten out of racing. And all automakers are reducing the number of models.

Putting the squeeze on overseas subsidiaries. Are overseas employees covered by the no-layoffs policy? Definitely not. Just a few weeks after Nissan in Tokyo promised to transfer, not lay off, workers at Zama, Nissan Motor Corp. USA announced it would fire 5% of its work force at corporate headquarters in Carson, California. Back in Tokyo, Nissan's Yasuda says: "It's an American company run by American people. Perhaps they could have depended more on attrition, but they chose layoffs. We asked them to meet the bottom line. The rest was their responsibility."

While their tactics range from the eccentric to the essential, the Japanese clearly aren't going far enough. Most of their restructuring falls short of even the most benign American definition. Many of their moves are reminiscent of ineffective attempts by companies like IBM to pare down while protecting employees and established business lines. One thing is certain: Whether Japanese companies take drastic steps or not, their comparatively freer American competitors will. Already Japanese companies are having trouble contending with U.S. computer, semiconductor, and even auto companies that have emerged from the cathartic late 1980s stronger than ever.

That's why the CEOs in MITI's study group are now methodically drawing up a blueprint for restructuring Japanese industry. Says Ushio, wearing a sly grin: "Enlightened people are studying quietly." The committee's goal is to devise politically and socially acceptable methods to use real layoffs and divestitures within a few years. Their models are companies such as General Electric and Intel, and the CEOs are ranking each stage of restructuring from least to most painful for Japan.

More difficult than understanding these cases will be convincing Japan Inc.'s loyal employees that their companies are in deep enough trouble to justify drastic action. Ushio's smile suddenly drops as he adds, "We have to persuade the older people and the masses so that they recognize Japanese corporations are in a bad position to compete in the international market."

He estimates that Japan's GNP would have to enjoy 5% growth to sustain the way Japanese companies do business now. Forget it. The present rate hovers around 2%. Ushio has written essays warning that everything unique about Japan Inc.—the lifetime employment system, cross-shareholding, even the cooperative relationship between business and government—will be endangered by 1995 if companies don't take stern action now. Nevertheless, he sighs, "almost 90% of Japanese people still say Japanese companies are strong."

Although Japanese companies are still wrangling over what *risutora* really is, American competitors should not take too much comfort in their struggle. All of Japan's industrial companies won't make it unscathed through the tough transition to slower growth. But the ones that do will be meaner and leaner than ever.

Source: Thornton, Emily. "Japan's Struggle to Restructure." *Fortune* 28 June 1993: 84–88. [© 1993 Time Inc. All rights reserved.]

1. Do the following thesis statements adequately focus the reader on the point of the article?

   a. In Emily Thornton's article "Japan's Struggle to Restructure," she states that the Japanese economy is in trouble.

   b. In Emily Thornton's article "Japan's Struggle to Restructure," she states that Japanese corporations are using *risutora*.

   c. In Emily Thornton's article "Japan's Struggle to Restructure," she states that Japanese companies are laying off workers to remain competitive.

   d. In Emily Thornton's article "Japan's Struggle to Restructure," she states that Japanese business is trying to return to its competitive instincts.

2. To formulate an effective thesis statement for Emily Thornton's article, what items must be included in it?

3. Write an effective thesis statement for Emily Thornton's article.

7.4: You can practice your abstract skills by first reading the article in box 7.5. Then, write both an informative and a descriptive abstract. Your intended audience is Robert Schules, CEO of your corporation. Schules is a white male of 68 who worked his way to the top by beginning in the mail room.

CHAPTER 8 · Doing Research

On occasion you will be asked to write longer, more complex, more detailed papers. You may be asked to analyze, to persuade, or to inform an audience. You will have to provide the facts that illustrate and support your conclusions. In such instances, you will write reports.

Chapters 8 through 10 show how to write a business report. Chapter 8 provides an overview of the research process, emphasizing the care that you must take in documenting your findings and sources. Chapter 9 suggests methods that you can use to organize your findings—both in outline and textual form. Chapter 10 illustrates how to put everything together into a neat and professional package.

The Research Process

Just as writing is a process, so is research. You need to organize your time as well as collect data. If you rush through either your research or your writing, you will make mistakes.

ORGANIZING YOUR TIME

Whatever the research topic, first make a simple chart that organizes your time. You know when the report is due, so organize your time between the receipt of the request for a report and when it is actually due. Divide this time according to the steps of the research process and the steps of the writing process. Then determine the weeks or days when certain aspects of the report's research and writing are to be completed. You might employ a Gantt chart, or you can simply use a calendar to indicate what will be done in what week. (See chapter 11 for details concerning the construction of a Gantt chart.)

If you have a plan, you will not be hurried and you will not procrastinate.

COLLECTING THE DATA

Before you can even begin to think about writing, you must gather the data. To gather the data efficiently, follow a pattern of organization and development. Whatever the research project, the following eight steps will help you complete it.

1. Limit the Topic of Research. Before you begin looking for information, first narrow down the research topic. Do not go to the library or log onto a database without first deciding what it is, precisely, that you need to know. Establish guidelines for yourself. Sometimes you will know exactly what the audience who requested the report wants to know; other times, the report request may be more general, and you will have to analyze the needs of your audience.

For example, if your boss wants to know the applicable legal guidelines with respect to sexual harassment, do not just search under the heading of *sexual harassment*. If you do, you may be overwhelmed by the amount of data available. Instead, ask yourself, "What does my audience really want to know?" In this case, the answer might simply be that your boss is interested in sexual harassment *in the workplace. The workplace* already represents a narrowing of the research topic. This is a beginning. On a notecard, write down all those subtopics required by your audience to fulfill its informational needs. Thus, on the notecard for this report, you could list the following:

Sexual harassment—workplace

Sexual harassment—women

Sexual harassment—laws

Sexual harassment—statutes

Sexual harassment—definition

Sexual harassment—legal decisions

Sexual harassment—Supreme Court decisions

Use this list throughout your research, and update it as you proceed. After all, you may find additional subtopics in the indices or databases that you search. If you do, add the new subtopic to the list. By following these steps, you ensure that your research is as complete and thorough as it can be.

2. Formulate the Research. Once you have narrowed your topic or issue, decide what research tools to use to begin the research. Box 8.1 lists just some of the many research tools available.

Begin with general indices, databases, and guides that you already know are on point with your research. For example, if you were asked to write a report on a particular corporation, you might begin with *Hoover's Handbook to American Business* or *Value Line Investment Survey*. Both of these would be good places to start because they each provide an overview of the corporation. Once you have an overview, you will know more precisely where to look and what to look for. For instance, let's say that you look up X Corporation in the two sources just mentioned. You discover that X Corporation is currently suffering legal problems because of disgruntled consumers and it is also having tax problems with the federal government. Based on such general information, you now know more precisely both what sources to begin with and what topics to search in indices and databases. Such topics might now include the names of cases involving X Corporation, the kind of consumer lawsuits involved, and the precise nature of the tax problem. You now also know some of the research tools that you can use to uncover more specific data: *Business Periodicals Index,*

BOX 8.1

List of Research Resources

ABI/INFORM

Accountant's Index

Ageline

Almanac of Business and Industrial Financial Ratios

Barron's Finance and Investment Handbook

Barron's Keys to Reading an Annual Report

Barron's Keys to Understanding Financial Forms

Business Database Plus [on-line service]

Business Information Sourcebook

Business Periodicals Index

CCH Product Liability Reporter

CCH Standard Federal Tax Reporter

CCH Trade Regulation Reporter

Computer Industry Almanac

Congressional Information Service: Information and Abstracts

Cracking Latin America

Credit Manual of Commercial Laws

Dialog Business Connection [on-line service]

Directory of American Firms Operating in Foreign Countries

Disclosure [computer database]

Dow Jones Guide to the World Stock Market

Dow Jones News / Dow Jones Free-Text Search [on-line service]

Dun and Bradstreet's Guide to Your Investments

Dun and Bradstreet's International Business

Dun and Bradstreet's Key Business Directory of Latin America

Dun and Bradstreet's Million Dollar Directory

Dun and Bradstreet's Principal International Businesses

Dun and Bradstreet's Reference Book of Corporate Managements

Dun's Business Month

Dun's Employment Opportunities Directory

Dun's Financial Profiles

Dun's Review

Dun's Review and Modern Industry

Dun's Statistical Review

European Business Services Directory

Fortune 500 Directory of U.S. Corporations

continued

General Business File Database

Guide to Doing Business in the European Economic Community

Hoover's Guide to Private Company Profiles of 500 Major U.S. Private Enterprises

Hoover's Handbook of American Business

Hoover's Handbook of Emerging Companies

Hoover's Handbook of World Business

Index of Economic Articles

Index to Legal Periodicals

Job Seeker's Guide to Private and Public Companies

Key to Economic Science and Managerial Science

Kompass-Mexico [database]

LAN database

Maquiladora Directory

Mexico Business

Mexico Company Handbook

Moody's Bank and Finance Manual

Moody's Handbook of Common Stock

National Accounts Statistics: Main Aggregates and Detailed Tables

National Directory of Corporate Public Affairs

National Directory of Minority-Owned Business Firms

National Trade and Professional Associations of the United States

New York Times Index

PAIS International—Public Affairs Information Service

Personnel Management Abstracts

Poor's Register of Corporations, Directors and Executives, United States and Canada

Price Waterhouse—Doing Business in Texas

Price Waterhouse—Guide to Doing Business in _____ [name of country]

Proquest [computer database]

Reader's Guide to Periodical Literature

Standard and Poor's

Standard and Poor's 500 Guide

Standard and Poor's Register / Standard and Poor's Industry Surveys

Standard and Poor's Stock and Bond Guide

Statistical Abstract of the United States

Texas 500: Hoover's Guide to the Top Texas Companies

Texas Road Map to Starting a Business in Texas

Thomas' Register Inbound Traffic Guide

Thomas' Register Mid Year Guide to Data Information Processing

Thomas' Register of American Manufacturers
United States Industrial Outlook
U.S.-Mexico Trade Pages
Value Line Investment Survey
Wall Street Journal Index
Who Owns Whom: North America
Who Owns Whom: Continental Europe
World's Emerging Stock Markets

CCH Product Liability Reporter, CCH Standard Federal Tax Reporter, Disclosure, Index to Legal Periodicals, New York Times Index, and Wall Street Journal Index.

Search these sources with your notecard of topics in hand. Remember, each source may suggest other sources that you can search for additional details. The beginning of any research is like a stone dropped in a pond: The expanding ripples are the sources and the data created by the initial plunge.

3. Gather the Data. Once you have decided where to begin, use your notecard of topics and begin to look up these topics in the various indices and guides. At this point in your research, simply go through your research tools and make a list of those articles and books that appear related to your topic. You are not yet taking notes; you are simply creating a list of sources that you will later look up.

You will find that the titles of most articles and books with respect to business are generally informative. You will seldom find, for instance, an article whose title is solely *Sexual Harassment.* Usually *sexual harassment* is only a part of the title, and the title specifies something about the general topic of sexual harassment. Therefore, be selective in the titles that you write down on your list: Select only those titles that appear related to the purpose of your report.

Search the computer databases such as Disclosure and Proquest following the same guidelines, and add what you find to your list of sources.

4. Use Notecards. Now that you have your list of sources, you are ready to take notes. You can use your PC to create a database, or you can use two sets of notecards. Use one set of notecards for sources, another for the actual notes. (Your database can be constructed in the same way.)

Use one source notecard for each source. Label each source with a letter of the alphabet. Beneath the letter, write a correct MLA bibliographic entry for that source. (You will see the benefit of this method when you write the works-cited page: all you need do is alphabetize the notecards by the author's last name and then type out the works-cited page.)

The other set of notecards is used for the actual notetaking. When you take notes, use the same letter that you gave to the source to number the cards. Thus, the notes taken from source A will be written on notecards numbered A1 through however many notes you take.

On each notecard only write one quote, one paraphrase, or one piece of data. In the bottom right-hand corner of each notecard, cite the page number or numbers where the information came from. Both of these pieces of data—the information and the page reference—will be used in creating an outline and in providing precise in-text documentation.

5. Read and Take Notes.   For efficient and effective notetaking, follow a strategy for reading as well as for taking notes.

When you read a document for the purpose of taking notes, do not read each and every word in it. Instead, read topic sentences. In a business article or book, the topic sentence is the first sentence of each paragraph. Therefore, read the topic sentence and decide whether the paragraph may contain information useful to the writing of your report. If it does, then read the whole paragraph and take notes relevant to your research in the form of paraphrases, quotes, or pieces of statistical data. (Get into the habit of paraphrasing information. This will save you time when you actually begin writing the report because no one wants to read a report that is merely a compilation of quotations. But more on this when the actual writing of the text is discussed.) Furthermore, when dealing with a book, use the book's index in conjunction with your list of subtopics. When you have discovered those subtopics in the index and noted their page numbers, then go to those pages and read them as you would any business document, taking the appropriate notes as you proceed. In this way, you will save yourself time and effort.

6. Add to the List of Sources.   In addition to taking notes from sources, also look for more possible sources by examining the bibliographies and sources that are cited in the book or article you are taking notes from. When you find a reference to a book or article that seems relevant to your research project, and it is not already listed on your sheet of sources, then by all means add that source to your list of sources.

7. Examine Financial Reports.   Business research often requires that you examine financial reports from a company or companies. These reports are usually quite detailed and sometimes quite lengthy; therefore, you must know how to discover the information that you are searching for.

Three of the most common types of financial reports are

Annual reports

Proxy statements

10-K forms

Annual Reports are sometimes available from libraries, from the company that you are researching, and from some computer databases such as Disclosure. Annual reports can be useful research tools because they provide financial information for a company. However, annual reports are not easy to read, nor should you read just one.

Annual reports are difficult to read not because they are complex, but often because vital information is hidden in selected areas throughout the report. Annual reports are written with the ordinary shareholder in mind. That is why the text of the report is written in general, nontechnical language. If you want to discover the real financial status of the company, you will not find it in the text.

Furthermore, you will not find it in the "Letter from the CEO" (which normally precedes the written text), nor will you discover the true financial status of the company in the "Report of the CPA" (which normally comes near the end of the annual report). Both of these items are written in general language, and they attempt to put the best possible light on the financial situation of the company. The "Letter from the CEO" normally speaks to the shareholders. Often this "letter" will address what the corporation has accomplished in the year just ended, and sometimes the CEO will forecast what the company hopes to accomplish in the future. Although this letter cannot be deliberately misleading, it can and often does attempt to speak in glowing terms of the company and its accomplishments, even when things are going badly. Likewise, the "Report of the CPA" speaks in general terms with respect to the financial status of the company, and it, too, will speak well of the company.

So where is the true financial picture of the company? It is found in three areas of the report: (1) footnotes, (2) balance sheet, and (3) income statement.

First, examine the footnotes for details concerning earnings. In particular, read them to determine the manner in which the profits and losses occurred. After all, a short-term loss may be a long-term gain, and a short-term gain may be a long-term loss.

Second, examine the balance sheet. From this sheet you can discover

Assets and current assets

Liabilities and current liabilities

Stockholder's equity

Debt

Third, look at the income statement for information on earnings per share and sales.

For a complete picture, look at more than one annual report for a particular company so you can make comparisons over a period of years. Such comparisons will give you a better understanding of the company's financial picture and will be more accurate than any one annual report.

Proxy Statements are difficult to find, but they are available in some databases. When companies solicit proxies, written agreements allowing the company to vote and act on the behalf of shareholders, SEC requirements state that companies must give shareholders specific reasons as to the reason for the proxy. Therefore, proxy statements sometimes disclose more information with respect to the operating procedures and financial strategies of the company than do annual reports. Corporations, however, do not have to make proxy statements public; thus their scarce availability to the researcher.

10-K forms are annual reports that publicly held companies must file with the SEC. As such, they contain more financial data than do annual reports. These financial forms are also difficult to find, though they are in some databases. Shareholders, of course, can get them when they ask, but it is up to the company whether to release them to the public.

With these financial tools, you should be able to get a good picture of a company's finances.

8. Complete the Research. You may wonder how you will know when your research is complete. This is a good question because in theory research can be almost never ending, but your research must end at some particular point in time. So how do you know when your research is completed? The answer to this question is twofold: When you have (1) answered all the questions that began the research project in the first place, and (2) noticed that sources are becoming repetitive and redundant.

At this stage of the report, then, you can begin to plan its organization. First, however, let us examine the rules of documentation that you must follow in citing your sources.

The Method of Documentation

Because reports are lengthy documents based on research, you must credit the sources of the information that you use in your report. If you do not do so, then you can and will be accused of plagiarism.

Many forms of documentation exist today, but the MLA method is best because of its ease of use and its precision. Many other forms of documentation, especially other forms of in-text documentation, are imprecise because they omit page numbers, authors, or titles. MLA documentation, by contrast, is so exact that the reader always knows precisely where the information came from.

To achieve its precision MLA documentation relies on two methods to arrange source material: a works-cited page (also known as the references page) and in-text documentation.

Footnotes are no longer necessary for documentation. With MLA, footnotes are used for explanation only.

The information in this chapter with respect to MLA documentation concerning the works-cited page, in-text documentation, and the use of footnotes can be found in Joseph Gibaldi's *MLA Handbook for Writers of Research Papers*, 4th ed., New York: Modern Language Association of America, 1984.

WORKS-CITED PAGE

Anything that you use as a source of information requires documentation. In your report, the two means of documentation, the works-cited page and in-text documentation, must work together to provide full details on the source of the information. The works-cited page, therefore, must present complete bibliographic information following MLA format.

The works-cited, or references, page lists in alphabetical order by the author's last name the sources that you have used and cited in the body of the report. In formatting this page, follow these guidelines:

- Begin each entry on the left-hand margin.
- If the entry is longer than one typed line, then indent the subsequent lines as you would for a paragraph.
- If the entry contains no author, then alphabetize it according to the first word in the title, unless the first word is *a, an,* or *the,* then alphabetize by the second word in the title.
- If there is more than one entry by an author, then give the author's name in the first entry only, and in all subsequent entries use three hyphens and a period in place of the author's name.

- Double-space within and between entries.
- Underline book titles and names of journals or magazines.
- Set off magazine and journal articles with quotation marks.
- Give complete page numbers of articles.
- If page numbers are cited consecutively, separate them with a hyphen.
- If page numbers are not consecutive, give the first number then a plus sign.
- Do not cite any source that you have not actually cited in the text.

There is an MLA format for virtually every kind of source; therefore, what follows is only a sampling of the more common forms of documentation that must be used precisely. For further examples and details concerning other kinds of sources that require documentation in the works-cited page, inspect sections 4.1 through 4.10.14 of the *MLA Handbook for Writers of Research Papers*. Formats for the most common kinds of sources that you will use—magazines, journals, newspapers, and books—are discussed here.

Magazine Article

Magazine as here used refers to a magazine for a general public that can be purchased on the newsstand. *Magazine* does not mean a publication written for a sophisticated audience.

A magazine article's entry contains the last and first name of the author; the article's title in quotation marks, the magazine's name, underlined; the date of publication; and the article's page numbers:

> Moore, Lisa J. "An Argument for Starting Small." *U.S. News and World Report* 26 Oct. 1992: 85–88.

Journal Article

A *journal* as here defined is a periodical publication written by experts in the field for the benefit of other experts or scholars in the field.

A journal article's entry contains the last and first name of the author; the article's title in quotation marks; the journal's name underlined; the journal's volume and issue number, separated by a period; the date of publication in parentheses; and the article's page numbers:

> Mascolini, Marcia. "Another Look at Teaching the External Negative Message." *The Bulletin of the Association for Business Communication* 57.2 (1994): 45–47.

Newspaper Article

A newspaper article must be documented by giving the last and first name of the author; the article's title in quotation marks: the newspaper's name, underlined; the date of publication; and the article's section and page numbers:

> O'Boyle, Thomas. "Working Together." *The Wall Street Journal* 5 June 1992: A1+.

Book

A sample entry for a book should contain the author's name; title of book, underlined; place of publication; name of publisher; and year of publication.

> Boone, Louis E., and David L. Kurtz. *Contemporary Business Communication.* Englewood Cliffs, NJ: Prentice Hall, 1994.

Book with Edition

Books are often published in more than one edition. If there is more than one edition, then note that edition:

> Black, Henry Campbell. *Black's Law Dictionary.* 5th ed. St. Paul, MN: West, 1979.

Book with Multiple Authors

Books sometimes have multiple authors. If this is the case, then give the last and first name of the first author listed on the title page and then the first and last names of the other authors, in the order they are listed on the title page, separating them with commas if there are more than two, with the conjunction *and* preceding the last named author:

> Parks, A. Franklin, James A. Levernier, and Ida Masters Howell. *Structuring Paragraphs: A Guide to Effective Writing.* 2nd ed. New York: St. Martin's, 1986.

Book with Author and Editor

If the book has both an author and editor, then cite both:

> Follett, Wilson. *Modern American Usage: A Guide.* Ed. Jacques Barzun. New York: Hill and Wang, 1966.

Book with Editors

If the book lacks an author but has an editor, then use the editor's name as you would the author's name, and place the abbreviation *ed.* after the editor's name. If there is more than one editor, give all their names in the order they appear on the title page, with *and* before the last name, and *eds.* following:

> Hoover, Gary, Alta Campbell, and Patrick J. Spain, eds. *Hoover's Handbook of American Business.* Austin, TX: Reference, 1994.

Book without Author

If a book has no author, then begin with the title:

> *The American Heritage Dictionary.* 2nd ed. Boston: Houghton Mifflin, 1991.

Book with Multiple Volumes

Some books have more than one volume. If you are using only one volume, give that volume number after the title. Then, after the publication date, you may indicate the complete number of volumes in the series:

> *Job Seeker's Guide to Private and Public Companies.* Vol. 4. Detroit: Gale Research, 1992. 4 vols.

Box 8.2 provides a sample works-cited, or references, page.

BOX 8.2

Works Cited

The American Heritage Dictionary. 2nd ed. Boston: Houghton Mifflin, 1991.

Black, Henry Campbell. *Black's Law Dictionary.* 5th ed. St. Paul, MN: West, 1979.

Boone, Louis E., and David L. Kurtz. *Contemporary Business Communication.* Englewood Cliffs, NJ: Prentice Hall, 1994.

Follett, Wilson. *Modern American Usage: A Guide.* Ed. Jacques Barzun. New York: Hill and Wang, 1966.

Gibaldi, Joseph. *MLA Handbook for Writers of Research Papers.* 4th ed. New York: Modern Language Association of America, 1984.

Hoover, Gary, Alta Campbell, and Patrick J. Spain, eds. *Hoover's Handbook of American Business.* Austin, TX: Reference, 1994.

Job Seeker's Guide to Private and Public Companies. Vol. 4. Detroit: Gale Research Inc., 1992. 4 vols.

Mascolini, Marcia. "Another Look at Teaching the External Negative Message." *The Bulletin of the Association for Business Communication* 57.2 (1994): 45–47.

Moore, Lisa J. "An Argument for Starting Small." *U.S. News and World Report* 26 Oct. 1992: 85–88.

O'Boyle, Thomas. "Working Together." *The Wall Street Journal* 5 June 1992: A1+.

Parks, A. Franklin, James A. Levernier, and Ida Masters Howell. *Structuring Paragraphs: A Guide to Effective Writing.* 2nd ed. New York: St. Martin's, 1986.

IN-TEXT DOCUMENTATION

All quotations, paraphrases, and ideas derived from a source must be cited both in the works-cited page and in the text. In-text documentation provides an abbreviated form of the source citation given in full in the works-cited page, and it provides the exact page number or page numbers from which the information is derived. The in-text citation follows the quotation, paraphrase, or idea to be cited, and it encloses one or all of the following in parentheses:

Author's last name

Title of source

Page number

In MLA in-text documentation only those sources listed in the works-cited page can be cited in the text. In other words, the works-cited page and in-text documentation work hand-in-hand: a source cannot be cited in the one without it also appearing in the other.

Sections 5.1 through 5.5.2 of the *MLA Handbook for Writers of Research Papers* provide the information for the following discussion of in-text documentation.

The rules for using MLA in-text documentation are straightforward and readily illustrated in a sample paragraph, as the following paragraph based on imaginary sources illustrates:

> **George Mayfield believes that all legal issues are essentially economic in nature (17). Robert Engles agrees with this view, and this leads him to imply that there is no real need for antitrust legislation *(The Antitrust Problems* 77). However, a number of prominent legal theoreticians continue to view legal problems in terms of bettering society (Howarth 15; Sinkle 276). To these theoreticians, legal issues cannot simply be economic; they see law as an outgrowth of society's moral purposes (Smith, *The History of Law* 2: 67–165).**

Before examining these sentences individually, note that each parenthesis is followed, not preceded, by the period. Further, a hyphen is used between the inclusive page numbers from which the material comes, and a semicolon is used to separate sources when more than one is cited for the same information.

Look at the first sentence:

> **George Mayfield believes that all legal issues are essentially economic in nature (17).**

Here, the author of the source is mentioned in the sentence: *George Mayfield*. Therefore, his name is not given inside the parentheses because it would be redundant. Note that no title is mentioned. When the author or authors have only one entry in the works-cited page, do not give a title in the in-text citation. In this instance all that need be placed in parentheses is the page number.

Look at the second sentence:

> **Robert Engles agrees with this view, and this leads him to imply that there is no real need for antitrust legislation *(The Antitrust Problems* 77).**

Here, the author of the source is mentioned in the sentence: *Robert Engles*. Again, it would be redundant to repeat his name in the parentheses. However, the title is given because Engles has more than one entry in the works-cited page. In the first mention give the complete title. Thereafter, shorten it to its significant nouns. Subsequent in-text references to *The Antitrust Problems* may be shortened to *Antitrust*. (Note that book titles are underlined and article titles are given in quotation marks.)

Look at the third sentence:

> **However, a number of prominent legal theoreticians continue to view legal problems in terms of bettering society (Howarth 15; Sinkle 276).**

Note that there are two authors from two separate sources, but that the authors are not mentioned in the sentence; therefore, the authors must be mentioned inside the parentheses. Titles are not given since each author has only one source listed in the works-cited page. Because there are two authors from two separate sources, a semicolon is used to indicate that these are two sources. By mentioning two authors in this manner, you are saying that both authors agree with the content of the sentence immediately preceding the parentheses.

Look at the fourth sentence:

> **To these theoreticians, legal issues cannot simply be economic; they see law as an outgrowth of society's moral purposes (Smith, *The History of Law* 2: 67–165).**

Here, no author is mentioned in the sentence, so the author must be mentioned in the parentheses. Further, because this author has more than one entry in the works-cited page, a title must be given. (Just as with authors, so with titles: if the title is mentioned in the sentence, then the title need not be given within the parenthesis. Such is not the case here, and thus the title must be given.) Note also that a number precedes the colon. This means that this is volume two of the author's work. If only one volume was cited in the works-cited page, then a volume number would not be given in the parentheses.

There are only a few other guidelines for in-text documentation to remember. First, if a source has no author, then you must cite in-text by title. Give the complete title the first time and the shortened form thereafter. Second, every sentence need not be documented. If you have a series of sentences in a paragraph that derive from the same source and from the same page number, then simply provide the in-text citation at the end of the last sentence. If an entire paragraph is derived from one source and from the same page number or page numbers, then simply provide the in-text citation at the end of the paragraph. However, you can only do this by paragraph; you cannot have five paragraphs, for example, and provide the in-text citation at the end of the last sentence of paragraph five. The reader will not understand that the citation applies to paragraphs one through five but will believe that the citation only applies to the fifth paragraph.

NOTES

MLA documentation using notes is explained in section 5.5 of the *MLA Handbook for Writers of Research Papers*. With MLA documentation, notes are only used for brief clarification, examples, or references and comments regarding other sources. The key word here is *brief*. If your examples, explanations, clarifications, references, or comments are lengthy, then use an appendix or glossary.

A note is indicated by a raised numeral placed beside that which requires the aforementioned examples, explanations, clarifications, references, or comments.[1] Notes can be presented either as footnotes, at the bottom of the relevant page, or as endnotes on a page placed at the end of the text entitled *Notes*. In either case, the explanatory text follows the note, and in-text documentation may be required. Notes are numbered consecutively throughout the text.

---

[1] A judgment awarded by the judge to the moving party when there is no issue of material fact, and the moving party must prevail as a matter of law (*Black's Law Dictionary* 1287).

If you use a notes page, center the title at the top of the page. Then, simply indent each entry five spaces from the right margin, give the footnote number as it appears in the text, provide your comments, and use in-text documentation if needed. The same information in the sample footnote would appear identically in a notes page, except that the page would contain double-spaced, numbered entries, with double-spacing between entries.

Exercises

8.1: Because business students must familiarize themselves with library resources to become effective in the business world, this assignment is designed to provide a more comprehensive look at what is available. To begin the assignment, each student is asked to choose one of the business research tools available in the library. Box 8.1 provides a list of these research tools, and students are to make their choices from this list. The assignment calls for one student per research resource. Each student is responsible for understanding this research resource. This understanding will then be presented to the class in two forms: one part written text and one part oral presentation.

1. *The Written Part:* Write a two-page memo addressed to your fellow classmates. (This memo will be handed out to the class before the oral presentation.) This memo will explain the library resource in terms of its location, coverage, organization, and updating. In addition, provide a visual that will further explain the text. The first page explains the location, coverage, organization, and updating. The second page provides the visual.

   a. **Location:** Provide the call number of the library resource and state its location in the library. (Essentially, this is a timesaving device for students who may have to use this resource at some point in their academic or business lives.)

   b. **Coverage:** Provide a detailed listing of the contents of this library resource. In other words, what information can be found by using this library resource? This information can be provided either in a detailed paragraph or in a precise list.

   c. **Organization:** Provide a concise explanation of the organization of the library resource. Not only state how the material is organized but also provide an example (or examples) to illustrate how information can be accessed. A list can be used quite effectively here.

   d. **Updating:** Provide information about how the library resource is updated. For example, is the resource updated weekly, monthly, or yearly? Is the updating accomplished through the publication of a new edition, or is it done with a pocket supplement?

   e. **Visual:** Provide a visual that demonstrates what information the library resource contains and how the information is organized. The easiest method for students to adopt is to copy all or a portion of a page of the library resource. This page should be a representative page of this resource in the sense that all other pages of this resource are organized in the same way.

   Refer to the visual in the text of the memo as Fig. 1, and provide a brief caption either at the top or at the bottom of the visual. Then provide arrows and captions on the visual itself, thus highlighting the important sections of the copied page. The arrows and captions should begin at twelve o'clock and move clockwise around the visual. Beside each arrow, provide a brief phrase that tells readers what it is that they are looking at.

2. ***The Oral Part:*** Present a five minute oral presentation that demonstrates your understanding of this library resource and your ability to pass this understanding on to your classmates. The oral presentation should contain an introduction, body, and conclusion.

    a. Introduction: Pass out your memo to your classmates before the oral presentation. Then introduce yourself and the library resource that is to be discussed. Next, state the location and call number of the resource and forecast the contents and arrangement of the talk.

    b. Body: The oral presentation must cover the items discussed in the memo. However, you cannot use any written text other than the visual and a small notecard with topic headings when you speak from the podium. This prohibition ensures that you will maintain eye contact and not simply read the memo to the class. In discussing the visual, you will orally demonstrate your understanding and grasp of the library resource.

    c. Conclusion: State how the library resource is updated and ask for questions from the audience. This call for questions is crucial for two reasons: first, answering questions forces you to make sure that you know your material; second, answering questions ensures that the audience understands the library resource that has been presented.

3. ***A Final Comment:*** By the time the oral presentations conclude, you will have a notebook-sized body of memos describing numerous library resources that you can use in writing and business classes.

CHAPTER 9

Analyzing and Outlining the Data

Once you have completed the research, perform a thorough audience analysis. You need to know as much as possible about your audience to tailor your report to its needs. Many questions concerning the arrangement and development of the text can then be answered. These questions range from what is the most effective format to what is the appropriate vocabulary to what are the most effective headings. Review chapter 1 to make sure that you properly take your audience's needs into account.

Once you know your audience, you can bring order to the chaos: your note-cards. The simplest way to accomplish this is to decide on the purpose of your report. In other words, is it informative, or is it an argument and thus persuasive? If you focus on your purpose, your goal or objective, then all the writing to achieve that end will be succinctly organized.

Developing a Plan of Action

Make sure that your data and your evaluation of that data match the audience's needs, in other words, that the report answers the audience's questions (Guffey 320). One way to ensure that your audience will have its questions answered is to evaluate your notecards or note database. Based on your evaluation, determine your goal.

If you have decided to make a recommendation, whether positive or negative, then determine what criteria led you to that recommendation. You have the data before you. What does it tell you, and how does it agree with your recommendation? Use a set of standards to evaluate the information you have found (Guffey 330). By articulating your criteria for judgment, you will avoid subjectivity, hyperbole, and understatement (Guffey 326–27). Furthermore, with these criteria, you can readily organize the body of your report.

Even if you are not recommending anything at all, but merely providing data that you will sum up at the end of the report, you can still, based on your data, provide yourself with a brief summary of the points that you would like to end with.

Once you have these concluding points written down, structuring the body of the report to match them makes writing the report easier.

Deciding How to Organize the Report

When you have your recommendations or conclusions set down in writing, once again review your notecards. Ask yourself what writing format will most easily and completely convey your data in a comprehensible form. In general, you have seven ways to organize your data:

1. Comparison / contrast
2. Problem / solution
3. Elimination of alternatives
4. General to specific, or specific to general
5. Spatial
6. Functional
7. Chronological. (Locker 423)

Choose one of these organizational patterns that fits your data and your audience's needs by using the following guidelines.

Use comparison and contrast when deciding between a number of possibilities, one of which is somehow better than the others. For example, should you adopt Word Perfect or AmiPro 3.1 as the word processing system for your office?

Use problem and solution when you have a problem that you can analyze, break down, and solve. The solution section should be the longest part of the report because it must resolve all (or at least as many as possible) parts of the problem (Locker 424–25). For example, how can you turn over your inventory more quickly and efficiently?

Use the elimination of alternatives pattern when you want to demonstrate the *best* solution to a problem. In proceeding by elimination, you are eliminating alternative solutions to arrive at the solution that you think is the best (Locker 425). For example, why is one medical plan for employees better than all the other medical plans?

Use the general to specific pattern when you wish to identify aspects of a problem and then the specific solution to each aspect (Locker 425). For example, why does your company require outside auditors?

Use the specific to general pattern when you want to discuss specific aspects of a problem, how they relate to a larger, more comprehensive problem, and how both the specific and general aspects can be solved (Locker 425). For example, why should Bob Jones, CPA, be your company's accountant?

Use a spatial organization when you want to describe something, when you want to describe how something works or functions, or when you want to break down something into geographical locations (Locker 426). For example, what is the chain of command in your company? How does a computer operate? How are your sales doing in various parts of the United States and Europe?

Use a functional organization when you want to divide up something, analyzing each part of that something to come to a conclusion about the viability of a solution, the cost of a solution, the impact of certain market strategies—anything that can be divided up and analyzed in terms of its parts (Locker 426). For example, what are the costs and benefits in expanding your advertising budget? Why is your marketing strategy working well in New York but ineffectively in Vermont?

Use a chronological organization when you want to show when things occurred or will occur (Locker 427). For example, how has your company grown over the last decade?

Look at your data and decide what organizational pattern will most completely and simply incorporate it. Of course, you may discover that not all the data will fit into one pattern. That's okay. Use one primary method of organization for your report, but also use any secondary ones that serve your purpose.

Outlining the Report

Having decided whether you will make a recommendation or whether you will simply supply a summary kind of conclusion, you will then know whether your report is informative or analytical and persuasive. With this goal in mind, take the data that you have categorized according to one of the seven organizational patterns and develop an outline.

When constructing your outline, devote the first section of the report to an introduction that (1) states why the report was written, for whom it was written, and who wrote the report; (2) describes, in general, what the report will cover; and (3) forecasts the major sections of the report (Locker 445). Of course, you can add much more than these three items. The introduction can also include (1) any limitations to research or to the report, (2) any assumptions that you have made in writing the report, (3) the methods used in conducting interviews or surveys, (4) the criteria used in analyzing or presenting the data, and (5) a few definitions that the audience might have to know to understand the report. (If you must define many terms, then use a glossary) (Locker 446).

The second section of a report usually gives background information, or the history of the problem (Locker 446). This is usually concise but informative, because "[e]ven though the current audience for the report probably knows the situation, reports are filed and consulted years later" (Locker 446).

The third section is the body of the report. Here, use one of the seven organizational patterns.

Finally, at the very end of the report, present your recommendations or conclusions.

INFORMATIVE REPORT

If the report is informative, then you will write a report that does not persuade or analyze; instead, such a report will only provide the data and answer those questions that the audience wants and needs answered to make a decision (Guffey 350). To effectively organize this information before writing, make an outline.

For the sake of illustration, let us assume that you are writing an investment report on a particular stock. Box 9.1 (page 114) provides a sample outline of an informative report.

The outline in box 9.1 is preliminary: It is the first but not the last outline that you will make before writing the rough draft and the report itself. This outline divides the information into general categories as well as subheadings, but you must now go further. Flesh out the subheadings. In other words, using your notecards, provide more specific details that support each of the capitalized letters in box 9.1. The higher the degree of specificity that you can provide for yourself in an outline, the easier becomes the writing of the rough draft.

Once you have achieved the necessary degree of specificity, organize the data according to one of the seven patterns of organization. Choose a method that achieves ease of comprehension. For the outline in box 9.1, the primary pattern of organization, based on ease of use, should either be general to specific or specific to general.

ANALYTICAL OR PERSUASIVE REPORTS

Analytical or persuasive reports seek to provide data to persuade an audience to take a particular action or view something in a particular way. As Guffey points out, "[i]nformational reports emphasize facts; analytical reports emphasize reasoning and conclusions" (360).

To develop an outline for a persuasive report, follow the same methodology employed in the informative report, but because the focus is persuasive rather than informative, use the persuasive techniques described in chapter 7. For example, adopting the same scenario as in box 9.1 but with the change that you argue for or against investment in a particular stock, the actual persuasion of the audience would occur in sections IV through VI. Let us assume here that you are not recommending investment. An outline for this argument is given in box 9.2 (page 115).

This outline represents an investment analysis that suggests investment should not occur. Note that section IV is the longest section, and it focuses on the reasons the investment should not take place. This is the heart of the report, and as such you would devote the most time to it. Sections I through III are merely the background information that section IV draws upon to present all of the reasons investment would be a poor decision. Here, you could use comparison and contrast, elimination of alternatives, general to specific, or specific to general methods of organization to illustrate why such an investment would be a bad move. Section V would, then, downplay any benefits that such an investment would offer, and you would end with a logical appeal using financial data and statistics demonstrating the unprofitability of such an investment.

The same format, however, could be used to argue for investing. In that case, section IV would deal with the benefits of investment in great detail, and, again, comparison and contrast, elimination of alternatives, general to specific, or specific to general organizational patterns could be used to illustrate why such an investment would be a fine investment decision. Section V would refute or downplay the potential risks

BOX 9.1

An Outline for an Informative Investment Analysis

I. Introduction

   A. Statement of purpose: what are you researching; who you are; why you are doing this?

   B. What you have used to arrive at your conclusions?

   C. Forecast of the major sections of the report

II. Corporate history

   A. What does this company do?

   B. Who are the corporate officers? Address of corporation?

   C. Principal shareholders?

   D. Is this corporation a subsidiary, or does it have subsidiaries?

III. Financial information

   A. What are the sales? How does the annual report look?

   B. What are the earnings per share?

   C. What is the stock selling for now and in the past?

   D. What are the corporation's assets and liabilities?

IV. Risks of investment: Identify and explain the risks

   A.

   B.

   C.

V. Benefits: Identify and explain the benefits

   A.

   B.

   C.

VI. Conclusion (summary of risks and benefits)

   A.

   B.

   C.

   D.

   E.

   F.

BOX 9.2

An Outline for Analytical or Persuasive Investment Analysis

I. Introduction

   A. Statement of purpose: what are you researching; who you are; why you are doing this?

   B. What you have used to arrive at your conclusions?

   C. Forecast of the major sections of the report

II. Corporate history

   A. What does this company do?

   B. Who are the corporate officers? Address of corporation?

   C. Principal shareholders?

   D. Is this corporation a subsidiary, or does it have subsidiaries?

III. Financial information

   A. What are the sales? How does the annual report look?

   B. What are the earnings per share?

   C. What is the stock selling for now and in the past?

   D. What are the corporation's assets and liabilities?

IV. Risks of investment: Identify and explain the risks

   A.

   B.

   C.

   D.

   E.

   F.

V. Benefits: Identify and refute the benefits

   A.

   B.

VI. Recommendations: Based on the foregoing, Professor Meaney should not invest

   A. Summary

   B. Logical appeal

BOX 9.3

An Outline for an Informative Investment Analysis with Visuals and Forecasting Statements

I. Introduction

    A. Statement of purpose: what are you researching; who you are; why you are doing this?

    B. What you have used to arrive at your conclusions?

    C. Forecast of the major sections of the report

II. Corporate History: **FS**

    A. What does this company do?

    B. Who are the corporate officers? Address of corporation?

    C. Principal shareholders?

        1. **V—pie chart**

    D. Is this corporation a subsidiary, or does it have subsidiaries?

        1. **V—pie chart or table**

III. Financial information: **FS**

    A. What are the sales? How does the annual report look?

    B. What are the earnings per share?

        1. **V—line graph or bar chart**

    C. What is the stock selling for now and in the past?

        1. **V—line graph or bar chart**

    D. What are the corporation's assets and liabilities?

        1. **V—table**

IV. Risks of investment: **FS:** Identify and explain the risks

    A.

    B.

    C.

V. Benefits: **FS:** Identify and explain the benefits

    A.

    B.

    C.

VI. Conclusion (summary of risks and benefits)

    A.

    B.

    C.

    D.

    E.

    F.

of investment, and you would end with a logical appeal using financial data and statistics demonstrating the profitability were an investment to be made.

USING VISUALS AND FORECASTING STATEMENTS

Once you have a good outline, consider where to place visuals and forecasting statements. In many business reports, visuals are extraordinarily useful because they can take complex financial data and present it in a straightforward way. Box 9.3 (page 116) presents an outline of an informative report that includes the locations of visuals (V) and forecasting statements (FS).

Conclusion

As you can see, the difference between writing a report or any other business document is merely one of degree. Reports demand more time and effort, but they follow remarkably similar guidelines to the other kinds of business documents described and detailed in this book.

Exercises

9.1: Assume that the data below is a summary based on a great deal of other information:

> **Six suppliers have made bids to sell your company the same number of computers. Computer Universe makes a bid of $450,000 with a 24-mo. warranty, but not including the cost of installation or on-site training. Computer Warehouse makes a bid of $520,000 with a 12-mo. warranty, including the cost of installation, but not including on-site training. New Age Electronics makes a bid of $600,000 with a 3-mo. warranty, including the cost of installation and on-site training. Low-Cost Computers makes a bid of $380,000 without a warranty and not including the cost of installation or on-site training. Supreme MicroSystems makes a bid of $700,000 with a 12-mo. warranty, including on-site training, but not including the cost of installation.**

If you are asked to write an informative report on which supplier to buy from, what primary organizational patterns can you use in writing the report?

If you are asked to write an analytical or persuasive report that recommends a particular supplier, what primary organizational patterns can you use in writing the report?

9.2: Write an outline for an analytical or persuasive report in which you have chosen Supreme MicroSystems as your supplier.

9.3: Write an outline for an informative report on choosing a supplier.

CHAPTER 10
Formatting the Report

After you have compiled your data and outlined it, you can then arrange it in a proper format. You want a format that is simple to skim as well as to read. A good format will allow your readers easy access to the information that they need. It will also make writing the text easier for you.

This chapter will illustrate the arrangement of those sections of the report that precede the written text, of those sections that come after the written text, and of the written text itself. The following lists the possible sections of the report in the order they are to be presented:

1. Title page
2. Letter of transmittal
3. Table of contents
4. List of illustrations
5. Informative or descriptive abstract
6. Text of the report
7. Notes
8. Glossary
9. Appendices
10. Works cited or references (Gibaldi 4.4; Guffey 388–91)

Some of these sections are required and some are optional, as will be discussed in due course.

Sections Preceding the Text

Five sections precede the text of the report itself:

1. Title page
2. Letter of transmittal
3. Table of contents

4. List of illustrations

5. Informative or descriptive abstract

TITLE PAGE

For the title page, use one-inch margins on the sides and two-inch margins on the top and bottom of the page. This design ensures that items will stand out on the page. The title page should provide the following blocks of information:

1. Title

2. Whom the document was prepared for: name, title, name of company, city, state, and zip code

3. Who prepared the document: name, title, name of company, city, state, zip code

4. Release date (Locker 439).

Title

The first item placed on the page is the title. Capitalize the first word, last word, and all principal words. Do not use all capital letters. Center the title on the page.

The title is the subject line for the report. It should tell the reader exactly what the document contains. Thus, titles such as *Financial Report* or *Research on Y Corporation* are useless. They tell the reader nothing. Like the subject line for a memo, the title must specifically tell the reader what will be forthcoming (Locker 439). The title must inform the reader with respect to content and purpose:

A Financial Report on the Advisability of Investing In Intel Corporation

Reader

After the title, skip a few spaces and provide information about the reader of the document. Spacing throughout the title page is a matter left to your own discretion, but you want to achieve a sense of balance upon the page. Type *Prepared for*, centered on the page, and double-space. Then, provide and center the following information about the reader:

1. Reader's name

2. Title (if the reader has one)

3. Name of company reader is employed by (if applicable)

4. City, state, zip code

Author

Skip more spaces and provide information about yourself. Type *Prepared by*, centered on the page, and double-space. Then, provide and center the following information about yourself:

1. Author's name

2. Title

3. Name of company author is employed by

4. City, state, zip code

Release Date

You have two choices here. Either give the date on which you presented the report, or, if others will read the report before taking action on it, then give the date when the public will have access to it (Locker 440).

Box 10.1 provides a sample title page.

LETTER OF TRANSMITTAL

The letter of transmittal introduces readers to the report and provides a positive view of the writer and of the report (Locker 441).

If you are an employee who is writing a report for your company, use a memo format for this letter. If, however, you are not an employee of the company, then use a letter format (Locker 440).

In writing the letter of transmittal do the following:

1. State who wanted the report and why.

2. Provide a concise but brief description of your conclusions or recommendations.

3. Note any areas of significance and any difficulties that you had to overcome.

4. Thank those who were involved in researching and preparing the report.

5. If there is any further investigation required, describe it.

6. Thank your reader and state your willingness to provide answers to any questions. (Locker 441)

BOX 10.1

The Title Page

A Financial Report on the Advisability of Investing
In Intel Corporation

Prepared for

Edward Jones
CEO
Xexon Corporation
El Paso, Texas 79912

Prepared by

John Maynard
Director of Accounting
Xexon Corporation
El Paso, Texas 79912

23 September 1994

Because the letter is not a part of the actual written text, paginate it with a small roman numeral *i*.

TABLE OF CONTENTS

The table of contents provides the reader with an outline and an overview of the report's contents. As such, it is best that you write the report first, and then write the table of contents. In this way, you will know exactly what your report contains and what occurs where in your report.

The table of contents is little more than a listing of headings and subheadings. To construct a table of contents, place the title *Table of Contents* at the top of the page, center it, and boldface it. Then, place the titles *List of Illustrations* and *Abstract* flush with the left-hand margin, and boldface them.

Then, beneath these items, flush with the left-hand margin, list headings and subheadings in the order that they appear in the report. If the text of the report has fewer than 25 pages, list all headings and subheadings. If the text of the report is much longer than 25 pages, then "pick a level and put all the headings at that level and above in the Table of Contents" (Locker 441). The headings and subheadings must appear as they do in the report's text. Boldface the major headings, and use a regular font for all subheadings.

Next, if your report has endnotes, use the caption *Notes* in the Table of Contents, and boldface it.

Then, if you have a glossary or appendices in your report, list and boldface them. Include the number or letter and caption when listing appendices.

After this, place the heading *Works Cited*. Boldface it.

After each one of these items, provide a series of dots to the right-hand margin. Beside or close to each series of dots place the page number on which this section of the report begins. Line the page numbers up evenly.

Throughout the table of contents, double-space between all boldfaced headings and single-space between subheadings.

The table of contents is actually the first page of your report; however, just like the title page, it has no page number.

Most word processors have a function that you can use to create a table of contents. Look under "Tools" on your command bar.

Box 10.2 (page 122) provides a sample table of contents.

LIST OF ILLUSTRATIONS

When the report contains more than one visual, provide a list of illustrations for the reader's benefit. The list of illustrations is the second page of the report. Because it precedes the report's text, however, it is paginated with small roman numerals beginning with *ii*.

Your visuals may be either figures or tables (Locker 441). Locker distinguishes figures from tables by saying that "[t]ables are words or numbers arranged in rows or columns" and "[f]igures are everything else . . ." (441).

BOX 10.2

Table of Contents

List the figures or tables, their numbers or letters, and their captions as they appear in your report (Locker 442). Boldface these entries and double-space between them. Paginate appropriately.

Box 10.3 provides a sample list of illustrations.

BOX 10.3

List of Illustrations

ABSTRACT

Depending on the length and nature of the report, you can provide the reader with either an informative or descriptive abstract. (See chapter 7 for discussion on how to write each.)

On a separate page or pages immediately preceding the report, prepare a page with the heading *Abstract* boldfaced, centered, and placed at the top of the page. In the abstract, continue to use roman numerals for pagination.

You will find it easier to write the abstract after the report has already been written. Then you are merely summarizing what you have already written.

Sections Succeeding the Text

Four sections may follow your report's text:

1. Notes
2. Glossary
3. Appendices
4. Works cited or references

These sections will continue the pagination with the arabic numerals that began with the first page of your report's text.

NOTES

Endnotes are explanatory, and they begin on the page immediately after the report's text has concluded. (See chapter 8 for further discussion of notes.)

GLOSSARY

A glossary is an alphabetical listing of words appearing in the report's text that require a definition. A glossary can be quite useful in limiting the amount of supplemental information in the report's text itself. A glossary ensures that you will not have to constantly stop and define words for the reader. But do not make a glossary if you have only a few words to define for your reader. In that case, place those words and their definitions in the introduction. It is only when you have a number of words to define that you might want to make a glossary.

If you are going to make a glossary for your reader, then you must alert the reader to the fact that a glossary is available. Thus, the first time that you come across a word in your text that requires a definition, **boldface** the word and follow it with parentheses. In the parentheses, tell your reader that boldfaced words are defined in the glossary on page whatever, and that from this point on, all defined words will be boldfaced in the text.

The glossary page should have the heading *Glossary* boldfaced, centered, and placed at the top of the page. The words or phrases to be defined should then be listed alphabetically and boldfaced with the first letter of each word capitalized. Place a boldfaced colon immediately after each boldfaced term. After the colon, place the definition of the word.

Definitions, if they are not common knowledge, may require in-text documentation. Box 10.4 illustrates a sample glossary.

BOX 10.4

Glossary

Expectation Damages: Awarded for breach of contract. Based on the difference between what the injured party would have received from performance of the contract and what the injured party actually received because of nonperformance of the contract (Black 352).

Malfeasance: Doing something that one should not do (Black 902).

Nonfeasance: Failing to act when one should do so (Black 902).

Misfeasance: Doing something improperly though one could have done it properly or legally (Black 902).

Negligence: Failure to act as a reasonable person would have acted under the same or similar circumstances.

Punitive Damages: Damages beyond the actual property loss that are meant to severely punish the offender for malicious or wanton or fraudulent conduct and to set an example for future wrongdoers (Black 352).

Shareholder: One who has an ownership interest in a corporation.

Summary Judgment: A judgment awarded by the judge to the moving party when there is no issue of material fact and the moving party must prevail as a matter of law (Black 1287).

APPENDICES

When you have a great deal of information that is important but supplemental, then consider placing it in an appendix. *Supplemental* means that you have already provided enough information on a topic in the text for the readers, but there is a lot more that could be said on the topic. Rather than overwhelming readers with too much information, place this information in an appendix. The readers can then refer to it at their leisure, or when they find the supplemental information necessary to their understanding of the text. The decision will be the readers', and you will not have alienated anyone with an overwhelming amount of information.

You may have any number of appendices, and each appendix may be of any length. However, remember to refer to the appendix in the text at the point where it is relevant. For example, in the report's text you might write a sentence like the following: *See Appendix A: "IBM's Annual Report" on page 42 for further information on this aspect of accounting.*

Assign the appendix a number or letter as well as a title that immediately tells the reader its contents, as follows:

Appendix A: IBM's Annual Report, 1990

In an appendix you may place anything that you think readers might like to know, but the information is supplemental to the report's text. The following list suggests items that could be placed in an appendix, but by no means is this list comprehensive, because the determination of what is supplemental is up to you as the writer of the report:

1. Statistics
2. Questionnaires
3. Applicable laws and regulations
4. Visuals
5. Financial data and forms
6. Prior research on the same topic

You may have to use in-text documentation, or you may have to write to the source to ask for permission to use the data.

WORKS CITED

The works-cited or references page lists in alphabetical order by the author's last name the sources that you have used and cited in the body of the report. See chapter 8 for guidelines on the arrangement and contents of this page.

Arranging the Report's Text

To arrange the report's text, review the guidelines for document design in chapter 3. With relatively few exceptions, the report as a business document differs little from other business documents.

HEADINGS

You may use any number of headings in a report, but the five illustrated in box 10.5 should be more than sufficient for your purposes. Just make sure that your headings are consistent throughout the report and that all major headings begin on a new page. The latter instruction will help the reader distinguish the sections of the report.

Major sections should contain forecasting statements that detail the upcoming subheadings. If subheadings contain complex information that is further subdivided, then also use forecasting statements in these subheadings. Forecasting statements will help ensure that the reader can easily follow each and every section of your report.

Headings should be placed in appropriate sections of the document, depending on their logical position in the divisions of the subject under discussion. You can break the position of headings down as follows in box 10.5.

The more complicated and lengthy the document, the more divisions may be necessary. But always remember, the fewer headings and subheadings there are, the less likely it is that the reader will become confused (Locker 438).

BOX 10.5

Heading Levels

1. Major headings are centered on the page, boldfaced, and capitalized:

    MAJOR HEADING

2. Subheadings to the major heading should be centered on the page, boldfaced, and the first letter of each word should be capitalized:

    First Subheading

3. Subheadings to the first subheading should be placed on the left margin, boldfaced, and the first letter of each word should be capitalized:

    Subheading to First Subheading

4. Subheadings to the subheading to the first subheading should be placed on the left margin, boldfaced, and followed by a period. The paragraph would begin on the same line as the heading:

    Subheading to Subheading to First Subheading.

5. **Subheadings to Subheading to Subheading to First Subheading** should be placed on the left margin, boldfaced, and they should be part of the opening paragraph of this section of the document.

Source: Locker, Kitty O. *Business and Administrative Communication.* 3rd ed. Boston: Irwin, 1995. Figure 16.3, page 438. Reprinted with permission.

PAGINATION

The initial page of the report's text is given an arabic numeral one. Paginate consecutively from here to the end of the entire report. Place all page numbers either at the center bottom of the page or in the upper right-hand corner. (Remember: The letter of transmittal, the list of illustrations, and the abstract are all paginated with Roman numerals; the table of contents and title page are unpaginated.)

MARGINS

Use justified margins to give your report that professional look. Use one-inch margins on the top, bottom, and sides of each page.

VISUALS

Visuals are a part of the text unless they are tangential or merely supplement what has already been explained and exemplified. If the visual is used as part of the text, then it should appear in the text itself. If the visual is tangential or supplemental, then place it in an appendix. See chapter 11 for a discussion of the use and placement of visuals.

PARAPHRASING AND QUOTING

Most of the information that you present in the written text should be paraphrased. By paraphrasing, you demonstrate that you know the material well enough to translate it for the reader. After all, anyone can quote, but paraphrasing demonstrates that you know what you are talking about.

Should you choose to quote—and these instances should be few and far between—then make sure that you only quote for one of the following reasons:

- To paraphrase the quote leads to a misconstruction in meaning, an unwarranted complexity, or an overly lengthy sentence longer than the original quote.
- To quote from the cited authority lends credibility to what you are saying.
- To quote the cited material adds force to your writing because the quote says something so well.

Quotes should be used according to the following seven guidelines.

First, introduce all quotations with a phrase or clause, such as the following: *Bill Gates believes,* ". . . ." Do not use a quote as a sentence unto itself.

Second, block quotes of more than four typed lines: The quote is indented one inch, or ten spaces, from the left margin; the quotation marks are omitted; and the in-text documentation follows after the period.

Third, indicate omitted portions of a quote with ellipsis marks (three spaced periods). If the quote also ends the sentence, then use three spaced periods and a fourth period indicating the termination of the sentence.

Fourth, use brackets to indicate that the quote has been shortened, as in the following sentence: *John Doe says, "[H]e is an evil man."* Here, the brackets around the *H* indicate that in the original quote the *H* was lowercase and thus part of a larger sentence.

Fifth, use brackets to indicate that the quote contains all of the original material right from the beginning. *John Doe said, "[s]he was evil."* Here, the brackets around the *s* indicate that in the original quote the *s* was uppercase and began the sentence.

Sixth, use brackets in conjunction with a quote to indicate that

the original quote contains a grammatical or spelling error: place *[sic]* after the error;

part of the quote requires explanation: place *[i.e., and the explanation]* after the portion of the quote requiring the explanation; and

part of the quote requires examples—place *[e.g., and the examples]* after the portion of the quote requiring the examples.

Seventh, place commas and periods inside quotation marks; place semicolons and colons outside quotation marks. Punctuation with quotes is simple to remember.

Ending the Report

When you have arranged the text, work again on your conclusions or recommendations section. Although you knew when you organized and outlined your data where your report would end and what it would say, you are now ready to clean up the ending to make it concise and effective.

Devote special care to the report's ending because it is the most widely read section of the report (Guffey 325; Locker 463).

CONCLUSIONS

Conclusions are most often used in informative reports. They summarize information that you have already presented in the body of the report. Conclusions do not add any new information or commentary.

You can order your conclusion into a series of paragraphs that summarize the major points, or you can use a list (Locker 463).

RECOMMENDATIONS

Recommendations are used in analytical or persuasive reports to "solve or meliorate the problem" (Locker 463). You may use a series of paragraphs to explain each recommendation if you believe that your audience may not readily accept them. On the other hand, if the recommendations are a logical and noncontroversial solution to the problem, then you could simply list them (Locker 463).

Some audiences require that recommendations be placed near the beginning of the report. In such cases, place your recommendations in the report's title, the letter of transmittal, or the abstract—and sometimes in all three (Locker 463).

Exercises

10.1: Choose one of the following stocks. Then read the assignment.

Stocks

Name	Market	Ticker Symbol
1. Motorola	NYSE	MOT
2. Dell	NASDAQ	DELL
3. Reebok Int'l	NYSE	RBK
4. Eaton Corp.	NYSE	ETN
5. Raytheon	NYSE	RTN
6. Genentech	NYSE	GNE
7. Gateway 2000	NASDAQ	GATE
8. Coca-Cola	NYSE	KO
9. Digital Equipment	NYSE	DEC
10. Enron Corp.	NYSE	ENE
11. Eli Lilly	NYSE	LLY
12. Sprint Communications	NYSE	FON
13. Adolph Coors Co.	NASDAQ	ACCOB
14. Seagate Technology, Inc.	NASDAQ	SGAT
15. Unisys Corp.	NYSE	UIS
16. Promus Companies, Inc.	NYSE	PRI
17. Office Depot	NYSE	ODP
18. Colgate-Palmolive Co.	NYSE	CL
19. Archer Daniels Midland	NYSE	ADM
20. PepsiCo	NYSE	PEP
21. Mattel, Inc.	NYSE	MAT
22. Spiegel, Inc.	NASDAQ	SPGLA
23. Dr. Pepper/Seven-Up Companies, Inc.	NYSE	DPS
24. Phillips Petroleum	NYSE	P
25. Advanced Micro Devices	NYSE	AMD
26. American International Group	NYSE	AIG
27. Time Warner, Inc.	NYSE	TWX
28. CBS, Inc.	NYSE	CBS
29. Toys "R" Us, Inc.	NYSE	TOY
30. Monsanto	NYSE	MTC
31. Lotus Development Corp.	NASDAQ	LOTS
32. Novell, Inc.	NASDAQ	NOVL

A Report Scenario: You are a stock consultant in Salmon Brothers, a growing investment corporation. Last week, one of your longtime clients, George Meaney, an economics professor, asked your firm whether your chosen stock from the list is a worthwhile investment. If your firm considers it worthwhile, Prof. Meaney would like to invest $180,000. However, Prof. Meaney isn't so easy to convince. His portfolio is worth $2.7 million, and he has accumulated this sum through shrewd investing, all of which has been done through your firm. Before he makes a decision with respect to making the investment, he would like a report that details the pros and cons of the investment. At the end of the report, he would like an overall recommendation as to whether he should invest.

Two days ago, Ms. Roberta Jackson, CEO, came into your office and dropped the problem of the investment analysis on your desk. She told you that although a $180,000 stock purchase would ensure a hefty commission, she wants an honest appraisal of the stock. She doesn't want to lose Prof. Meaney as a client because of a "skewed" investment analysis. Furthermore, she has told you that you will present your analysis both in written and oral form. The latter event will take place in her office. She has also forewarned you that, in her words, "Prof. Meaney hates BS, and he always has questions that hurt your head."

This morning, Prof. Meaney has sent you a memo asking you to answer the following questions in your stock analysis:

1. What is the stock selling for?
2. How has the stock performed in the last ten years?
3. What are the earnings per share?
4. Who are the principal shareholders?
5. What are the risks in investing in this stock?
6. What are the long range predictions for this stock?
7. Would you recommend this stock?

Ms. Jackson has asked you to answer the professor's questions and to provide any other relevant information that you think the professor would need to make an informed decision. She has asked that the report's written text be about five pages in length.

10.2: Write a report on one of the following business concepts:

1. Soft manufacturing
2. Stretch targets
3. Laffer curve
4. Griffen good
5. Bust-outs
6. Bleed-outs
7. Dead net pricing
8. Forward Buying
9. Global marketing
10. Euro branding

Your report should

1. define the concept,
2. provide examples of its use,
3. explain how and why businesses use it, and
4. explain its effectiveness in terms of
   a. sales,
   b. efficiency,
   c. profits, and
   d. earnings per share.

CHAPTER **11**

Creating Visuals

Many business texts spend a great deal of time and effort discussing how to create and use visuals. However, with the availability of computer software, the creation of graphics and visuals no longer requires a great effort on your part nor a lengthy discussion here. You can create powerful visuals by using software such as Harvard Graphics, Lotus 1-2-3, CorelDraw!, MacPaint, and Visio.

Although you can now easily create visuals using computer software, the software will not answer questions concerning what should be in a visual, nor will it tell you how to use a visual in a written text. In brief, you must know how to choose the right visual for your data, when to use a visual, how to identify it, and what it should contain.

Guidelines for Using Visuals

A good visual helps the reader, but it also aids you in imparting information because a good visual can

>   summarize information
>
>   emphasize and display crucial facts
>
>   compare and contrast data
>
>   illustrate complex ideas

WHEN TO USE A VISUAL

The primary point to remember about visuals is that they are not merely supplementary to the text; they are not decorative devices that can be used to fill empty space. Visuals are part of the text. They are not to be used to explain information that is readily understood by the reader. Instead, "restrict your use of visual aids to situations in which they do the most good" (Bovee and Thill 458).

Use a visual only when you need one; that is, when your reader may need help in understanding the information because of its complexity or abstractness. You must create a visual "that communicates your message most clearly to your audience" (Bovee and Thill 461). Of course, this means that you must know your audience: You must know the level at which your audience thinks, and you must use the visual that will be most appreciated by the audience because it is the one the audience can readily grasp.

HOW TO IDENTIFY A VISUAL

Once you have determined that a visual is necessary, you must identify it correctly. First, designate the visual as a figure or table. (That which is not a table is a figure.) Then assign it a number or letter (Bovee and Thill 472), as in the following examples: *Figure A, Figure 1, Table C.*

Second, immediately after the figure designation, place a colon, and then add a caption that describes what the reader is looking at in this particular visual. The caption should be a phrase, and it should not exceed one line, nor should it exceed the width of the visual itself. The caption must be specific; readers must know what they are looking at without undue questioning or guesswork: "[o]ne of the best ways to tie your visual aids to the text is to choose titles and captions that reinforce the point you want to make" (Bovee and Thill 474). For example, if Figure A provides a graph displaying IBM's growth in sales over the past decade, the caption following the colon should be *IBM's 10-Year Sales Growth.* Capitalize the first letter of each word in the caption, and boldface the entire visual designation:

Figure A: IBM's 10-Year Sales Growth

This visual designation should appear either above or below the visual itself.

If you used or adapted a visual from some other source, then cite that source. In such a case, provide the visual designation as illustrated, and directly beneath the designation on a separate line write *Source*, followed by a colon and a correct bibliographic citation.

HOW TO ACCURATELY INCORPORATE
THE VISUAL IN YOUR TEXT

Once you have determined the need for a visual and have created it, use it properly. Improper use of the visual may result in reader confusion. Use the following twelve guidelines to ensure that the visual is useful both to you and your reader.

First, use a visual that is appropriate to your purpose. Make sure that the data contained in the visual is formatted into the best visual for that data. For example, do not use four pie charts when one bar chart or graph would do.

Second, before the actual display of the visual, always refer to it and introduce it (Bovee and Thill 472). For example, you might write, *Figure A below displays IBM's ten-year sales growth.* The visual would then follow.

Third, because visuals are part of the text, place them where they would most effectively aid the reader: in the text itself (Bovee and Thill 474). Avoid placing visuals in an appendix or notes because this arrangement will simply irritate readers; after all, they will be forced to flip back and forth between sections of the text. (The only exception to this rule is information that is supplementary or of a nature that only a part of your audience will appreciate. In this one instance, place these visuals in appendices or notes. Should you use this approach, refer to the appendix or note by number or letter and page number. For example, you might write, *See Appendix A, which details IBM's ten-year sales growth.*)

Fourth, surround your visual with adequate space. Do not crowd visuals onto the page. If the visual cannot be placed on the page without crowding, then simply place it on the next page. Make sure that the visual is balanced on the page; in other words, neatly center the visual.

Fifth, after presenting the visual, briefly explain it to the reader. You should be able to do this in a few sentences by either highlighting significant points contained in the visual or by making general comments about the data that it contains. Do not assume that readers will focus on data that you find particularly significant; as the writer, it is your task to point out the significance to the reader. Moreover, "[s]ome people ignore the visuals and focus on the words; others do the opposite. If you know that your audience prefers one form of communication over the other—or has special communication needs—you can adjust the balance accordingly" (Bovee and Thill 460).

Sixth, repeat the visual if necessary. Some visuals may contain a great deal of data that your text may refer to again and again. In such instances, you should not hesitate to repeat the visual. If you do not repeat visuals, especially in lengthy documents, readers will become confused.

Seventh, keep the visual simple. Visuals should not be overly complex. Therefore, do not load the visual with too much data. There is no rule that says that you may use only one visual to encompass data. If the data contained in the visual is lengthy and complex, then simply use more than one visual.

Eighth, emphasize the significant information in the visual. Visuals sometimes provide a lot of data, and what you consider truly important may be lost if you do not point the significant items out to the reader. You can do this in one of two ways. First, as mentioned previously, you can highlight significant features of the visual in the explanatory text following or preceding the visual. Second, you can use prose captions in the visual itself to point out significant aspects. For these captions, employ a smaller font size than that used in the visual or the text, underline or italicize them, and make a line from the caption to the significant feature in the visual so that the reader will know what you are referring to.

Ninth, present data accurately. Make sure that your visual does not distort data. For example, good news should not appear gigantic and bad news infinitesimal (Locker 485–86). It is easy to distort data, but it is unethical.

Tenth, exercise care when using colors. Colors signify ideas. For example, the color red usually signifies a deficit or danger, while black signifies a credit or profit. Readers are attracted to colors because colors are another easy way to suggest ideas. On the other hand, do not overuse color. Too many colors will distort information because readers will be distracted by the colors rather than focusing on the data they provide (Locker 484).

Eleventh, be cautious when using the three-dimensional effect currently in vogue. The three-dimensional effect can sometimes confuse the reader, as it does frequently with line graphs. Which line should the reader focus on: the actual line or the three-dimensional shadow line? The reader may not be able to distinguish between the two (Locker 486).

Twelfth, use the standard rule of thumb for all visuals: A good visual should be able to stand on its own without explanation. Thus, if you show your visual to a colleague, that colleague should understand what is displayed in the visual without any questions. If there are questions, or if you must explain the visual, then you have created a bad visual.

Formats

We use certain kinds of visuals because of the information they contain; therefore, we must choose the visual that best suits the information that we wish to present.

TABLES

We use tables when we want the audience to focus on specific numbers, but, at the same time, we want an easily grasped presentation of the numbers. Tables are arranged by columns and by rows (Bovee and Thill 461).

A good table should accomplish six objectives. First, a table should have what is called a boxhead. This is the top section of the table; it tells the reader what the numbers in the columns of the table represent (Bovee and Thill 462; Locker 479). The names in the boxhead can be italicized, boldfaced, underlined, or capitalized, but whichever you choose, the names must stand out.

Second, a table must also have what is called a stub. The stub names the items listed in the first row flush with the left margin (Locker 477). Like the boxhead, the stub should be highlighted in some fashion. Each item listed in the stub can then be read across to see the figures displayed in the corresponding columns.

Third, the figures represented beneath each column should not exceed three figures (Locker 477). If they do, they will confuse readers because they will be too complex to understand.

Fourth, if a column contains numerous pieces of data, then provide subtotals (Locker 477). What the subtotal represents should be named in the stub column.

Fifth, items in each column can be given subheadings that will more easily facilitate the readers' understanding of the table.

Sixth, if your table has many rows of data, then double-space after every five entries (Locker 477).

Tables come in a variety of forms, and they can present much in addition to numbers. As stated previously, tables can be used to present specific numbers, as in box 11.1 (page 136).

Tables can include information in addition to numbers, such as the type of industry and trade assignment, as in box 11.2 (page 137).

BOX 11.1

ious e-mail services and measuring the time

The Price of E-Mail

We calculated how much time it would take to send 10, 50, 100, and 200 messages per day, then how much that online time would cost you each month. The result: If you're unfailingly efficient, you can send 100 messages a day for less than $5 a month.

	Cost to send/receive 10 messages per day	Cost to send/receive 50 messages per day	Cost to send/receive 100 messages per day	Cost to send/receive 200 messages per day
America Online [1]	$9.95	$9.95	$9.95	$16.71
CompuServe [1]	$9.95	$9.95	$9.95	$10.64
Internet [2]	$4.95–$30	$4.95–$30	$4.95–$30	$4.95–$30
MCI Mail [3]	$11.20	$14.20	$17.95	$22.50
The Microsoft Network [4]	$4.95	$4.95	$4.95	$8.99
Prodigy [1]	$9.95	$9.95	$11.32	$25.48

[1] $9.95-per-month base rate includes 5 free hours, $2.95 per hour thereafter

[2] Monthly fees and terms of service vary by vendor, but prices generally range from $20 to $30 for unlimited access; CompuServe's Spryte service costs $4.95 per month for 3 free hours, $1.95 per hour thereafter.

[3] $10-per-month base rate Includes unlimited incoming messages and 40 outgoing messages; thereafter, 50 cents for the next 100 to 500 characters, 10 cents for characters 501 to 1000, 10 cents for characters 1001 to 10,000, and 5 cents for each additional 10,000 characters after that.

[4] $4.95-per-month base rate includes 3 free hours, $2.50 per hour thereafter.

METHODOLOGY We measured how long on average it took to log in to each service and transmit a series of 1000-character messages. In each case, we used a 14.4-kbps connection and the most efficient mailing method (most services offer utilities that let you compose mail offline and then automatically log in and upload your mail). Using these figures, we calculated how much it would cost for four levels of e-mail usage (10, 50, 100, and 200 messages a day) billed at each service's base rate. Be warned: These are best-case scenarios, and your mileage will no doubt vary.

Source: Heim, Judy. "The Great E-Mail Shoot-Out." *PC World* February 1996: 184. Reprinted with the permission of PC WORLD Communications, Inc.

BOX 11.2

Cheap Companies With Excellent Prospects

These companies scored high relative to their rivals with respect to projected earnings growth, return on equity and balance sheet strength. Yet they trade at 1996 price/earnings ratios at least 15% below the typical company in their industry. Dominated by cyclicals, it's a good portfolio if you believe the economy will continue to expand next year.

COMPANY	INDUSTRY	FW FORECAST GRADE[1]	ESTIMATED P/E — 1996 MEAN	DISCOUNT TO INDUSTRY[2]	RECENT STOCK PRICE	EPS 1996 MEAN[3]
BMC SOFTWARE	Computer Software and Services	B	11	−52%	$33.50	$2.91
RAYTHEON	Aerospace•Defense	B	6	−50	43.38	7.17
AMR	Transportation•Freight Forwarding	A	8	−38	66.25	8.18
GENERAL MOTORS	Auto•Truck	B	6	−37	44.13	7.82
MICRON TECHNOLOGY	Electrical Equipment•Electronics	B	9	−37	69.38	7.36
COMPUTER ASSOCIATES INT'L	Computer Software and Services	B	15	−36	51.38	3.37
BEAR STEARNS	Financial Services•Brokerage	B	8	−29	19.38	2.47
DELTA AIR LINES	Transportation•Freight Forwarding	A	9	−28	66.00	7.05
REEBOK INT'L	Apparel•Textiles	A	11	−24	35.25	3.32
CHRYSLER	Auto•Truck	B	7	−23	53.25	7.65
PPG INDUSTRIES	Chemicals	B	10	−22	43.00	4.24
HASBRO	Leisure•Entertainment	B	12	−22	29.38	2.51
FMC	Chemicals	B	10	−21	71.13	6.92
APPLIED MATERIALS	Electrical Equipment•Electronics	A	12	−20	46.50	3.74
ALUMINUM CO. OF AMERICA	Metals•Mining	B	8	−20	49.63	6.20
PHILIP MORRIS	Beverages•Tobacco	B	11	−20	84.63	7.54
DEERE	Machinery•Industrial Products	B	10	−20	89.25	9.25
GANNETT	Media	B	15	−19	54.38	3.72
ARMSTRONG WORLD INDS	Building Materials	A	11	−18	55.38	5.22
LOEWS	Insurance	B	9	−17	146.00	16.09
CSX	Transportation•Freight Forwarding	B	11	−17	83.00	7.68
COMPAQ COMPUTER	Computer Hardware	B	12	−17	53.00	4.55
LUBRIZOL	Chemicals	B	11	−15	29.63	2.69
BRISTOL-MYERS SQUIBB	Drugs	B	14	−15	77.63	5.37
GATEWAY 2000	Computer Hardware	A	12	−15	31.31	2.63
CONSOLIDATED EDISON	Utilities	B	11	−15	31.00	2.80

1. Based on estimated earnings growth, return on equity and financial strength, relative to the other companies in its industry. A=excellent, B=above average. 2. Based on the companies

Source: Owens, Sondra D., and Michael K. Ozanian. "Peer Preview: How the 500 Most Valuable Companies in the U.S. Should Perform Next Year." *Financial World* 5 Dec. 1995: 57.

Telephone numbers can even be added to the data, as in box 11.3.
Tables can be used to present product surveys, as in box 11.4.
Finally, tables may lack numbers altogether, as in box 11.5 (page 140).

PIE CHARTS

We use pie charts to compare a part to the whole, for example, the distribution of my monthly income (Bovee and Thill 467).

A good pie chart fulfills four requirements. First, the pie chart begins with the largest section at twelve o'clock and moves clockwise with each slice of the pie becoming smaller (Bovee and Thill 467; Locker 479).

Second, make the pie a perfect circle. Many pie charts today are constructed elliptically; this merely distorts information as the readers may not be able to determine which slice is greater or smaller (Locker 479).

BOX 11.3

Ten Largest Ginnie Mae Funds

Ginnie Mae Fund	Yield	1990-1994 Total Return	Annual Expense Ratio	Total ▪ Assets ($bil.)	Telephone
AARP GNMA	6.8%	+27%	0.68%	5.57	800-253-2277
Benham GNMA	7.6%	+31%	0.54%	1.03	800-331-8331
Dreyfus GNMA	6.7%	+27%	1.28%	1.51	800-645-6561
Federated Inst Ginnie Mae	7.4%	+27%	0.57%	1.75	800-245-2423
IDS Federal Income	7.2%	+25%	0.76%	1.01	800-437-4332
Kemper "A" U.S. Government	5.4%	+26%	0.71%	5.08	800-621-1048
Kemper "B" U.S. Mortgage	4.6%	+23%	1.70%	3.91	800-621-1048
Liberty Financial U.S. Government	6.0%	+26%	1.00%	0.78	800-872-5426
Price GNMA	7.3%	+28%	0.77%	0.79	800-638-5660
Vanguard Fixed-Income Sec. GNMA	7.8%	+31%	0.28%	5.81	800-523-1184

Funds that invest principally in Ginnie Maes; other government agency funds also own Ginnie Maes as part of diversified portfolios.

Source: Metzner, Douglas E. "Time for Ginnie Maes?" *Mutual Funds* March 1995: 23.
Courtesy of *Mutual Funds.*

BOX 11.4

Network Operating Systems

DATAMATION's Feature Summary: Network Operating Systems

For more information on all the products listed, circle 213 on the Reader Service Card	Banyan 800-222-6926 VINES 6.0	IBM 800-426-4329 OS/2 LAN Server 4.0	Microsoft 206-882-8080 Windows NT Server 3.51	Novell 800-638-9273 NetWare4.1
Circle Number	210		211	212
Price One server, 10 users	$3,995	$1,009-$2,189	$999	
One server, 250 users	$14,995	$12,605-$18,345 (5 servers)	$7,199	$12,495
Two servers, 1,000 users	$49,995	$50,381-$71,281 (20 servers)	$26,398	$95,990
Supported processors	Intel	Intel, RISC AS/400, VM, MVS	Intel, Alpha, PowerPC, Mips	Intel
SMP support/Number of processors	✔/2	✔/4	✔/32	in Q4/32
Maximum number of concurrently active users per server	1,000	1,000	Unlimited	64,000
Maximum directory entries	Unlimited	Unlimited	40,000 users/ groups per domain	64,000 entries or 2 million files
Server RAM (minimum/maximum)	12/256MB	12MB/hardware limit	16MB/4GB	8MB/4GB
Maximum hard disk per server (TB)	20GB	Hardware limit	408 million	32
File compression on server			✔	✔
Disk/storage management features	Disk mirroring, duplexing	Disk mirroring, optional disk striping, duplexing	Disk mirroring, disk striping	Disk mirroring, disk striping, duplexing
Supported RAID levels	All	1,3,5 (opt)	Via SCSI hardware	0, 1, others via 3rd parties
Server duplexing		opt.	Via 3rd party	✔
Maximum printers per server	400	24	Unlimited	56
Maximum number of servers	Unlimited	Unlimited		Unlimited
Communications protocols supported: Shipping with NOS	VINES IP	TCP, NetBIOS, Named Pipes, TCP Sockets	NetBEUI, TCP/IP, IPX, PPP, SLIP	IPX/SPX, AppleTalk, TCP/IP
Available as extra-cost add-ons	TCP/IP	802.2, SNA (LU6.2), AppleTalk		
Available through 3rd-party vendors	IPX/SPX	IPX/SPX		
Remote access via ISDN	✔	✔	✔	✔
Remote access via X.25	✔	✔	✔	
Security protocols on remote link	Encryption	None	C2 security level	None
Protocols with native dial-up support	TCP/IP, VINES IP	All protocols on top of 802.X	PPP	SLIP/PPP, dumb terminal emulation
Software compression for remote access	✔		✔	✔
Auto address configuration on remote link (supported protocols)	VINES IP	None	None	PPP
Resource names stored in single hierarchical database	✔			✔
Supported log-in scripts	System, group, user	Group, user	User (file and print services for NetWare)	System, group, user, object, containers
Supports nested scripts	✔	✔		✔
Automatically detects and updates out-of-date workstation shells	✔			✔
Administrator can install NOS from one server onto another		✔	✔	✔
Administrator can set maximum disk space limits per user account	✔	✔	via 3rd party	✔
Administrator can reboot server remotely	✔	✔	✔	✔
Supported resources	Connect time, server requests, reads, writes, disk space	Connect time, server requests, buffers	Connect time, server requests, reads, writes, disk space	Connect time, server requests, reads, writes, disk space, user audits, file archiving
Chargeback-accounting functions			via 3rd party	✔
APIs exposed to developer	File and print, e-mail, audit, application, APPC	File and print, audit, application, RPC, IPC	File and print, e-mail, audit, application, resource accounting, RPC,network administration, LPC	File and print, e-mail, audit, application, resource accounting, RPC, network administration
Imports user information from other NOSs	via ENS	NetWare	NetWare to Windows NT Server	LAN Manager, LAN Server, NetWare 3.1

Chart compiled by Susan Mael and Charles B. Darling

Source: Darling, Charles B. "VINES Makes the Grade." *Datamation* 1 Sept. 1995: 76.

FRANCHISING

SUCCESS SELECTS
Maintenance Masters

SOME OF THE MOST DRAMATIC GROWTH in franchising is taking place in building and maintenance businesses. Patrick Swisher, president of Swisher International Inc., defied conventional wisdom to transform his industry and was chosen as a SUCCESS Renegade earlier this year. When he started his company in 1983, "no one had heard of a restroom hygiene company," says Swisher. Today the company is growing 50 percent annually. Its $20 million national network includes about 500 employees and 92 franchise branches across America and Canada.

The following list of building and maintenance providers is taken from our 1994 Franchise Gold 100 survey. □

Company Name	Product Category	Number of Units	Year Founded	Investment	Location	Phone Number
ABC Seamless	Building Services	137	1978	Under $75,000	Fargo, ND	800-732-6577
Decorating Dan	Decorative Services	1,112	1969	Under $75,000	Bethesda, MD	800-428-1366
Dynamark Security Centers Inc.	Security Systems	143	1975	Under $75,000	Hagerstown, MD	301-797-2124
Floor Coverings International	Decorative Services	387	1988	Under $75,000	Forest Park, GA	404-361-5047
Harris Research Inc. (Chem-Dry)	Maintenance Services	4,000	1975	Under $75,000	Logan, UT	800-541-6553
Jani-King International Inc.	Maintenance Services	4,033	1968	Under $75,000	Dallas, TX	800-552-5264
Mr. Rooter Corp.	Maintenance Services	250	1968	Under $75,000	Waco, TX	800-582-8003
Servpro Industries Inc.	Maintenance Services	875	1987	Under $75,000	Gallutin, TN	615-451-0200
Steamatic Inc.	Maintenance Services	370	1948	$76,001 to $150,000	Fort Worth, TX	800-527-1296
Swisher International	Maintenance Services	89	1983	$75,001 to $150,000	Charlotte, NC	800-444-4138

BOX 11.6

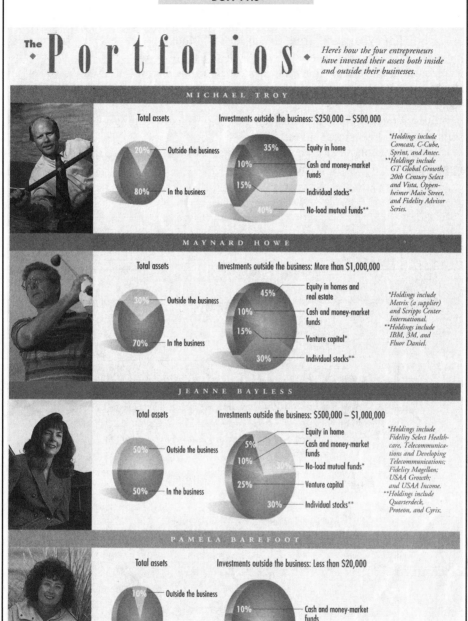

The·Portfolios·

Here's how the four entrepreneurs have invested their assets both inside and outside their businesses.

MICHAEL TROY

Total assets
- 20% Outside the business
- 80% In the business

Investments outside the business: $250,000 – $500,000
- 35% Equity in home
- 10% Cash and money-market funds
- 15% Individual stocks*
- 40% No-load mutual funds**

*Holdings include Comcast, C-Cube, Sprint, and Antec.
**Holdings include GT Global Growth, 20th Century Select and Vista, Oppenheimer Main Street, and Fidelity Advisor Series.

MAYNARD HOWE

Total assets
- 30% Outside the business
- 70% In the business

Investments outside the business: More than $1,000,000
- 45% Equity in homes and real estate
- 10% Cash and money-market funds
- 15% Venture capital*
- 30% Individual stocks**

*Holdings include Metrix (a supplier) and Scripps Center International.
**Holdings include IBM, 3M, and Fluor Daniel.

JEANNE BAYLESS

Total assets
- 50% Outside the business
- 50% In the business

Investments outside the business: $500,000 – $1,000,000
- 5% Equity in home
- Cash and money-market funds
- 10% No-load mutual funds*
- 25% Venture capital
- 30% Individual stocks**
- 30%

*Holdings include Fidelity Select Healthcare, Telecommunications and Developing Telecommunications; Fidelity Magellan; USAA Growth; and USAA Income.
**Holdings include Quarterdeck, Proteon, and Cyrix.

PAMELA BAREFOOT

Total assets
- 10% Outside the business
- 90% In the business

Investments outside the business: Less than $20,000
- 10% Cash and money-market funds
- 90% Equity in home

Source: Ochsner, Neal. "In Search of the Perfect Portfolio." *Inc.* Nov. 1995: 30.

Reprinted with permission, *Inc.* magazine, November, 1995. Copyright 1995 by Goldhirsh Group, Inc., 38 Commercial Wharf, Boston, MA 02110.

Third, limit your slices from five to seven. If your pie chart exceeds seven slices, then add a miscellaneous category (Bovee and Thill 467; Locker 479).

Fourth, place the percentages or numbers in the slices, but label the slices outside the pie. This will make reading the pie chart easier (Bovee and Thill 467; Locker 479).

Box 11.6 (page 141) provides a series of pie charts dealing with entrepreneurs' assets and outside business investments.

Because of computer graphic capabilities, pie charts can even take on eye-catching and innovative forms, as in box 11.7.

BOX 11.7

BENCHMARK
The Cost of Fast Growth

By a wide margin, sales-force compensation ranked as the top sales and marketing expense among this year's Inc. *500 (featured last month in our special issue). There's hope, however, for entrepreneurs possessing a smart idea and savvy marketing instincts: 135 companies on the list achieved success without spending a lot on sales salaries.*

Expense

Percentage of companies that ranked it as the number one or number two expense

Market research 4%
Public relations 8%
Promotional material 23%
Advertising 31%
Customer service 42%
Sales-force compensation 67%

Source: *Inc.* survey of the 500 fastest-growing small companies, 1995.

Source: "The Cost of Fast Growth." *Inc.* Nov. 1995: 92.

Reprinted with permission, *Inc.* magazine, November, 1995. Copyright 1995 by Goldhirsh Group, Inc., 38 Commercial Wharf, Boston, MA 02110.

BAR CHARTS

We use bar charts "to compare items, to compare items over time, and to show correlations" (Locker 479).

A good bar chart should fulfill the following five requirements. First, make the bars in the chart the same width. Otherwise the reader will wonder what the significance of the distortion is when there really is no significance (Locker 480).

Second, place the bars fairly close beside one another so that the reader can easily measure the differences (Locker 479).

Third, place the bars in a logical order. Many bar charts are chronological, but they could also be alphabetical or any other logical order appropriate to the data (Locker 479).

Fourth, label each axis of the bar chart. Most bar charts place numbers on the vertical axis with the other axis employing chronology or alphabetization (Locker 479).

Fifth, use colors appropriately. Do not overuse colors. Again, remember that colors signify ideas (Locker 479).

The bar chart in box 11.8 uses bars of only two colors to illustrate dividend yields.

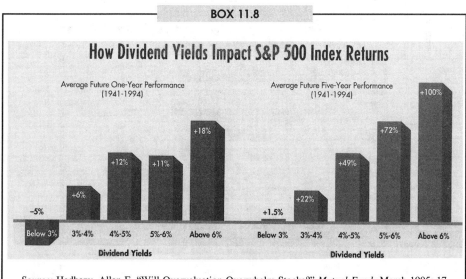

BOX 11.8

How Dividend Yields Impact S&P 500 Index Returns

Source: Hadhazy, Allan E. "Will Overvaluation Overwhelm Stocks?" *Mutual Funds* March 1995: 17. Courtesy of *Mutual Funds*.

Bar charts can also be created horizontally, as in box 11.9.

In box 11.10 the numerous horizontal bars are actually easier to read than vertical ones because the eye moves down and across, as if it were reading a page of written text.

LINE GRAPHS

We use line graphs or charts to show distribution, correlation, and frequency, and to compare items over time.

A good line graph should fulfill the following three requirements. First, label both the horizontal and vertical axes. As with bar charts, so with line graphs: The horizontal axis should refer to time (Bovee and Thill 463).

Second, limit yourself from three to five lines (Bovee and Thill 464). If you

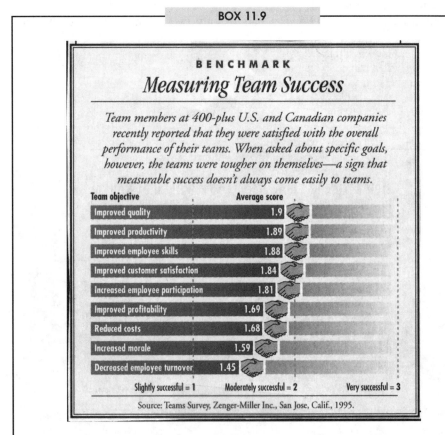

BOX 11.9

BENCHMARK

Measuring Team Success

Team members at 400-plus U.S. and Canadian companies recently reported that they were satisfied with the overall performance of their teams. When asked about specific goals, however, the teams were tougher on themselves—a sign that measurable success doesn't always come easily to teams.

Team objective	Average score
Improved quality	1.9
Improved productivity	1.89
Improved employee skills	1.88
Improved customer satisfaction	1.84
Increased employee participation	1.81
Improved profitability	1.69
Reduced costs	1.68
Increased morale	1.59
Decreased employee turnover	1.45

Slightly successful = **1**   Moderately successful = **2**   Very successful = **3**

Source: Teams Survey, Zenger-Miller Inc., San Jose, Calif., 1995.

Source: "Measuring Team Success." *Inc.* Nov. 1995: 94.

Reprinted with permission, *Inc.* magazine, November, 1995. Copyright 1995 by Goldhirsh Group, Inc., 38 Commercial Wharf, Boston, MA 02110.

BOX 11.10

Family Values

Average performance of domestic diversified
open-end and closed-end stock funds for 1994

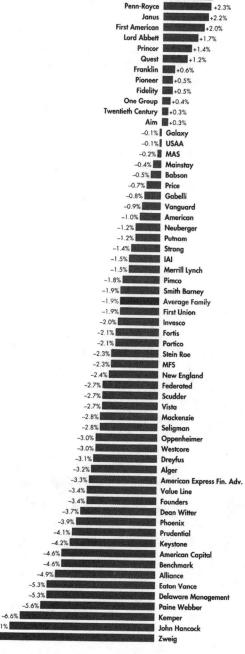

United	+2.4%
Penn-Royce	+2.3%
Janus	+2.2%
First American	+2.0%
Lord Abbett	+1.7%
Princor	+1.4%
Quest	+1.2%
Franklin	+0.6%
Pioneer	+0.5%
Fidelity	+0.5%
One Group	+0.4%
Twentieth Century	+0.3%
Aim	+0.3%
Galaxy	−0.1%
USAA	−0.1%
MAS	−0.2%
Mainstay	−0.4%
Babson	−0.5%
Price	−0.7%
Gabelli	−0.8%
Vanguard	−0.9%
American	−1.0%
Neuberger	−1.2%
Putnam	−1.2%
Strong	−1.4%
IAI	−1.5%
Merrill Lynch	−1.5%
Pimco	−1.8%
Smith Barney	−1.9%
Average Family	−1.9%
First Union	−1.9%
Invesco	−2.0%
Fortis	−2.1%
Portico	−2.1%
Stein Roe	−2.3%
MFS	−2.3%
New England	−2.4%
Federated	−2.7%
Scudder	−2.7%
Vista	−2.7%
Mackenzie	−2.8%
Seligman	−2.8%
Oppenheimer	−3.0%
Westcore	−3.0%
Dreyfus	−3.1%
Alger	−3.2%
American Express Fin. Adv.	−3.3%
Value Line	−3.4%
Founders	−3.4%
Dean Witter	−3.7%
Phoenix	−3.9%
Prudential	−4.1%
Keystone	−4.2%
American Capital	−4.6%
Benchmark	−4.6%
Alliance	−4.9%
Eaton Vance	−5.3%
Delaware Management	−5.3%
Paine Webber	−5.6%
Kemper	−6.6%
John Hancock	−7.1%
Zweig	−7.8%

Source: Metzner, Douglas E. "All in the Family." *Mutual Funds* March 1995: 27.
Courtesy of *Mutual Funds*.

145

have more than five lines, then simply make more line graph visuals. No one says that everything must be contained in one visual. Also make each line different so that it stands out. You can use color to accomplish this, or each line can be constructed differently: One line may be solid, another dashes, yet another dots, and so on, as illustrated in boxes 11.11 and 11.12.

Third, where lines intersect at important points, those that represent significant facets of the data, draw the readers' attention to them. You can readily do this by providing a brief caption in the visual and drawing a line from the caption to the intersection, as in box 11.13 (page 148).

MAPS

We use maps to indicate the distribution of things, products, people, and activities in a geographic area (Bovee and Thill 468).

The map must encompass the area indicated in the visual's caption. Maps normally contain a legend at the bottom that tells the reader what the numbers or figures

---

BOX 11.11

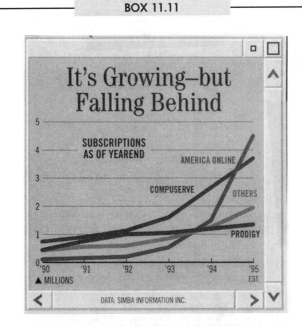

Source: Eng, Paul M., and Susan Chandler. "Prodigy: A 5-Year-Old Underachiever." *Business Week* 30 Oct. 1995: 150.

Reprinted from October 30, 1995 issue of *Business Week* by special permission, copyright © 1995 by the McGraw-Hill Companies.

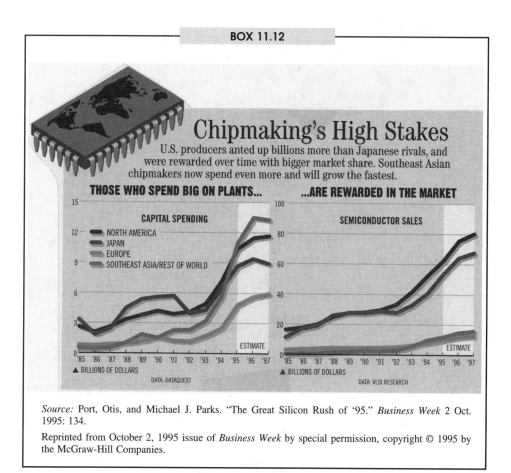

BOX 11.12

Chipmaking's High Stakes

U.S. producers anted up billions more than Japanese rivals, and were rewarded over time with bigger market share. Southeast Asian chipmakers now spend even more and will grow the fastest.

THOSE WHO SPEND BIG ON PLANTS...

...ARE REWARDED IN THE MARKET

CAPITAL SPENDING
- NORTH AMERICA
- JAPAN
- EUROPE
- SOUTHEAST ASIA/REST OF WORLD

SEMICONDUCTOR SALES

▲ BILLIONS OF DOLLARS

DATA: DATAQUEST

▲ BILLIONS OF DOLLARS

DATA: VLSI RESEARCH

Source: Port, Otis, and Michael J. Parks. "The Great Silicon Rush of '95." *Business Week* 2 Oct. 1995: 134.

contained in the areas of the map signify, for example, "Number of people in thousands eating out twice a week."

Box 11.14 (page 149) shows the most economically free countries in the world (the lower the number, the greater the freedom).

PHOTOGRAPHS

We use photographs to depict how things are arranged, how they look, or how they work. The caption is crucial here as it will tell readers what they are looking at and why: "Zero Lawnmowers Really Cut Down the Competition."

Items in the photograph can be highlighted by captions and lines that tie the items to their respective captions. As Bovee and Thill put it, "[n]othing can demon-

BOX 11.13

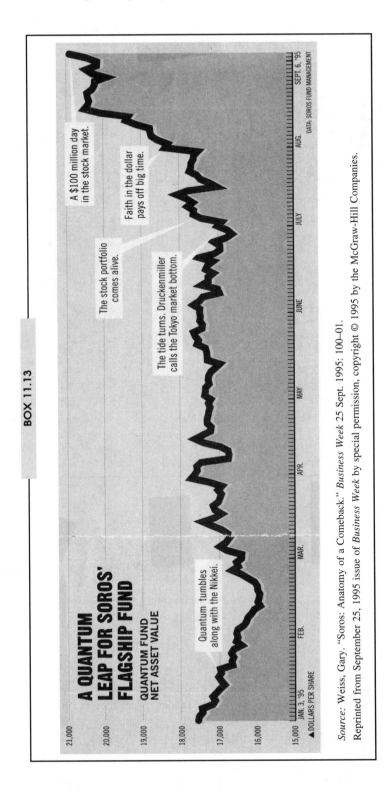

A QUANTUM LEAP FOR SOROS' FLAGSHIP FUND

QUANTUM FUND NET ASSET VALUE

▲ DOLLARS PER SHARE

A $100 million day in the stock market.

Faith in the dollar pays off big time.

The stock portfolio comes alive.

The tide turns. Druckenmiller calls the Tokyo market bottom.

Quantum tumbles along with the Nikkei.

DATA: SOROS FUND MANAGEMENT

Source: Weiss, Gary. "Soros: Anatomy of a Comeback." *Business Week* 25 Sept. 1995: 100–01.

Reprinted from September 25, 1995 issue of *Business Week* by special permission, copyright © 1995 by the McGraw-Hill Companies.

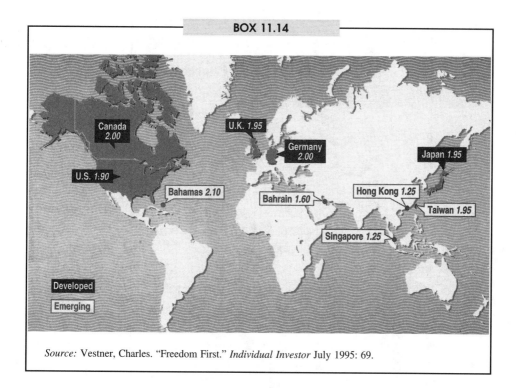

BOX 11.14

Source: Vestner, Charles. "Freedom First." *Individual Investor* July 1995: 69.

strate the exact appearance of a piece of property or equipment, or a new product the way a photograph can" (469).

GANTT CHARTS

We can use Gantt charts to measure and organize our work. They are most often used in business proposals or progress reports (Bovee and Thill 466; Locker 482).

A Gantt chart looks very much like a table but for two qualities: (1) It does not contain numerical data, and (2) each item in the column is boxed in. Other than that, the Gantt chart, like a table, contains rows, columns, a stub, and a box-head.

The boxhead contains dates arranged either daily, weekly, or monthly. The stub refers to the work that will be accomplished. In each row and beneath each column, a box is blacked out, indicating the time for the completion of that task (Locker 482). Box 11.15 (page 150) provides a sample Gantt chart.

DRAWINGS

Use drawings "to show how something looks or operates" (Bovee and Thill 468). Drawings can be quite effective when you want to show specific details (Locker 480).

Box 11.16 (page 151) shows an effective drawing that illustrates new oil-drilling techniques.

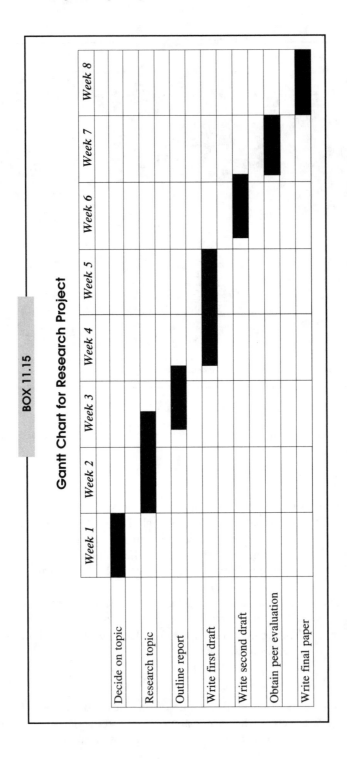

BOX 11.15

Gantt Chart for Research Project

BOX 11.16

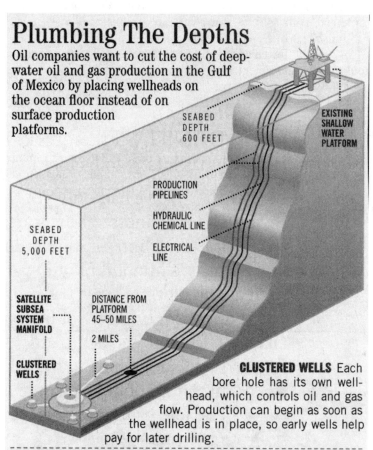

Plumbing The Depths

Oil companies want to cut the cost of deep-water oil and gas production in the Gulf of Mexico by placing wellheads on the ocean floor instead of on surface production platforms.

SEABED DEPTH 600 FEET

EXISTING SHALLOW WATER PLATFORM

PRODUCTION PIPELINES

HYDRAULIC CHEMICAL LINE

ELECTRICAL LINE

SEABED DEPTH 5,000 FEET

SATELLITE SUBSEA SYSTEM MANIFOLD

DISTANCE FROM PLATFORM 45–50 MILES

2 MILES

CLUSTERED WELLS

CLUSTERED WELLS Each bore hole has its own wellhead, which controls oil and gas flow. Production can begin as soon as the wellhead is in place, so early wells help pay for later drilling.

MANIFOLDS More adaptable than older manifolds, these hubs can gather oil and gas from wells as far as two miles away, then send the flows up to the surface.

EXISTING SHALLOW-WATER PLATFORMS These play a new role as way stations for the new fields. They separate the oil from the gas and send them down separate pipelines.

DATA: TEXACO INC.

Source: McWilliams, Gary. "Pulling Oil From Davy Jones' Locker." *Business Week* 30 Oct. 1995: 74. Reprinted from October 30, 1995 issue of *Business Week* by special permission, copyright © 1995 by the McGraw-Hill Companies.

FLOWCHARTS

Flowcharts are useful when you want to show "processes, procedures, and relationships" (Bovee and Thill 467). A flowchart can demonstrate "a sequence of events from start to finish" (Bovee and Thill 467).

Box 11.17 uses a flowchart effectively to show "what there is to manage" when it comes to desktop management.

ORGANIZATION CHARTS

Organization charts show "the positions, units, or functions of an organization and the way they interrelate" (Bovee and Thill 467). For example, organization charts can illustrate a corporation's executive hierarchy or the relationship between subsidiaries and the parent company. Organization charts can show how a system operates.

BOX 11.17

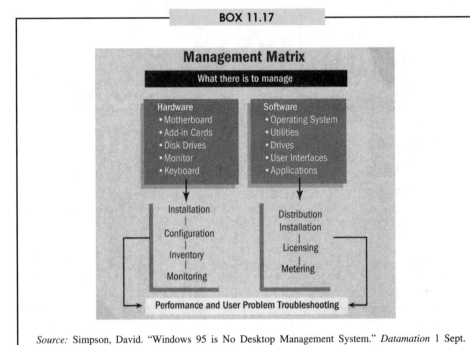

Source: Simpson, David. "Windows 95 is No Desktop Management System." *Datamation* 1 Sept. 1995: 50.

Reprinted with permission of DATAMATION Magazine, September 1, 1996 © by Cahners Publishing Company.

Conclusion

Although visuals are now easier to construct than at any time in the past, this does not mean that they are losing their effectiveness. We are a visually oriented society. We demand visuals to entertain us and to inform us.

This is equally true in business. Your topic may appear dry, but you can enliven it with visuals. As Bovee and Thill put it, "[I]n the numbers-oriented world of work, people rely heavily on visual images. They think in terms of trend lines, distribution curves, and percentages. An upward curve means good news in any language, be it English or Japanese" (458).

But visuals are also more than tools to make comprehension easy: Studies suggest that visuals are highly effective in helping an audience reach a decision, and they are highly persuasive (Bovee and Thill 458).

Box 11.18 provides a checklist to consult when you design a visual.

BOX 11.18

A Checklist for the Creation of Visuals

If you answer *no* to any of the questions below, then revise your visual according to the guidelines given in the preceding text.

1. Do you really need a visual?
2. Is the visual attuned to the audience's level of understanding?
3. Have you designated the visual as a figure or table and assigned it a number or letter?
4. Do you have a precise caption that tells the audience what the visual contains?
5. Is the caption a short but concise phrase?
6. Is the caption capitalized appropriately?
7. Do you need to cite a source?
8. If applicable, does the source citation follow proper bibliographic form?
9. Is this the best visual for the data?
10. Do you refer to and explain the visual?
11. Is the visual balanced on the page in the text? Or should it be placed in an appendix?
12. Is the visual overly crowded with data?
13. Are important features of the visual highlighted by caption or by text?
14. Does the visual distort data?
15. Is color used appropriately and with care?
16. Does the visual employ the proper format?
17. Can the visual stand on its own merits, without further explanation?

Exercises

11.1: Create visuals to fit the data below. Provide figure or table numbers or letters, captions, internal captions when necessary, and proper source citations. (Library research is necessary.)

1. Market share of the leading computer corporations
2. The sales growth of Intel over the last six years
3. The sales growth of Intel versus the sales growth of Microsoft over the last five years
4. The sales growth of Compaq versus the sales growth of Microsoft, Packard Bell, and Dell
5. How to use one of the following databases:
   a. Disclosure
   b. Proquest
   c. LAN
6. Dell's corporate hierarchy
7. A breakdown of the assets and liabilities of Novell
8. The number of home-owned PCs state by state
9. The subsidiaries of GM
10. How a computer processes information
11. Schedule for the completion of your research project
12. The inner components of a PC
13. The increase in the number of maquiladoras over the last decade
14. Leading microchip producers by nation
15. Cost of PC to consumer by Microsoft, Dell, Packard Bell, IBM, and Gateway 2000 over the last five years
16. Percentage increase in on-line services over the last five years
17. Market share of major computer book publishers
18. How to use Lotus 1-2-3 graphics
19. The major components of a 486 motherboard [do not use a photograph]
20. Packard Bell earnings per share over the last five years versus four other PC manufacturers
21. Clock speed of Intel's CPU starting with the 8086

CHAPTER 12

Presenting Information Orally

The key to presenting a speech is preparation. You can give a fine speech if you just devote a little time to preparing yourself and what you want to say. To help you prepare, this chapter provides general guidelines for organizing and presenting a speech, followed by a hypothetical situation taking you through the process.

General Guidelines

To ensure a successful speech, do the following: (1) know your audience, (2) outline your presentation, (3) rehearse what you want to say, and (4) anticipate questions.

KNOWING YOUR AUDIENCE

Knowing your audience is crucial to giving a good speech. If you know your audience, you will know what vocabulary to employ, how to behave, and what to focus on. Do not approach all audiences the same! Different audiences possess different levels of experience and expertise. Therefore, ask yourself the following questions:

- What members compose my audience?
- What is the audience's primary age group?
- What profession do most members of the audience practice?
- What is the audience's level of education?

Questions such as these will help you keep an audience before your mind. You cannot and should not prepare for an unknown audience; unpleasant surprises may be the only result. Tailor your speech for a particular audience whose needs and expectations you must fulfill (Bovee and Thill 593).

OUTLINING YOUR SPEECH

When making oral presentations, "[y]ou define your purpose, analyze the audience, and develop a plan for presenting your points" (Bovee and Thill 592). Prepare the speech both for yourself and your audience by making an outline. You must come

155

across as knowing what you are talking about, and providing a guide in the form of an outline will help your credibility enormously.

When you outline your speech, use notecards or a single sheet of paper (Bovee and Thill 609). These items should contain only the headings that divide the sections of your speech. You may add notes to these headings to tell you where visuals are to come in your speech, and you may even include transitions or transitional sentences between major points in your speech (Bovee and Thill 596–97). This need for transitions is especially crucial in longer speeches because the audience may not grasp the connection between your ideas unless you make those connections explicit (Bovee and Thill 603). (Signposting your main ideas throughout the speech is one simple way to make sure that the audience can easily follow along.)

Outlining ensures that your speech will have a spontaneous and extemporaneous air. You want your audience to believe that although you are prepared, you are not reciting by rote. For the same reason, do not attempt to write out the speech and take it with you to the podium. This will only lead to reading to the audience—the worst thing that any person making a speech can do. In a sense, you have a crutch. You can use the cards or paper should you forget a part of the speech. On the other hand, you may never use them. But why take the chance that you will forget and mess up?

REHEARSING THE SPEECH

To achieve spontaneity and extemporaneity in your speech, you must rehearse it. Stand before a mirror and observe yourself: your gestures, facial features, body movements. Also time yourself because most speeches are given a set time for their performance (Bovee and Thill 609). This is a key word: *performance*. You are giving a performance, and, like any actor, you must rehearse if you want the audience to be affected by what you have to say. Once you have the speech ready, practice it before friends or family and ask them what they think. And just as importantly, ask them to formulate questions that they would like answered.

ANTICIPATING QUESTIONS

The most difficult part of your preparation process will be in anticipating the audience's questions. For most people this is extraordinarily difficult because we all know quite well our own perspective on something, but to separate ourselves and see the speech and the information it presents from the audience's point of view is difficult. This is why rehearsing is so important. You need to know what could possibly be asked so that you can prepare answers beforehand that will make you look sharp and on top of things (Bovee and Thill 612).

Organization

Think of your talk as you would a paper. It should have a beginning, a middle, and an end.

INTRODUCTION

Beginnings and endings are especially important because most of your audience will not be paying strict attention to your speech (Locker 505). Intrigue your audience from the very beginning. Make them listen to what you have to say with introductory material that precedes the actual beginning of the speech itself. You can begin with an anecdote or humor; the only requirement is that the anecdote or humor should lead into the beginning of the speech itself. You can also begin with a question or a quotation (Locker 505–06).

The beginning of your speech should accomplish three objectives: introduce yourself, introduce the topic of discussion, and forecast the organization of your talk.

First, introducing yourself is important because good credibility, or ethos, will make you more persuasive, and your audience will pay more attention to what you have to say. After all, if the audience fails to believe in your expertise in the matter at hand, why should it listen (Bovee and Thill 601–02). To establish your credibility, all you need to do is state "your position in an organization, your profession, [and] the name of your company" (Bovee and Thill 602). You want to establish your credentials at the very beginning of the speech, but if you are worried about looking egotistical, then have someone else introduce you (Bovee and Thill 602).

Second, identify the subject and main idea that you will be discussing.

Third, forecast the points that your speech will cover. These points can be signposted as the speech progresses. Tell your audience that you will discuss *x* number of items in relation to the subject of the speech, and then take them up in the order in which you forecasted them. As Bovee and Thill state, tell the audience, "This is the subject, and these are the points I will cover" (603).

BODY

Once you have forecasted the organization of your speech, take up the forecasted items one by one. Signpost each section of the speech as it was forecasted. Then provide details that support or illustrate each topic sentence. Provide details that are concrete and specific because you need to give details that the audience can identify with and visualize.

Also, use visuals to enhance the effect of your speech. Audiences love visuals because they condense information into a comprehensible form. Visuals wake audiences up, so if you are presenting complicated information, a visual will keep the audience's attention.

You can use visuals in two ways. If you have an overhead or slide projector available, use that. Otherwise, use the visual in the form of a handout. Either way, refer to and explain the visual. Use the following guidelines to ensure the effective use of visuals in a speech:

- Be sure that all members of the audience can see the visual aids.
- Allow the audience time to read a visual aid before you begin your explanation.
- Limit each visual aid to one idea.
- Illustrate only the main points, not the entire presentation.

- Use no visual aids that conflict with your verbal message.
- Paraphrase the text of your visual aid; don't read it word for word.
- When you've finished discussing the point illustrated by the visual aid, remove it from the audience's view. (Bovee and Thill 607)

CONCLUSION

To make sure that the audience pays attention to the conclusion of your speech, use a phrase such as *in conclusion, to conclude,* or *to sum up* (Bovee and Thill 604).

To end your speech effectively, you can do three things. First, you can summarize key information for your audience (Bovee and Thill 604). This is particularly useful when the speech has been long and complex. Second, you can ask the audience to do something, for example, fill out a questionnaire or write its Congressman. Third, in the case of a persuasive speech, you can end with a logical or emotional appeal. A logical appeal tries to convince the audience that it is in its best interest to accept or adopt what you have been saying: for example, because the audience will save money, make money, or generally benefit in some way. An emotional appeal tries to persuade your audience to accept your viewpoint because good things would result if your viewpoint were accepted and bad things would occur if your viewpoint were ignored. (For a more detailed discussion of persuasion, see chapter 6, "Writing the Persuasive Message.")

The ending you choose will depend on your audience and your topic of discussion. At the very end of your speech, thank the audience for its attention and ask whether there are any questions.

Presenting the Speech

When it is time to present your speech, be sure to interact with your audience. Do not robotically present information, for if you do, you will certainly alienate and maybe even antagonize your audience. Your speech may possess the necessary content that the audience wants to hear and you may structure your speech effectively, but all is lost if this is all you do. You want your audience to pay attention and to be interested in you and your speech, and you want to impress it.

Although good content and a fine structure are necessary attributes of a speech, you must do certain things as well as avoid others if you are to be effective in fulfilling the audience's needs and demonstrating your expertise.

EYE CONTACT

When giving a speech, maintain eye contact. Eye contact is crucial if you want to build a rapport with your audience. If you do not have eye contact, or if you stare at a spot behind the audience, you will bore the audience and antagonize it. With eye contact you will appear relaxed and spontaneous; without it you will bore and alienate the audience (Bovee and Thill 611).

VOICE

When you speak *with* (not *to*) your audience, speak loudly enough so that everyone can hear you. And speak slowly enough so that all your words are heard clearly. Avoid meaningless words and phrases such as *you know, okay, like*, and *um* (Bovee and Thill 612). If you speak softly or quickly, you will not achieve a rapport with your audience because it may not hear you, or it may think the effort required to focus on your voice is not worthwhile.

In addition, display enthusiasm and interest in your subject. If you speak in a monotone and appear bored with your subject, your audience will view the presentation as you do: an unpleasant experience. One way that you can create the appearance of enthusiasm for your subject (even if you do not possess it) is by "varying your pitch and speaking rate to add emphasis" (Bovee and Thill 612).

BODY MOVEMENTS AND GESTURES

Smile when delivering your speech. You do not want to appear frightened or corpse-like. Demonstrate to your audience that not only do you know your material but you enjoy presenting it. Again, display enthusiasm for the subject. After all, if you appear nervous, ill at ease or grumpy, what is the audience to think of your subject but that it holds little value for you? Should the subject then hold any value for the audience? Smiling is a sign of enthusiasm, and if you use it, you will increase your rapport and your credibility.

Also downplay unnecessary body movements. There is nothing wrong with the occasional hand gesture or body movement, but if there are too many of these, the audience will begin to focus on your movements rather than on the content of your speech. Some of the most typical unnecessary body movements include the following:

Rocking back and forth in front of the podium

Dancing your feet around

Grasping the podium with a death grip

Jingling the coins in your pocket

Wandering about the stage

Wiping your hand or forehead

MISTAKES

Do not worry about messing up in the presentation of your speech. Everyone messes up a bit. Just watch the evening news for a good demonstration of this fact. The real key is to avoid drawing attention to your mistakes.

Too often, when speakers mispronounce a word, or if they have to go back over something they have missed, they spend time correcting the error and even letting the audience know that they are making a correction! Speakers will sometimes state that they are nervous in a feeble attempt to gain the audience's sympathy. What they do not realize is that they will not gain sympathy for their nervousness, but they will gain the audience's attention with respect to the error, and the audience may begin to think that the speaker is ill-prepared.

When you make a mistake, such as a mispronunciation, correct it immediately and go on. But do not go back to the mistake and thus draw attention to it. If you do so, you will more than likely confuse yourself, so there is no benefit to doing it. And, by all means, avoid those long pauses that often occur when a mistake has been made. Often, a speaker will stop with the mistake, think about how to correct it, and finally attempt the correction; meanwhile, audiences sit there and watch the speaker squirm— all the while inwardly debating the speaker's credibility.

HUMOR

A business speech is a formal and serious event. Therefore, while humor can be useful at the outset of the speech and occasionally thereafter, avoid being too funny. You are not a stand-up comedian. Too many jokes will result in a good time for you and your audience, but aren't you there to provide important information? Not everything can be a joke (Bovee and Thill 601).

QUESTIONS

If there are questions, answer them as directly as possible. Audiences easily recognize dissembling, and if the audience thinks that you have no answer, you will look foolish, and you will hurt the credibility of your speech. Of course, there will be occasions when a question is asked and you don't know the answer. Rather than saying "I don't know" or making something up, say something to the effect that that is a good question, and you would like to take the time to research it more thoroughly before giving the questioner an answer at a later time (Locker 517).

AUDIENCE BOREDOM

Sometimes you will find yourself before an audience that you know is bored with the subject under discussion, maybe even before you begin discussing it. Perhaps the boredom is simply a result of too many speakers on the same subject, or perhaps it is just the nature of the subject itself that is boring. Whatever the reason for the audience's boredom, strive to overcome it.

You can overcome boredom in a number of ways. First, you can relate the subject to the audience members on a more individual level: Show them how the subject can affect them (Bovee and Thill 601). Second, use precise and concrete language to explain concepts. Third, if the subject is dull, abstract, or highly complex, then use analogies between the subject and something more easily understood by the audience (Bovee and Thill 604). Fourth, you can use visuals "to maintain and revive audience interest" (Bovee and Thill 611).

AUDIENCE HOSTILITY

On occasion, you will be asked questions that are meant to be antagonistic. An audience member may want to put you on the spot, and one of the surest ways to do this is for the audience member to ask a complex or provocative question that strikes at the foundation of your presentation.

You can deal with such hostility in a number of ways. If the question is complex, answer it part by part. You can even involve the audience member who asked the question by asking for clarifications when necessary. In any event, answer calmly, thoroughly, and with a smile. This will help to put off antagonistic questioners because they were looking for a response filled with embarrassment or anger, not friendliness and concision (Bovee and Thill 613).

If the question is obviously meant to provoke you, answer it in a straightforward and professional manner and move on (Bovee and Thill 613).

Whatever the case, do not engage the audience member in a debate. You are there to provide information, not entertainment.

NERVOUSNESS

When you give a speech, it is inevitable that you will be somewhat nervous. You cannot overcome all nervousness, but you can certainly control and diminish its impact on your performance.

One way to avoid appearing overly nervous is to visit the room where you will be giving the speech. Stand at the podium and note the arrangement of the room. Where will people be sitting? Is there an overhead available? Where are the light switches? Is there a blackboard and chalk? Is there a microphone? Just by visiting the room before giving your speech you will lessen nervousness because you will have familiarized yourself with the surroundings (Bovee and Thill 610).

You can also lessen the fear of an oral presentation by

1. Having more information on hand than you can possibly use,
2. Knowing that your audience *wants* to hear what you have to say,
3. Psyching yourself up prior to speaking,
4. Inhaling deeply prior to speaking,
5. Committing your opening to memory,
6. Using visuals to lend an air of spontaneity and audience involvement, and
7. Maintaining a steady pace in the presentation of materials. (Bovee and Thill 611)

A Hypothetical Situation

Now that you have seen how to give a speech and some of the variables involved, let us take a hypothetical situation and see how to approach it.

Let us assume that the manager, a close friend of yours, at a local department store has asked you, an investment manager, to give a speech to employees with respect to stock investments. You will give this speech at the annual year-end dinner for all employees, and the speech is to last about an hour.

As with any speech, you must

Know your audience

Outline your presentation

Rehearse what you want to say

Anticipate questions

Because the speech is for all employees, you already know that the speech cannot be overly complex with a lot of sophisticated jargon. Your audience is diverse with respect to its educational level and to its grasp of business concepts, and you must speak so that all can understand you. Therefore, speak to the lowest level but without being condescending. Avoid condescension by speaking of your topic in terms that either your audience can readily understand or that you can define as the speech progresses.

Once you have your audience in mind, outline what you want to say. The subject is stocks, so you must mention this topic in your introduction. Because many people may not know what a stock is, or even how stocks work as investments, you will have to define and explain these concepts to the audience. You will have to discuss the risks and benefits of investment as well as how to know which stocks to invest in. You also need a good opening, perhaps an anecdote, and a conclusion.

At this point, you already have a sketchy outline:

I. Introduction
    A. Yourself and the topic
    B. Anecdote
    C. Forecast of speech
II. Stocks
    A. Defined
    B. Risks
    C. Benefits
    D. Determining a Good Stock
III. Conclusion

Now that you have a working outline, flesh it out. Don't worry about the forecasting statement just yet; first try to develop what you have. With the above outline before you, ask yourself a number of questions:

- What anecdote will you use?
- How will you define a stock?
- What are the risks inherent in stock investing?
- What are the benefits inherent in stock investing?
- How does one determine a good stock for investment?
- What kind of conclusion is most effective and appropriate?
- What kinds of questions are you likely to be asked?

The answers to these questions will give you enough information to write out a more detailed outline. Write down your answers to your questions, and then organize these answers by arranging them into headings. Once you have the headings, you can then create a forecasting statement, which you can use in section II of your outline as signposts. In this hypothetical situation, you also need a conclusion that summarizes your key points with respect to risks, benefits, and determining a good stock—the items that the audience will probably be most interested in.

Once you have written out your answers and provided yourself with a more detailed outline, rehearse it according to the guidelines given previously. When you have your speech down, in the sense that you are comfortable with it, you are ready to present it. However, one cautionary note: when you rehearsed your speech, you probably had the detailed outline before you; when you stand behind that podium, the sheet of paper you have in front of you should contain only headings, not details. If you use the detailed outline, you will probably read from it and thus hurt your effectiveness. Thus, use an outline sheet giving only a series of headings, as shown in box 12.1.

Conclusion

As you can see from box 12.1, you must be prepared in order to be effective. And with a good informational and organizational foundation, your confidence should be high. Furthermore, remember that you are the one in charge. You are the one with the knowledge and expertise, not the audience. Therefore, take charge and pursue the speech as you would any other business task: with enthusiasm and professionalism.

BOX 12.1

Sample Outline of Speech

I. Introduction

    A. Myself and the subject of discussion

    B. Anecdote

        1. How bad things happen to good people when they plan too late

    C. Forecast of speech

        1. What is a stock?

        2. What are the risks of stock investing?

        3. What are the benefits of stock investing?

        4. How can one determine a good stock?

II. Stocks

    A. Defined

        1. A stock represents an ownership interest in a company

            a. Interest in profits and losses

            b. Interest in management of company

B. Risks

    1. Inflation

    2. Debt

    3. Competition

C. Benefits

    1. Outperforms savings

    2. Negotiable for loans

    3. Inheritance

    4. Long-term growth

    5. Liquidity

D. Determining a Good Stock

    1. History of stock

    2. Earnings per share

    3. Shareholders

    4. Debt to equity ratio

    5. See a broker like me!

III. Conclusion

A. Summarize B, C, and D in section II

B. Thank the audience for its attention

C. Ask for questions

Exercises

12.1: In a ten-minute presentation, define one of the terms below. You must use a visual in your speech.

1. Mortgage
2. Equity
3. Punitive damages
4. Surety
5. Assignment
6. Real versus personal property
7. Earnings per share
8. Timeliness

9. Beta rating
10. Dividend
11. Share
12. Junk bond
13. Long-term debt
14. Short-term debt
15. Liquidity
16. Option
17. License
18. Franchise
19. Trademark
20. Copyright
21. Consideration
22. Annual report
23. 10-K form
24. Proxy statement
25. Capital gain
26. Derivatives
27. Amortize
28. Depreciation

CHAPTER 13

Selling Yourself: Resumes

When you begin looking for a job, the search may at first appear frightening. After all, you may fear that you won't be able to find a job that suits you, or you may fear that in today's economy jobs are scarce commodities. But just as you have fears, so do employers. Employers seek motivated and intelligent people who possess the technical skills they need. To find such people, employers spend about $11.5 billion a year (Bovee and Thill 352).

If you look at employers as the buyers in a market, then you are the seller. What you are selling are your skills, talents, intelligence, enthusiasm, motivation, and ambition. These are the qualities employers seek; your task is to convince them that you possess what they need. Viewed from this perspective, writing a good resume is your first step in convincing employers that you are who they are looking for.

A resume is a tool to demonstrate your aptitude for a particular position. A resume does not get you a job, but it may lead to an interview; it "can . . . get you in the door" (Bovee and Thill 353). And that is precisely what you want: the opportunity to make contact with a real person whom you can impress on an intellectual and human level. You want the opportunity to be something more than sheets of paper, more than simply one of hundreds of job applicants. You want the opportunity to make contact and get a job. Writing a good resume is the initial step in the hunt for employment.

But remember, it is only the first step. You must still write an effective cover letter, prepare and go through the interview, and maintain contact with the prospective employer after the interview—but these steps will be discussed in due time. For now, let us focus on creating an image of you that will show employers that you possess the skills that they need and must have. To do this, Henry Halaiko of Mobil states that a good resume must demonstrate that a prospective employee " '(1) thinks in terms of results, (2) knows how to get things done, (3) is well-rounded, (4) shows signs of progress, (5) has personal standards of excellence, (6) is flexible and willing to try new things, and (7) possesses strong communication skills' " (Bovee and Thill 353).

Introduction

To write a fine resume, you must do so with the interview in mind. In other words, the resume does not get you the job, but it might lead to an interview.

Although there are many kinds of resumes, the kind of resume that will be discussed here is one that is effective for the graduating college student. This kind of person is one who has a lot of education, but perhaps not much job experience. Because of the lack of job experience, many graduating students are apprehensive about applying for a job that they really want and thus settle for less than they may be qualified for. This need not be the case.

As stated previously, if you want that job, you must think in terms of selling yourself. This is the primary purpose of the resume. But before you even begin to think about writing one, you must have a position in mind. You want to apply for a particular position because the resume that you will write will be used again and again. You simply do not have time to tailor a resume for every employer; therefore, if you have a position in mind, the same resume can be sent to a host of potential employers without having to change anything at all. In addition, the job search may require that you send resumes to numerous employers, and it may take some time. In both cases, you want a resume that focuses on a particular position because it can be reused constantly, and, over time, it can be easily updated.

To begin writing your resume, ask yourself three preliminary questions:

- Is there a position open whose criteria you meet?
- Specifically, how do you qualify for that position?
- What can you offer the employer that sets you apart from most other applicants?

Write the answers to these questions down. You will incorporate these answers into your resume.

Remember, you are trying to fill an employer's needs. You want to come across as a person who has something to offer. You want to appear knowledgeable in your field of expertise, even if the expertise results only from academic study. The methods by which you can accomplish this are explained in the rest of this chapter.

Writing Guidelines

Your resume will employ a number of grammatical constructions that you normally would not use. You must write it

1. using sentence fragments,
2. omitting personal pronouns, and
3. using verbs that are not a form of *be*.

These three rules are necessary if you want to write an effective resume. First, write in sentence fragments because you want the essential and primary message laid bare before the reader. You will also avoid unnecessary verbiage if you write in fragments. Second, if you omit personal pronouns, you will avoid the impression that this is a self-centered document: Too many *I*'s alienate readers from you. Third, use strong verbs, rather than weak ones. Weak verbs consist of the forms of the verb *be: is, am, are, was, were, being* and *been*. Instead, use verbs that are more aggressive, such as the following: *prepared, conducted, coordinated, analyzed, planned, accomplished, produced, originated, facilitated*. Use strong verbs to begin each and every sentence in your resume (Bovee and Thill 354). By beginning every sentence in this way, you will produce maximum reader impact; in sum, the action that you performed will present itself immediately before each reader.

Appearance

Your resume must have an immediate impact. You will be competing with numerous other applicants for the same position, and you must stand out from the crowd. Bovee and Thill point out that "[y]our resume probably has less than 30 seconds to make an impression" (353). Thus, your resume better look good if you want someone to analyze your qualifications for the position (Bovee and Thill 354). If your resume looks sloppy, if the print is too light or blurred, if it looks crowded, the person looking at it may give its contents little more than a glance. You have a number of ways available by which you can make your resume attractive.

First, provide enough space between headings and between items that you want to stand out. In the resume, spacing is up to you, but don't crowd items together.

Second, make sure that your printer has a new ribbon or enough ink. Using a laser printer would be best, of course. You want to achieve that crisp, professional look.

Third, boldface major headings.

Fourth, align items properly. Begin major headings on the left margin and indent subheadings. Make sure to align sentence and subheadings properly. You should have an invisible margin that aligns each item beneath its corresponding heading.

Headings

Your resume is divided into the following parts:

Name

Address and phone number

Career objective statement

Education

Work experience

Awards or honors (optional category)

Special skills

Activities (optional category)

References

Earlier, you were told that the resume sells you. As every salesperson who has ever written a sales letter can tell you, the longer you can keep people interested, the more likely it is that they will buy. (Have you ever noticed that sales letters are rather long? Or have you noticed that salespeople who telephone you want to speak for a period of time before they get to the selling point?) With this in mind, try to come up with enough information that will fill two typed pages. You want to engage the reader's attention and differentiate yourself from those who have purchased those one-page resume computer programs. Two pages will allow you enough time to sell yourself and enough information to differentiate you from the mass of other job applicants.

Now, let's look at each heading and note what information each should contain. An example will follow each explanation to give you an idea of what should be included and discussed, so that you will know how the information should look when presented. After this discussion of the various headings, all the examples will be brought together to illustrate the resume format. For the sake of the following discussion, let us assume that Jonathan Smith, a recent graduate of The University of Texas, wants to find an accounting position.

NAME

At the top of the first page, type your name in capital letters and boldface it. Center your name (Bovee and Thill 354):

JONATHAN SMITH

ADDRESS AND PHONE NUMBER

Beneath your name, double-space and type your address. Immediately beneath your address, type your area code and phone number. Center this information beneath the name.

4513 Alto Way

El Paso, TX 79912

915-533-8090

CAREER OBJECTIVE STATEMENT

This is the first of six major headings to follow. All major headings other than your name are placed at the left margin and boldfaced, with only the first letter of each word capitalized. Depending on the amount of space available, either double- or triple-space between the last line of the information in a major heading and the next major heading itself.

The career objective statement is your first opportunity to sell your talents to a business; therefore, it must be precise and inviting to the potential employer. One way to accomplish this sales pitch is to focus on the needs of the potential employer. Focus on what you can offer the employer, not what you expect the employer to do for you. For example, do you have a special talent that the employer may need? Can you offer the employer versatile skills? Try to appear knowledgeable in your field and be specific.

You can easily write an effective career objective statement if you do the following:

1. Begin with a verbal infinitive.
2. State the position that you want.
3. Offer the employer information that distinguishes you from most other job candidates.

Career Objective Statement: To work for IBM as an accountant in the auditing division where skills in computer programming are necessary.

If you break Jonathan Smith's career objective statement down according to the three requirements, you can see that all three requirements have been met:

To work [number 1] for IBM as an accountant [number 2] in the auditing division where skills in computer programming are necessary [number 3].

This is a pretty good career objective statement, but it could be improved. The writer, Jonathan Smith, could specify the computer knowledge he possesses. As an accountant, computer skills are essential, but Jonathan Smith's career objective statement doesn't specify them. For example, what computer programs or languages does Smith know and use? Is he expert using Peachtree? Specifics derived from these questions would significantly improve Jonathan Smith's career objective statement. (But even as it stands, this writer has made a statement that tells the employer that he has something specific to offer.)

Note that Jonathan Smith refers to IBM in his career objective statement. However, he need not do so; after all, he may want to use a resume that he can use for all prospective job applications. He can accomplish this by omitting the reference to the particular company.

When you write these statements, pay attention to a few other guidelines as well.

First, make your career objective statement no more than three typed lines. You don't want to begin the resume with an essay.

Second, avoid vagueness. Don't tell the potential employer that you want a "challenging position." What does this mean? Isn't just getting the job challenge enough?

Third, avoid speaking of the future. Don't tell the employer that you want a job with "upward mobility" or that you want this job so that you can gain experience. The former suggests that you are already eyeing positions above you when you haven't even attained this job yet; the latter suggests that this job may be only temporary. Employers find neither prospect appealing.

Once you have your career objective statement, everything in the resume must be related to it. The resume validates or more fully explains the career objective statement. Anything that does not validate or further explain the career objective statement must be omitted. All parts of the resume must cohere. In this sense, your career objective statement is the thesis statement for your resume. If you think of the career objective statement in this way, you will not tire or confuse the reader with tangential or irrelevant material. As Bovee and Thill state, "[b]y including too much information, a resume may actually kill the appetite to know more" (353).

EDUCATION

Because you are a recent college graduate, this section will most likely be your most important selling point. You may lack experience, but you can make up for this if you can demonstrate knowledge and skills that the employer needs, knowledge and skills that your career objective statement has already, to a degree, forecast.

This heading contains three subheadings indented from the left margin:

Degree

GPA

Relevant Courses

Degree

Give the title of the degree, the field in which it was earned, and the date you received it:

Education
  Degree
    B.B.A., Accounting, University of Texas, 1995

If you have other degrees, list them as well, but do so in a reverse chronological order. If you want to include a minor field, simply double-space beneath your degree entry and place the word *Minor* before your entry:

Education
  Degree
    B.B.A., Accounting, University of Texas, 1995
    Minor: Marketing

If you have such a minor, include it. Diversity is a big selling point.

GPA

If you have a fine grade point average (GPA) for students in your field, include it. If not, then do not put this subheading in your resume:

GPA: 3.8

Don't bother telling the potential employer that this is on a four-point scale. If the employer has questions, well, that's what an interview is for. In addition, avoid using a category for GPA in Major. This will only make the potential employer suspicious about why you are creating this category: Is it to avoid mentioning your overall GPA?

Relevant Courses

This subheading is the most important of the three. You want to demonstrate what you know and can do if given the employment opportunity. Don't list courses. After all, most people with the same degrees will have taken the same or similar courses. Thus, listing courses will not distinguish you from other job applicants. Instead, categorize your courses and explain what you can offer the employer.

Relevant Courses

Accounting: Worked with all accounting spreadsheets that IBM now uses. Excellent skills in cost accounting, standard-base accounting, and auditing. Employed programs to efficiently process accounts. Created database accounting system for a small business.

Computer Information Systems: Learned all relevant programs for accountants. Used IBM models to learn methodology. Analyzed accounting spreadsheets and their interaction with computer programs.

Note that these descriptions elaborate on Jonathan Smith's career objective statement. The two categories contain within them many courses, but Jonathan Smith doesn't cite the courses, nor should you; instead, elaborate concerning what you can offer the employer. Always have the employer's needs foremost in your mind.

WORK EXPERIENCE

You may have some work experience, but maybe you think that menial or manual work is frowned upon. This is not true. If you worked and went to school, this displays your fortitude. And even if the jobs were not sophisticated, you can still demonstrate that you learned something that the potential employer might value.

For example, maybe you worked in a fast food restaurant. How this relates to accounting is the key question that you must ask yourself. At this fast food place you might have handled money, supervised employees, performed inventory, or balanced the books. Certainly, all of these tasks are related to accounting. Your job is to make sure that every position you list on the resume bears relevance to the job that you are now seeking.

Under this heading and in the right margin, use a reverse chronological order and give the dates of employment. Indent, and give the employer's name. Next, highlight your job title and provide a colon. Then describe your duties, using power verbs:

Work Experience

9/94–5/95   Furr's Foods. Assistant Bookkeeper: Provided weekly and monthly statements. Coordinated inventory control and purchasing. Set up new computer accounting program that saved two working days and hundreds of dollars per week.

4/93–8/94   Discount Records. Salesclerk: Operated cash register and provided accounting of daily receipts. Supervised two employees, and trained another.

8/92–3/93   McDonald's. Clerk: Operated cash register. Provided accounting of daily receipts. Supervised semiannual inventory process.

Do not worry about gaps in employment. You are a student, and such gaps are to be expected. The employer, however, may ask about them at the interview, but such questions are easily answered based on your student status.

AWARDS OR HONORS

This is an optional category, but almost everyone has received an honor of some sort. Items that fall in this category include making the Dean's List and receiving scholarships or awards for academic or work achievement.

When you cite these items, use a reverse chronological order with the dates beneath the heading in the margin. If the award is for something more than making the Dean's List, then give the title of the award, who gave it, and why the award was given:

Honors

1994–95	Kappa Kappa Chi Award, University of Texas, awarded to most outstanding accounting student.
1994–95	Omega Scholarship, Ford Motor Company, awarded to best business student.
1993–95	Dean's List, University of Texas.

SPECIAL SKILLS

Every person possesses special skills. Each one of us can do something better than another person. For the purpose of the resume, special skills can be categorized into three subheadings:

Language skills

Computer skills

Writing skills

Because these are subheadings, they are indented from the left margin. You may include any or all of these subheadings. Again, make sure that what you write is relevant to the position you are seeking.

Language Skills

In a diverse and international economy, employers are finding it necessary to hire people who have foreign language skills. If you have such skills, then use the term *bilingual* and cite the languages that you know:

Language Skills
Bilingual English/Spanish

That is all you have to say. After all, either you are bilingual or you are not. There is no in-between. Therefore, do not use terms as *have knowledge of* or *am familiar with*. The employer may then wonder, "How much knowledge," or "how much familiarity?" Such language is evasive; it demonstrates nothing and can only lead to suspicion; that is, are you suggesting a skill where there really is none?

Computer Skills

Computer skills are mandatory in today's world. Simply list the programs you can run and the computer languages that you know:

Computer Skills
MS-DOS
Lotus 1-2-3
Microsoft Windows for Accountants

Again, avoid phrases such as *familiar with* or *have knowledge of*.

Writing Skills

Writing skills are much sought after in the business world because so few people possess them. If you have taken writing classes beyond the freshman level that are relevant to the position being sought, then list and explain them:

> **Writing Skills**
> Business Writing: Learned proper formats and organizational criteria for business memos, letters, and analytical reports. Analyzed corporate records and provided both an oral and written report.

ACTIVITIES

Activities is another optional category. When you think of activities, think of professional activities. Do not list hobbies or sports. Activities include memberships in academic or professional organizations. When you write these in your resume, place them in reverse chronological order beneath the major heading. Then, write *member* or give the title of the position that you hold (e.g., president, treasurer), the title of the organization, and, if in an academic setting, the name of the university. If you were more than a member, then you should give a description of your duties in that organization:

> **Activities**
> 1994–95 Treasurer, Accounting Society, University of Texas: Responsible for fund-raising activities and maintaining proper records with respect to members' dues.
> 1993–95 Member, Marketing Society, University of Texas.

REFERENCES

Too often people write *available upon request* beneath this heading. But why do they do this? Does it serve any purpose, and does it help the employer evaluate your resume? In fact, Bovee and Thill state that "[m]any potential employers prefer to have actual references in the resume" (357).

Ask three professional people to write letters of recommendation for you. Make sure that these people are related to the job field that you are pursuing.

You want professional people because you are often known based on who recommends you. Choosing professional people will thus lend an aura of professionalism to your resume. Choose three people, and make sure that they are not related to you. Keep these letters on file. You then may list their names, addresses, and phone numbers on your resume:

> **References**
> Dr. Robert Cason, Professor of English, University of Texas, El Paso, TX, 79968, Tel. # 915-747-8876.
> Dr. James Edwards, Professor of Accounting, University of Texas, El Paso, TX, 79968, Tel. # 915-747-5608.
> Dr. Mary Trello, Professor of CIS, University of Texas, El Paso, TX, 79968, Tel. # 915-747-7677.

You may string the names, addresses, and phone numbers as illustrated in the example, or you may use blocks, depending on how much space is left to you.

Finally, at the very end of the resume, you may state, if you think it will help, that transcripts, work product, or letters of recommendation are available upon request (Bovee and Thill 357).

Box 13.1 provides Jonathan Smith's resume.

BOX 13.1

Jonathan Smith's Resume
JONATHAN SMITH

4513 Alto Way
El Paso, TX 79912
915-533-8090

Career Objective Statement: To work for IBM as an accountant in the auditing division where skills in computer programming are necessary.

Education

Degree

B.B.A., Accounting, University of Texas, 1995
Minor: Marketing

GPA: 3.8

Relevant Courses

Accounting: Worked with all accounting spreadsheets that IBM now uses. Excellent skills in cost accounting, standard-base accounting, and auditing. Employed programs to efficiently process accounts. Created database accounting system for a small business.

Computer Information Systems: Learned all relevant programs for accountants. Used IBM models to learn methodology. Analyzed accounting spreadsheets and their interaction with computer programs.

Work Experience

9/94–5/95 Furr's Foods. <u>Assistant Bookkeeper</u>: Provided weekly and monthly statements. Coordinated inventory control and purchasing. Set up new computer accounting program that saved two working days and hundreds of dollars per week.

4/93–8/94 Discount Records. <u>Salesclerk</u>: Operated cash register and provided accounting of daily receipts. Supervised two employees, and trained another.

8/92–3/93 McDonald's. <u>Clerk</u>: Operated cash register. Provided accounting of daily receipts. Supervised semiannual inventory process.

Honors

1994–95 Kappa Kappa Chi Award, University of Texas, awarded to most outstanding accounting student.

1994–95 Omega Scholarship, Ford Motor Company, awarded to best business student.

1993–95 Dean's List, University of Texas.

Special Skills

Language Skills
Bilingual English/Spanish

Computer Skills
MS-DOS
Lotus 1-2-3
Microsoft Windows for Accountants

Writing Skills
Business Writing: Learned proper formats and organizational criteria for business memos, letters, and analytical reports. Analyzed corporate records and provided both an oral and written report.

Activities

1994–95 Treasurer, Accounting Society, University of Texas: Responsible for fundraising activities and maintaining proper records with respect to members' dues.

1993–95 Member, Marketing Society, University of Texas.

References

Dr. Robert Cason, Professor of English, University of Texas, El Paso, TX, 79968, Tel. # 915-747-8876.

Dr. James Edwards, Professor of Accounting, University of Texas, El Paso, TX, 79968, Tel. # 915-747-5608.

Dr. Mary Trello, Professor of CIS, University of Texas, El Paso, TX, 79968, Tel. # 915-747-7677.

Conclusion

Jonathan Smith's resume illustrates a kind of resume useful for the recent college graduate. There are, of course, many other kinds of resumes, and as you advance in the business world you will become familiar with them. Box 13.2 (page 178) provides a review sheet that you can use when you complete your own resume.

BOX 13.2

Resume Review Sheet

1. Does the resume look attractive?
2. Does the career objective statement state the position the writer is seeking? Does it specify what this writer could do for the potential employer?
3. Does the writer state the degree held?
4. Does the writer categorize courses taken? Does the writer specify what skills and knowledge have been acquired by taking these courses?
5. Are the jobs listed in reverse chronological order?
6. Are the job descriptions related to the position that the writer is seeking?
7. Do the job descriptions begin with power verbs?
8. If the writer has an awards section, are dates given? Are award descriptions given?
9. Does the writer list references with addresses and phone numbers?
10. Does the writer avoid the use of personal pronouns?
11. Are all items related to the career objective statement?

You leave this chapter with an understanding of the elements of a good resume, but you need to consider the ethics of writing a resume. First, do not exaggerate or lie about your qualifications. If you do so and are later discovered, you will probably be fired. You may have problems finding another position because the employer who fired you will probably not recommend you to another potential employer.

Second, choose your words with care. You obviously want to avoid words with negative connotations, but it is easy to use power verbs that may suggest more than you actually did. For example, if you were part of a team that analyzed a CIS program, your resume should reflect that a team was involved, not just you. You can't say *analyzed x* when you and a team analyzed x. In this instance, you would be embellishing your qualifications.

Third, do not list people as references whom you did not ask whether it was okay to do so. If you don't ask these people, they may be surprised and then a bit angered if an employer calls to ask about you. Both their surprise and their anger may cause them to say things about you that may have a detrimental effect on your job prospects.

Exercises

13.1 Power Verbs: The following kinds of sentences often appear in resumes. Employ power verbs to change the sentences and thereby make them more effective.

1. Was responsible for collecting data in market survey analysis.
2. Have some experience with software design.

3. Am responsible for doing inventory at the end of every month.

4. Have developed new system for inventory oversight and control.

5. Sought out new customers by canvassing neighborhoods with door-to-door advertisements.

6. Was manager at local store and had five employees working for me.

7. I was part of a team that helped to install a new computer system at our store.

8. Had to provide supporting data for a research project on managers' behavior.

9. Had a project to analyze the accounting methods for a major department store.

10. I was a computer systems analyst at a computer store where I debugged many programs.

13.2: Now that you have rewritten the sentences, what else would you change or add to make them more effective? Write down your revised sentences.

1.

2.

3.

4.

5.

6.

7.

8.

9.

10.

13.3 Career Objective Statements: What is wrong with the following career objective statements?

1. I am looking for a job that will give me the experience to begin my own business.

2. I am looking for a position that has upward mobility.

3. I am seeking a job in which I can use my skills to their fullest.

4. I am looking for a job that is demanding and pays well.

5. Would like to work as a manager so that I can demonstrate my worth.

6. To work as a marketing executive.

7. Seeking a position that is challenging and exciting.

8. Desire a position where I can use my computer skills.

9. Require job where interpersonal skills are mandatory.

10. Would enjoy a job that allows me to travel.

13.4: Separate into groups of two. Each person should write a career objective statement for a job for which he or she is qualified. Then, exchange statements and discuss their positive and negative aspects. Taking into account the other person's comments, rewrite the career objective statement.

13.5: The education section of the resume is often the most difficult part to write because many people have the tendency merely to list their coursework. As noted in the preceding chapter, you should categorize your coursework into two or three parts and then describe what you learned and can do, bearing in mind, as always, the career objective statement. Use power verbs. Do so here.

13.6: You must also emphasize what you learned and can do in the employment section of your resume. Write a description of the last three jobs that you held. Focus on using an emphatic order. Begin your sentences with power verbs.

13.7: Let us now write a rough draft of a resume. Use the guidelines given in the chapter. Find a real job in a business magazine or newspaper for which you believe that you are qualified. Use the guidelines given for the position to help you in determining the most effective presentation of information. Once you have completed your rough draft, use the attached review sheet to evaluate your work. After you have done this, it is time to look at job application letters. And to that end, we can move to the next chapter.

CHAPTER **14**

Writing the Cover Letter

When you have written your resume, then, and only then, are you ready to write your job application letter. The reason for this is simple: While the resume summarizes all of your accomplishments, the job application letter selects and specifies aspects of it; therefore, it is only logical to begin with the resume and then select what you want to specify in your letter.

The job application letter should only contain information that is already in your resume. In other words, the job application letter and the resume work together. You cannot know whether the prospective employer will look at one or the other, or both. Thus, you must make sure that both of these documents contain identical information.

Like the resume, the purpose of the job application letter is to get you to that interview. Therefore, keep your prospective employer's needs foremost in your mind. Select and highlight information that not only is relevant to the position sought but also fulfills the needs of the potential employer (Guffey 470). To do this, of course, some library research is mandatory. As Bovee and Thill state, "Getting the job that's right for you takes more than sending out a few letters and signing up with the college placement office. Planning and research are important if you want to find a company that suits you" (348).

Do not generalize about the position you are seeking or about your prospective employer. If you do, your letter will appear generic, and this will suggest an uncaring attitude on your part.

This does not mean, however, that you must write a different letter to each potential employer. This would be far too time-consuming. Instead, you can write a letter that will appear original for every prospective employer whom you contact, yet only you will know that it is generic. But before you learn how to accomplish this appearance of originality, ask yourself what position you want and for whom you want to work.

As Guffey states, "[y]ou can't hope to find the position of your dreams without first (1) knowing yourself, (2) knowing the job market, and (3) knowing the employment process" (452).

Searching for a Job

When you begin your job search for prospective employers, first decide on the position that you want. Be specific in determining not only what position you want but what you can offer the prospective employer. This will be crucial in the development and force of your job application letter. But more on this in due time.

The first task is to find an employer for whom you would like to work. Numerous sources exist for this kind of search. Unfortunately, too many graduating college students, and even those already employed but entertaining a job move, always think in terms of the big company. It is not a local small business that many seek, but rather the IBMs or the Exxons. This may be a disastrous move. To limit yourself to the huge companies is to limit your opportunities for employment. Few people are hired right out of college by major corporations. Those who are hired by these corporations are often at the top of the class, and they may even have job experience in terms of summer employment or internships. Obviously, you can always apply to these kinds of businesses, but do not limit yourself to them. Many small businesses offer enormous opportunities, especially to those who lack job experience. In a small business, you will have a greater opportunity to garner financial and supervisory experience. Once you have this, then you will look more appealing to those larger corporations. (Read Lisa J. Moore's article "An Argument for Starting Small" in box 14.1 before you limit your job search to major corporations.)

Once you have decided on the kind of job you want, you must find the companies, large and small, that are seeking people like you. Many sources exist for this search. Obviously, you can consult your (1) local paper, (2) financial newspapers and magazines, and (3) college recruiting office.

But don't limit yourself to advertised positions. Many companies will take unsolicited resumes and application letters. In fact, 67% of employers in a recent survey analyzed the qualifications of unsolicited applicants. In the same survey, 18% of graduating students found a job in this way (Bovee and Thill 353). If you are making an unsolicited job search, the following sources available in any library will help you:

Lisa Birnbach, *Going to Work*

Career Information Center Encyclopedia

Career Placement Annual

Career: The Annual Guide to Business Opportunities

Another valuable source for this kind of search is *Job Seeker's Guide to Private and Public Companies*. This source consists of four volumes, one volume for each region of the United States. This is an especially useful source if you have a particular company or companies in mind for whom you would like to work. This guide is indexed by subject as well as by company. Therefore, if you would like to know whom to contact with respect to future employment and what the company offers employees, then this guide is a must. It is updated yearly, and it is also commonly available in the reference sections of libraries. Box 14.2 (pages 186–187) provides a representative listing in *Job Seeker's Guide to Private and Public Companies*. Box 14.3 (pages 188–189) then explains the various aspects of the entry displayed in box 14.2.

BOX 14.1

Lisa J. Moore's Article "An Argument for Starting Small"

If job-hungry graduates had a nickel for each *Fortune* 500 job that has vanished over the past several years, they wouldn't *need* to work. Downsizing has claimed more than 750,000 such jobs since 1988, when the class of '92 arrived as freshmen, and last spring's on-campus recruiting effort showed it. "It's the worst job market we've seen in 30 years," says Victor Lindquist, Northwestern University's placement dean, who tracks hiring among large and mid-size companies. At many schools, the number of such firms giving interviews this year dropped by as much as half.

The gloomy statistics have made headlines, but they are also misleading. Yes, it's taking students "two or three months longer to find work," says Linda Clay, associate dean of career services at St. Norbert College in De Pere, Wis. But many colleges and graduate schools around the nation are reporting that job-placement rates for graduates several months after commencement are on a par with the best of years. A part of the explanation: Students are knocking on different doors. "Smaller companies are where the action is, and it's a trend we see into the future," says Larry Simpson, university director of career planning and placement at the University of Virginia.

At the same time that whale-size firms are whacking away the blubber, a net of 1.9 million new jobs will be created this year, estimates Dun & Bradstreet, and 80 percent of them will be at companies with fewer than 100 employees. The 500 fastest-growing private companies identified this month by *Inc.* magazine have an average of 145 workers. Despite the rocky economy, many such outfits are thriving, often because they serve an ignored niche market or because they are being hired by downsizing giants to handle work that once was handled in-house. At New York University's Leonard N. Stern School of Business, job postings from smaller firms are up roughly 20 percent over this time last year, with openings in small accounting offices, investment banks, manufacturing plants, brokerages and insurance and real-estate firms. Truly Lilliputian firms with just a handful of employees are also creating jobs, but many of those that serve the public directly are suffering from sluggish consumer spending.

Young, energetic companies value recent graduates for, well, their youth—read flexibility—and energy. (Not to mention that they generally come cheaper than applicants accustomed to corporate pay.) But few lean-staffed firms have either the time or the training budget to bother with raw inexperience—and with so many downsizing victims making the rounds, the competition is stiff. At Stowe Engineering Corp., a 90-person firm in Quincy, Mass., that serves the electric utility industry, one entry-level engineering opening this year drew

continued

some 200 resumes—most from people with as much as 20 years' experience. "That's how desperate things are," says President Bob Hunt.

So serious younger applicants need to show relevant work history or specialized training in such disciplines as physical sciences, computer applications or business. "We looked for people with experience longer than a three-month internship, where they really had their hands around trying to get consumer goods into market," says Denise Smith-Hams, human resources director at the Learning Company, a 130-person educational-software firm in Fremont, Calif., that recruited on campus for the first time this year, at Stanford and Berkeley. Students "who have some environmental expertise have gotten fantastic jobs," says Sue Cohn, career counselor at New York University's Stern school and author of "Green at Work" ($16), a book about environment-related jobs, just out from Island Press, (800) 828-1302.

Risk vs. payoff.   For twentysomethings not yet burdened with minivans and mortgages, the risks of signing on with a small company often pale beside the payoff. Small companies, it is true, are far more prone to going under. And one individual's decisions, right or wrong, can weigh heavily—and visibly—on the bottom line. On the other hand, the lack of a bureaucracy forces rapid professional development. "We're growing so fast, my job description changes almost weekly," says Jim Gorka, an accounting major from the University of Akron who got a job in January with Steris Corp. in Mentor, Ohio, a 165-person maker of medical-sterilization equipment. After rejections from about 70 large companies, Gorka read in the local paper that Steris earned tax breaks for hiring area talent; he called and landed a job in accounting. Though the starting salary was less than he had hoped, Gorka was pleased not to be "stuck in accounts receivable," as he might have been at a mammoth firm. Instead, he also handled fixed assets, payroll and SEC filings and has recently been promoted from accountant to supervisor of information systems.

Such versatility may eventually get you further, faster with a big corporation than you would have got had you started at one. "With a small company background, it's easier to show us that you were able to get things done," says Mike Murray, vice president of human resources for Microsoft, the Redmond, Wash., software giant with 12,000 people and $2.7 billion in annual sales. Someone who came to him having designed, tested and marketed products, say, would carry more clout than someone who had specialized on "the fingernail of an 800-pound gorilla," says Murray.

New resources.   The challenge for students and still unemployed graduates is to root out small companies where opportunity exists. Beyond the obvious sources like the local Chamber of Commerce, professional directories and trade journals, a return to your college career center may be worthwhile. Many schools are launching new programs to help students and alumni target small fry. The University of Virginia has just bought a mailing list of 10,000 area firms employing 200 or fewer workers; the school will solicit job listings from the firm and send out resumes of qualified students or alumni. Duke's Fuqua School of Business recently started an on-campus research center for smaller businesses, where students and alumni can schmooze with business owners. Cornell's Johnson Graduate School of Management now has a fund that pays up to $2,000 toward the salary of M.B.A. students who choose internships with small companies that otherwise couldn't afford the outlay. And several schools are setting up phone-line job banks that students and alums can tap by dialing a special code. San Francisco State University's phone bank, for example, now bulges with about 500 jobs a month. Recently, its listing included openings for a chemist, nursing attendant, sportswriter and for a real-estate financial analyst paying $45,000 to start.

Ten colleges, including Oberlin, Babson, Cornell and the University of Miami, offer students and alumni on-campus access to the new database "Career Search," a massive directory of employers. Students log on free; alums may pay a nominal fee. The service profiles 210,000 banks, insurers and other companies, including 34,000 high-tech firms (30 percent of which have 10 or fewer workers) and 110,000 manufacturers employing 25 or more. Users target companies by product or service, then winnow the list by location, size, sales—even commuting distance from major cities. The listing is updated monthly, so names of contacts should be current.

Though such traditional legwork is generally a must, less conventional approaches may work well with small employers. Scott Wollschlager, a 1991 University of Wisconsin graduate in food-service administration, spent about $3,800 on his job search, which included travel to eight food-industry trade shows, where he passed out "business cards" imprinted with his condensed resume. The effort landed him a job this August with Prime Label, a small Washington, D.C., consulting firm that serves meat and poultry producers.

Students with the luxury of a couple of years until graduation should start plotting for that first job and snagging some experience *now*. But with many employers reluctant to pay even the modest salary of an internship, getting actual business experience is increasingly difficult. One strategy: Try a so-called externship, typically a one-week, unpaid stint at a company that provides a snapshot of various careers and a chance to network with insiders. Externships can be particularly useful for liberal-arts majors without a clear career track. Sociology major Marneia Gravely tackled three externships—doing public relations for a hospital, the Virginia governor's office and 20th Century Fox—before graduating from U.Va. last spring. Though none resulted in a job offer, her initiative impressed a vice president of

continued

personnel with Saks Fifth Avenue in New York. "It showed I was assertive enough to look at the career world on my own," says Gravely, now an assistant retail buyer.

While U.Va. helps place the students, anyone can craft an externship by simply calling a company and offering no-cost labor. Small firms in particular may be flattered at the interest. And if a job is extended you may wind up like Jim Gorka at Steris, who says, "I'm getting enough experience to open my own business." There's one more future employer of eager new grads.

Source: Moore, Lisa J. "An Argument for Starting Small." *U.S. News and World Report* 26 Oct. 1992: 85–88.
Copyright, Oct. 26, 1992, U.S. News & World Report.

BOX 14.2

A Representative Entry in *The Job Seeker's Guide to Private and Public Companies*

2238
Intel Corp.

5200 NE Elam Young Pkwy.
Hillsboro, OR 97124
Phone: 503/681-8080

Founded: 1968. **Type of Company:** Public. **Stock Exchange:** NASDAQ. **Ticker Symbol:** INTC.

Business Description: Engaged principally in the design, development, manufacture, and sale of microcomputer components and related products. Major operations outside the United States include manufacturing facilities in Israel, Malaysia, the Philippines, and Singapore, and sales subsidiaries in Japan and throughout Europe and other parts of the world. A plant is also being built in Ireland. Principal United States locations are Santa Clara, Livermore, and Folsom, California; Portland, Oregon; Phoenix, Arizona; Albuquerque, New Mexico; and Princeton, New Jersey. The company ranked number 266 on the 1989 "*Forbes 500: America's Largest Firms*"; ranked 65 on the 1990 "*Business Week 1000: America's Most Valuable Companies*"; ranked 119 on the 1990 "*Fortune 500: The Largest U.S. Industrial Corporations*"; ranked 52 on the 1991 "*Business Week 1000: America's Most Valuable Companies*".

Major Products/Services: microprocessors; microprocessor peripherals; *DVI Technology* brand or trade name; microcontrollers; *EPROMS* brand or trade name; *ASICs* brand or trade name; *OEM modules and systems* brand or trade name; systems interconnect; scientific computers; personal computer enhancement products.

Operating Units:
* Chandler Branch—4000 W. Chandler Blvd., Chandler, AZ 85226. Phone: 602/554-5705.

Corporate Officers:

Craig R. Barnett . . . . Exec. VP
Frank C. Gill . . . . Sr. VP of Sales & Mkt.
Andrew S. Grove . . . . President & CEO
Robert W. Reed . . . . CFO
Leslie L. Vadasz . . . . Sr. VP

Financial Information:

1989 Net Income: $391,000,000
1989 Revenues: $3,126,833,000
1988 Net Income: $452,922,000
1988 Revenues: $2,874,769,000
1987 Net Income: $248,055,000
1987 Revenues: $1,907,105,000

Employees: 29,000

Benefits/Features of Employment: Benefits include employee pension plan

Application Procedures: Contact the company for more information.

Source: Job Seeker's Guide to Private and Public Companies. Vol. 4. Detroit: Gale Research 1992. 561.

Format

Once you have your position in mind and a list of potential employers, it is time to design your letter. Write in single-spaced block paragraphs and limit yourself to one typed page. The following guidelines for your letter's focus, grammar, and content will help you compose your letter.

BOX 14.3

How to Use the Entry in *The Job Seeker's Guide to Private and Public Companies*

This box duplicates the information found in box 14.2, except that the numbers found in the margin explain the various parts of the guide. These explanations are found after the last entry on the next page.

1. **2238**

2. **Intel Corp.**

3. 5200 NE Elam Young Pkwy.
   Hillsboro, OR 97124
   Phone: 503/681-8080

4. **Founded:** 1968. **Type of Company:** Public. **Stock Exchange:** NASDAQ. **Ticker Symbol:** INTC.

5. **Business Description:** Engaged principally in the design, development, manufacture, and sale of microcomputer components and related products. Major operations outside the United States include manufacturing facilities in Israel, Malaysia, the Philippines, and Singapore, and sales subsidiaries in Japan and throughout Europe and other parts of the world. A plant is also being built in Ireland. Principal United States locations are Santa Clara, Livermore, and Folsom, California; Portland, Oregon; Phoenix, Arizona; Albuquerque, New Mexico; and Princeton, New Jersey. The company ranked number 266 on the 1989 "*Forbes* 500: America's Largest Firms"; ranked 65 on the 1990 "*Business Week* 1000: America's Most Valuable Companies"; ranked 119 on the 1990 "*Fortune* 500: The Largest U.S. Industrial Corporations"; ranked 52 on the 1991 "*Business Week* 1000: America's Most Valuable Companies".

6. **Major Products/Services:** microprocessors; microprocessor peripherals; *DVI Technology* brand or trade name; microcontrollers; *EPROMS* brand or trade name; *ASICs* brand or trade name; *OEM modules and systems* brand or trade name; systems interconnect; scientific computers; personal computer enhancement products.

7. **Operating Units:**
   * Chandler Branch—4000 W. Chandler Blvd., Chandler, AZ 85226. Phone: 602/554-5705.

8. **Corporate Officers:**

   Craig R. Barnett . . . . Exec. VP
   Frank C. Gill . . . . Sr. VP of Sales & Mkt.
   Andrew S. Grove . . . . President & CEO
   Robert W. Reed . . . . CFO
   Leslie L. Vadasz . . . . Sr. VP

9. Financial Information:

1989 Net Income:	$391,000,000
1989 Revenues:	$3,126,833,000
1988 Net Income:	$452,922,000
1988 Revenues:	$2,874,769,000
1987 Net Income:	$248,055,000
1987 Revenues:	$1,907,105,000

10. **Employees:** 29,000

11. **Benefits/Features of Employment:** Benefits include employee pension plan

12. **Application Procedures:** Contact the company for more information.

Source: Job Seeker's Guide to Private and Public Companies. Vol. 4. Detroit: Gale Research 1992. 561.

Each numbered item below corresponds to the one in the entry, and it describes what that part of the entry does:

1. Matches the entries in the subject index; in other words, if you looked up Intel or accounting, this number would be one of those given
2. Gives the name of the corporation
3. Provides the corporation's address and phone number
4. States the date on which the corporation was founded; type of corporation; traded on which exchange; ticker symbol for that exchange
5. Provides a description of the corporation's business, its locations, and corporate ranking
6. States major products and services of corporation
7. Provides address and phone number of a division, operating group, regional or branch office, a plant, or a retail outlet
8. Lists the corporate officers and their positions
9. Provides financial information with respect to the corporation
10. Gives the number of employees in the corporation
11. States some of the details of employment with the corporation
12. Tells who to contact when seeking a job with the corporation

FOCUS

You can achieve the proper focus in your letter in three ways. First, address your letter to someone in particular. Do not use *to whom it may concern*. If you do, then you are already indicating from the very outset that the letter is generic. Find out the person's name to whom you are writing. This is especially simple if a name is given in the ad or the job listing, but even if it's not listed in either of these, then you can do it by using a business directory or just picking up the telephone and calling the company. You must have a name if the letter is to appear personal. Of course, sometimes this is just impossible. If this is the case, then use a job title: *Dear Personnel Director; Dear Vice President of Personnel; Dear Human Resources Officer.*

Second, make sure that your letter is positive throughout. One way to do this is to avoid using qualifying statements that may make you appear less qualified than you really are. For example, don't say, "I have some experience with Lotus programs"; instead, state it assertively: "I have used Lotus programs." The former sentence suggests mere familiarity; the latter affirms expertise.

Third, avoid listing your jobs or courses. A list will not help the potential employer determine what it is that you know and can offer. Instead, focus on particular courses and training by specifying what you know and can do.

GRAMMAR

Grammar is crucial in a job application letter. The letter demonstrates your ability to communicate effectively. If you are ungrammatical, the prospective employer may think that you have a potential communication problem, that even if you are qualified and exceptionally bright, you may lack the ability to communicate your knowledge to others.

First, you can avoid many problems by writing in the active voice. If you do, the reader will always know the subject under discussion, and sentence length will be reduced.

Second, make sure that all sentences are grammatically correct. Unlike in the resume, there should be no sentence fragments.

Third, use the spell-check on your PC. There is no excuse for misspellings in today's world of computer technology.

Finally, have someone else proofread your letter. A person can catch misspellings the computer program misses. For example, a spell-check program will okay *form* when you wanted to say *from*, but an alert proofreader will correct the error. A proofreader is also necessary because writers cannot often see their own obvious mistakes. They may have worked on the document so long that everything looks correct.

CONTENT

The content and structure of the letter must follow a format that businesspeople expect. If your letter is to be effective, you must fulfill their expectations.

You can fulfill the reader's expectation in three ways. First, make sure that paragraphs two and three begin with a topic sentence. This topic sentence should provide the reader with a general statement concerning the contents of the paragraph. It should also indicate the method of organization that the paragraph will employ. It may even signpost the parts of the paragraph itself:

I received my B.B.A., Accounting, from Wisconsin University in May, 1994.

This sentence indicates the subject of the paragraph, education, as well as the method of organization, chronological. This sentence could easily be specified to include signposting:

I received my B.B.A., Accounting, from Wisconsin University in May, 1994, and I have learned four methods of accounting principles that your corporation employs.

This paragraph is identical to the previous one except that the writer has changed the method of organization from chronological to emphatic. In other words, the writer will take up the four accounting methods in some order of importance: either from most important to least important or vice versa. Furthermore, because the writer has stated that four methods will be discussed, the reader would expect sentences to be signposted as *First, Second, Third*, and *Fourth*.

Second, avoid the "me" attitude. No one wants to read a letter filled with *I*'s and *me*'s. If you do this, you will sound arrogant and egotistical. You can easily cut down on these pronouns by focusing on the subject under discussion. For instance, in the sentence in the previous example the writer stated that four methods of accounting will be discussed. Why not focus on what those methods are and what was learned and thereby avoid the intrusive pronoun *I*?

Finally, avoid repeating yourself. If you have said and explained something once, then that is all that is necessary. Because the letter will only be one page long, needless repetition will stand out.

Working with the Resume

Once you have these guidelines in mind, and you know the position and employer you desire, you are then ready to work on your job application letter. The first step is to use your resume. Go through it and highlight those aspects of it that you think would interest your employer. After all, the cover letter is a sales letter: You are selling yourself and your talents. As some human personnel professionals put it: " 'I want you to tell me what you can do for my organization. This is much more important to me than telling me what courses you took in college or what 'duties' you performed on your previous jobs' " (Guffey 474).

When you go through your resume, focus on what you can offer the employer, not on past accomplishments (Guffey 473).

For the purposes of illustration, let us use Jonathan Smith's resume from the previous chapter, omitting the specific reference to the company he wants to work for. Box 14.4 (pages 192–193) provides Jonathan Smith's resume.

Writing the Job Application Letter

Now that you have highlighted those aspects of the resume that you consider to be strong selling points for yourself and your talents, and now that you have a list of prospective employers on hand, you can begin writing the letter. The letter will con-

---

BOX 14.4

Jonathan Smith's Resume

JONATHAN SMITH

4513 Alto Way
El Paso, TX 79912
915-533-8090

Career Objective Statement: To work as an accountant in the audit-ing division where skills in computer pro-gramming are necessary.

Education

Degree

B.B.A., Accounting, University of Texas, 1995
Minor: Marketing

GPA: 3.8

Relevant Courses

Accounting: Worked with all accounting spreadsheets that IBM now uses. Excellent skills in cost accounting, standard-base accounting, and auditing. Employed programs to effi-ciently process accounts. Created database ac-counting system for a small business.

Computer Information Systems: Learned all relevant programs for accountants. Used IBM models to learn methodology. Analyzed accounting spreadsheets and their interac-tion with computer programs.

Work Experience

9/94–5/95 Furr's Foods. <u>Assistant Bookkeeper</u>: Provided weekly and monthly statements. Coordinated inventory control and pur-chasing. Set up new computer accounting program that saved two working days and hundreds of dollars per week.

4/93–8/94 Discount Records. <u>Salesclerk</u>: Operated cash register and pro-vided accounting of daily receipts. Supervised two employ-ees, and trained another.

8/92–3/93 McDonald's. <u>Clerk</u>: Operated cash register. Provided account-ing of daily receipts. Supervised semiannual inventory process.

Honors

1994–95   Kappa Kappa Chi Award, University of Texas, awarded to most outstanding accounting student.

1994–95   Omega Scholarship, Ford Motor Company, awarded to best business student.

1993–95   Dean's List, University of Texas.

Special Skills

Language Skills

Bilingual English/Spanish

Computer Skills

MS-DOS
Lotus 1-2-3
Microsoft Windows for Accountants

Writing Skills

Business Writing: Learned proper formats and organizational criteria for business memos, letters, and analytical reports. Analyzed corporate records and provided both an oral and written report.

Activities

1994–95   Treasurer, Accounting Society, University of Texas: Responsible for fund-raising activities and maintaining proper records with respect to members' dues.

1993–95   Member, Marketing Society, University of Texas.

References

Dr. Robert Cason, Professor of English, University of Texas, El Paso, TX, 79968, Tel. # 915-747-8876.

Dr. James Edwards, Professor of Accounting, University of Texas, El Paso, TX, 79968, Tel. # 915-747-5608.

Dr. Mary Trello, Professor of CIS, University of Texas, El Paso, TX, 79968, Tel. # 915-747-7677.

---

sist of four parts: an introduction, a paragraph dealing with your education, a paragraph dealing with your job experience, and a conclusion. To make illustration simple, let us assume that Jonathan Smith wants to work at Intel as an accountant. He has a resume, and he has found Intel in *Job Seeker's Guide to Private and Public Companies*. He will thus be writing an unsolicited cover letter with his resume attached to it.

INTRODUCTION (PARAGRAPH ONE)

Because you do not want to write a different letter for each prospective employer, you must devise a method by which the letter will appear original when it is actually generic—so that only you can tell that it is generic.

To accomplish this feat, only change the first paragraph of each letter that you send to prospective employers. Everything else will remain the same. Thus, at the outset, each letter will appear to be tailor-made for every prospective employer.

Jonathan Smith will tailor his opening paragraph in four ways. First, he will address the letter to someone specifically, and his opening sentence or sentences will state the position that he wants and how he found out about it (Bovee and Thill 367):

Dear Director of Personnel:
I was recently looking through *Job Seeker's Guide to Private and Public Companies* **when I came across your corporation's entry. I was excited by what I read, and I would relish the opportunity to work for Intel as an accountant in your auditing division.**

Apparently, Jonathan Smith could not find out the personnel director's name, so he uses the title instead. In all else, Jonathan Smith here fulfills our criteria for the start of his letter. Note that he mentions the source of his information. This is an extremely good idea; you want the prospective employer to know that you took the initiative to seek him out in a respected business publication. This will enhance your credibility immediately.

Second, add a few sentences that demonstrate why you want to work for the corporation. What Jonathan Smith has said about Intel—that he was excited about what he read with respect to the corporation—is not enough. You must say something specific! If you do not, then the letter will look generic. You must again show that you have taken the initiative to find something out about the corporation (Guffey 471). The simplest way to find such information is to use a business research resource such as *Hoover's Handbook of American Business*.

Hoover's Handbook of American Business is published yearly. It is alphabetically arranged by the corporation's name. Each corporation is then briefly analyzed under the following headings:

1. **Overview:** Provides information with respect to the corporation's major products, current and future marketing and financial strategies, and ownership
2. **When:** Gives a history of the company
3. **Where:** Provides the address of the corporate headquarters as well as the phone and fax numbers
4. **What:** Lists what the company produces
5. **Key Competitors:** States names of key competitors
6. **How Much:** Displays a chart detailing sales, net income, earnings per share, stock price, book value, number of employees—a period covering ten years

Section 6 is the one to focus on. It provides easily accessible numbers that you can use to impress the potential employer. In Jonathan Smith's case, when he must say something about why he wants to work for the company, he can cite and use the following figures:

- Sales have increased 20.1% each year over the last nine years.
- Net income has increased 27.9% each year over the last nine years.
- Earnings per share have increased 24.3% each year over the last nine years. (Hoover, Campbell, and Spain 634–35.)

With this information, Jonathan Smith can write a few lines to indicate why he wants to work for Intel:

Over the past nine years, Intel has shown a growth of more than twenty per cent in sales, net income, and earnings per share.

Jonathan Smith must now not only show his enthusiasm at the thought of working for the company but also why he believes that he is qualified to do so. As mentioned previously, the cover letter is a sales letter, so advertise what you can offer the potential employer (Bovee and Thill 364). To accomplish this task, Jonathan Smith can use the career objective statement listed in his resume:

To work as an accountant in the auditing division where skills in computer programming are necessary.

For the purposes of the resume, such a career objective statement was appropriate. But it is unsatisfactory here. Jonathan Smith must specify what he can offer the corporation. Remember, he is selling his talents, and such talents must be specified if they are to be strong selling points. In the above career objective statement, Jonathan Smith said that he possessed computer programming skills. He must now specify them at the same time that he displays his enthusiasm for this job opportunity:

I would like to be a part of Intel's tremendous growth, and I can offer you my skills in computer accounting techniques: I have studied and used all computer programs currently used by major corporations such as yours.

Note that Jonathan Smith does not repeat his career objective statement word for word. Instead, he has used the statement as a foundation on which to build a more specific assertion. Further, he has displayed his enthusiasm for the company and provided a neat transition from the preceding sentence. Finally, Jonathan Smith also shows that he is a team player. He wants to be a part of something, a contributor, not an egomaniac who thinks of his talents so highly that by hiring him the company will receive a tremendous boon.

Jonathan Smith is now finished with his first paragraph. This will be the only paragraph he will have to change when he applies to other companies for a job.

If Jonathan Smith had been asked to apply for the position, then he would be writing a solicited letter. In such a letter, the first line would state how and where he found out about the position and the fact that he is applying for it (Bovee and Thill 366; Guffey 471). All else in the paragraph would remain the same.

EDUCATION (PARAGRAPH TWO)

The topic sentence for paragraph two will deal with your education. If you have little job experience, this will be the longest and most detailed paragraph in the letter (Guffey 474). This paragraph and the one that follows are the most difficult to write because you must pay attention to transitions between sentences. You must structure it so that it is easy to read. The simplest way to begin this paragraph is to state your degree, the institution that gave it, and the year it was given. If you have a particularly high GPA, mention it as well. In Jonathan Smith's case, his opening to paragraph two could appear as follows:

> **I received my B.B.A. in Accounting from the University of Texas in 1995 with a GPA of 3.8.**

Once you have this beginning, you must then think how you are going to structure the rest of the paragraph. In the opening paragraph you stated in general terms what you could offer the prospective employer were you to be hired. This paragraph, while focusing on education, should also specify what you can offer (Bovee and Thill 367). To accomplish this task, look at three sections of your resume: relevant courses, special skills, and awards. Determine what to highlight in terms of its attractiveness to the prospective employer, and decide how to organize this material.

To organize this paragraph, use an emphatic order and signpost its sections. Jonathan Smith could write the following:

> **I believe that my coursework, computer knowledge, and language skills make me an excellent candidate for a position in your corporation.**

Having forecasted the structure of the paragraph, Jonathan Smith can now move on and flesh out what he has asserted. He must, however, be selective. If he merely recounts the information contained in the resume, then he may wind up listing, rather than explaining, and stating his qualifications, rather than showing how these qualifications are related to the position he is seeking (Bovee and Thill 367). Thus, when Jonathan Smith begins to write this paragraph, he must keep in the forefront of his mind the career objective statement that he used to end paragraph one.

If he is to look logical, then his writing must be organized. Jonathan Smith must write the paragraph in the order he forecast it. Hence, the first paragraph should deal with relevant coursework, relevant in the sense that it demonstrates how he is qualified for the position:

> **My coursework has focused on accounting and CIS. I am skilled in using the accounting spreadsheets employed by major corporations. I even created a database accounting system for Exco Industries, a major distributor of electronic equipment. To date, I have learned all the relevant CIS programs for accountants, but I have gone further than this: I possess the ability to analyze spreadsheets and their interaction with computer programs. This is a particularly useful skill, especially in today's high tech industries where accounting has reached extraordinary levels of complexity. As a reward for my talents, I received the Omega Scholarship, awarded to the best business student. In addition to my accounting and computer skills, I can also offer you diversity: I am bilingual, English/Spanish, and thus I would be an asset in providing accounting skills for your international work. Lastly, I have taken a number of writing classes, and I have learned how to present my work and ideas in formats and styles that are readily understandable to everyone.**

Several qualities stand out about this paragraph. First, the paragraph does have a recognizable structure. Jonathan Smith even employs transitional expressions to assure the effectiveness of his paragraph's structure: *to date, in addition*, and *lastly*. These expressions help to tie the paragraph together. And it must be tied together. If it is not, then you are forcing the reader to make the transitions for you. Not only would this demonstrate poor communication skills, but even worse, it would allow the reader to pause and perhaps question what you are saying. Second, Jonathan Smith repeatedly ties his skills to what he thinks the corporation is looking for. This is crucial. You cannot simply give your resume in written form; you must sell yourself. Third, this paragraph will be Jonathan Smith's longest paragraph because he possesses more education than job experience. Fourth, Jonathan Smith has demonstrated that he is team oriented, assertive, creative, responsible, and well trained—all attributes that employers want in their employees (Guffey 474).

WORK EXPERIENCE (PARAGRAPH THREE)

Once you have completed the education paragraph, you are ready to start the paragraph that deals with work experience. Begin this paragraph with a transitional expression. This will make the reader immediately aware that a new topic is now under discussion. In Jonathan Smith's case, the opening sentence will begin with a transitional expression that introduces the paragraph's topic of discussion:

> **In addition to my education, I also possess work experience relevant to the position that I am seeking with your corporation.**

As with the preceding paragraph, Jonathan Smith must now forecast the structure of the ensuing paragraph, and he must focus on what he can offer his prospective employer. When you write this paragraph, be selective (Bovee and Thill 367). You may have had any number of jobs, and they may all be listed in your resume, but you cannot discuss them all with any degree of specificity. Therefore, choose one or two jobs that you believe demonstrate your skills and responsibilities, and discuss them with the prospective employer's needs in mind.

Jonathan Smith has had two jobs. One was relatively minor; the other was a more responsible position. Because the latter will be more developed and specified than the former, it is the more important position. Jonathan Smith should employ an emphatic order: moving from the least important item to the most important. He should also forecast the structure of the paragraph:

> **I have had two jobs while attending college: one as a salesclerk at a record store, the other as a bookkeeper with a major supermarket.**

Jonathan Smith has forecast the positions he has had, and he will take them up in the order in which he stated them. Further, he pointed out that these were jobs held while he was attending school. The prospective employer will understand two things from this point, both of which make Jonathan Smith appear more favorable. First, Jonathan Smith is a hard worker: After all, he worked while attending school and this had no detrimental effect on his GPA. Second, the prospective employer will assume that these positions were not all that important; therefore, Jonathan Smith's task is to demonstrate that despite his hard labor at school, he nonetheless fulfilled a noteworthy position at work.

The rest of Jonathan Smith's paragraph looks like this:

> **I was a salesclerk at Discount Records for over a year. I supervised two employees, trained another, and provided a daily accounting of receipts. I left this position when a more challenging position opened up at Furr's Foods. There, I was in charge of providing the monthly statements and coordinating inventory control and**

purchasing. But even more importantly, I established an accounting program that currently saves the company hundreds of dollars a week. At both of these stores I held responsible positions that demanded not only good accounting and computer skills, but also communication skills so that I could work well with my supervisors and fellow employees.

Note that Jonathan Smith has focused on only two jobs. This allows the degree of specificity necessary to demonstrate both what he did and can do, if given the opportunity. Also, Jonathan Smith ends the paragraph with a summary sentence: He makes a general assertion about his own job performance, but he can comfortably do so since the rest of the paragraph provides a foundation for the assertion.

CONCLUSION (PARAGRAPH FOUR)

The last paragraph is the easiest to write. It should accomplish two things:

- Tell the reader that your resume is enclosed.
- State your availability for an interview. (Bovee and Thill 368; Guffey 474)

You can begin your last sentence with a power verb such as *enclosed*, state what is enclosed, and make a general statement that the enclosure contains more details with respect to your qualifications, as Jonathan Smith does here:

Enclosed is my resume, which further details my qualifications.

The second sentence is a bit trickier because you must tread that fine line between appropriate business aggression and obsequiousness. In other words, you do not want to appear too demanding to your prospective employer. The employer may see your aggressiveness as egotistical or arrogant. On the other hand, you do not want to appear lacking a backbone. You must find the appropriate tone to take.

You have two options available to you. One is to simply state that you are available for an interview on particular days and times. Be sure to give a phone number where the prospective employer can reach you (Bovee and Thill 368; Guffey 474–75). Jonathan Smith can then write sentences like the following:

I am available for an interview any Tuesday or Thursday after two o'clock. I can be reached at 756-8765.

Do not say something to the effect that you are available any time for an interview. This just makes you look desperate. At the other extreme, don't state that you are available Mondays from ten to ten-thirty. This is overly demanding because you are leaving the prospective employer with no option but that time. The employer will most likely view such a time as an attempt on your part to set the terms of the interview from the very start. Furthermore, what if the employer can't meet your time? Do you really want to risk missing an interview because you set times that were too constrained for any employer to meet?

The second option may be the more effective of the two. In this option state that you will call to arrange an interview (Bovee and Thill 369). This is indeed aggressive, but what you are really telling the prospective employer is that based on the information provided in the letter, you deserve an interview. Jonathan Smith can write this sentence as follows:

I will call your office next Tuesday to arrange an interview.

This is the preferred option. You display here confidence and aggression: two sought-after business attributes. Besides, the worst that can happen to you is that the prospective employer will not give you an interview. But isn't this a better scenario than waiting around for weeks for a response?

One final caution here is appropriate: Never end the letter by asking for the job. People aren't hired on the basis of their resumes and letters; interviews and discussions normally precede any hiring. To ask for the job in your letter makes you sound unprofessional, as if you don't know the steps involved in gaining a job (Guffey 474–75).

Conclusion

You can now construct a letter that will appear genuine—only you will know that it is only the first paragraph that is original.

With a good resume and letter, you may get that interview. But the job search is for the long-winded; don't be disappointed easily. Continue applying and forcing your skills upon those whom you believe need them.

Box 14.5 presents Jonathan Smith's completed job application letter. Box 14.6 (page 201) provides a review sheet to be used when you write your cover letter.

BOX 14.5

The Completed Job Application Letter

19 Nov. 1994

Intel Corporation
Director of Personnel
5200 NE Elam Young Pkwy.
Hillsboro, OR 97124

Dear Director of Personnel:

I was recently looking through *Job Seeker's Guide to Private and Public Companies* when I came across your corporation's entry. I was excited by what I read, and I would relish the opportunity to work for Intel as an accountant in your auditing division. Over the past nine years, Intel has shown a growth of more than twenty per cent in sales, net income, and earnings per share. I would like to be a part of Intel's tremendous growth, and I can offer you my skills in computer accounting techniques: I have studied and used all computer programs currently used by major corporations such as yours.

continued

I received my B.B.A. in Accounting from the University of Texas in 1995 with a GPA of 3.8. I believe that my coursework, computer knowledge, and language skills make me an excellent candidate for a position in your corporation. My coursework has focused on accounting and CIS. I am skilled in using the accounting spreadsheets employed by major corporations. I even created a database accounting system for Exco Industries, a major distributor of electronic equipment. To date, I have learned all the relevant CIS programs for accountants, but I have gone further than this: I possess the ability to analyze spreadsheets and their interaction with computer programs. This is a particularly useful skill, especially in today's high tech industries where accounting has reached extraordinary levels of complexity. As a reward for my talents, I received the Omega Scholarship, awarded to the best business student. In addition to my accounting and computer skills, I can also offer you diversity: I am bilingual, English/Spanish, and thus I would be an asset in providing accounting skills for your international work. Lastly, I have taken a number of writing classes, and I have learned how to present my work and ideas in formats and styles that are readily understandable to everyone.

In addition to my education, I also possess work experience relevant to the position that I am seeking with your corporation. I have had two jobs while attending college: one as a salesclerk at a record store, the other as a bookkeeper with a major supermarket. I was a salesclerk at Discount Records for over a year. I supervised two employees, trained another, and provided a daily accounting of receipts. I left this position when a more challenging position opened up at Furr's Foods. There, I was in charge of providing the monthly statements and coordinating inventory control and purchasing. But even more importantly, I established an accounting program that currently saves the company hundreds of dollars a week. At both of these stores I held responsible positions that demanded not only good accounting and computer skills, but also communication skills so that I could work well with my supervisors and fellow employees.

Enclosed is my resume, which further details my qualifications. I will call your office next Tuesday to arrange an interview.

Sincerely,

Jonathan Smith

4513 Alto Way
El Paso, TX 79912
915-533-8090

enc.

BOX 14.6

Job Application Letter Review Sheet

Paragraph One

1. Does the letter follow the correct format?
2. Is the letter addressed to a specific person?
3. Does the first sentence introduce the writer, the position sought, and where this position was advertised or discovered?
4. Does the opening paragraph demonstrate knowledge of the corporation?
5. Does the last sentence of paragraph one make an assertion with respect to what the writer can offer the potential employer?

Paragraph Two

6. Does this paragraph state the writer's degree? Does the first sentence or two provide a forecast of the paragraph?
7. Does the writer give detailed descriptions of specific coursework? Does the writer relate these descriptions to the job sought?
8. Does the writer demonstrate possession of special skills related to the job sought?
9. Is there an order of emphasis?

Paragraph Three

10. Does the writer specify job experience? Does the first sentence or two provide a forecast of the paragraph?
11. Is this job experience given an emphatic order? Is it related to the job sought?
12. Does the last sentence make a summary assertion with respect to the writer's skills and qualifications?

Paragraph Four

13. Does the writer refer to the enclosed resume?
14. Does the writer state a date and time for an interview, or does the writer state that a call will be made to the secretary at a specific time in the future? Which would be more effective?

Additional Comments

15. Are there transitions between all paragraphs?
16. Do paragraphs two and three have good topic sentences?

Exercises

14.1: Assume that you have graduated from college. Find an advertised position or a position listed in the *Job Seeker's Guide* for which you believe you are qualified. Find out additional information concerning the employer from *Barron's, Hoover's,* or *Value Line*.

14.2: Look at your resume. What educational qualifications can you offer the potential employer? What jobs have you held that will sell you? Highlight them.

14.3: Write the opening paragraph to your cover letter. Exchange it with the person sitting next to you. Make constructive comments regarding the cover letter: What needs to be changed? What is good about the paragraph? How can it be improved?

14.4: Write the topic sentence to paragraph two and list your qualifications and skills. Exchange the topic sentence and the list with the person sitting next to you. Make constructive comments regarding the topic sentence and the list: What is good about the topic sentence? What needs to be changed? How can it be improved? Are all the items in the list effective? Which ones aren't? What should be added to the list? Are the items listed in an emphatic order?

14.5: Write the topic sentence to paragraph three listing your qualifications and skills. Exchange the topic sentence and the list with the person sitting next to you. Make constructive comments regarding the topic sentence and the list: What is good about the topic sentence? What needs to be changed? How can it be improved? Are all the items in the list effective? Which ones aren't? What should be added to the list? Are the items in an emphatic order?

14.6: Complete steps 14.1 through 14.5. Write the complete cover letter.

CHAPTER 15

Interviewing and Pursuing That Job

If you have written a good resume and job application letter, the odds are that you will be asked to interview for the sought-after position. Remember that you are still selling yourself. You must make the prospective employer understand just how qualified you are for the position. Bovee and Thill point out that "[t]he organization's main objective is to find the best person available for the job; the applicant's main objective is to find the job best suited to his or her goals and capabilities" (380).

To make your prospective employer aware of your qualifications and talents, you must approach the job interview as a process. The job interview does not begin and end with your conversation with the interviewer. In reality, the interview is only the midpoint of the process.

You must approach the job interview with the idea that you will do all that is possible and necessary to get that job. If you think of the interview as part of an ongoing process, you will more likely than not be prepared for the interview and, at the very least, assure yourself that you have done everything possible to make yourself the best job candidate you can be. But from the employer's perspective, "[t]he purpose of the interview is to:

- select a good performer
- educate him [or her] as to who you and the company are
- determine if a mutual match exists
- sell him [or her] on the job. (Grove 203)

With these prefatory comments in mind, think of the job interview process as having three distinct phases:

1. Preinterview
2. Interview
3. Postinterview

Preinterview

One of the ongoing difficulties that you—like every other job applicant, for that matter—faces is the uncertainty about what the interviewer may ask or demand. Although you cannot anticipate every possible question or scenario, it is possible to provide yourself with a foundation from which you can build responses to the interviewer's questions. With this in mind, before the actual interview, do a little research and thinking about the prospective employer.

The following subheadings are typical questions that interviewers ask. Advice about how to deal with such questions follows.

WHY DO YOU WANT TO WORK FOR THIS COMPANY?

Know the business for which you want to work: Understand its history, its financial standing, and its potential for future growth. You can readily use three sources to find this information: *Job Seeker's Guide to Private and Public Companies, Value Line Investment Survey*, and *Hoover's Handbook of American Business*. Any one of these sources should provide you with enough information to answer a typical interview question: Why do you want to work for this corporation? You will be able to provide a specific answer, rather than a generic one. Your prospective employer will also be impressed that you took the time to find out something about the business. Moreover, you will appear less desperate for a job because you will appear to be seeking a position with the company because you know something about the company, not simply because this company is now hiring.

WHY SHOULD THIS COMPANY HIRE YOU?

Know what the company is looking for, what it needs. Mentally prepare answers that demonstrate that you have something to offer the company. (Of course, if such a question were to occur in the interview, do not provide a quick response. If you do, the interviewer will know that you have anticipated the question, and the interviewer will not be overly impressed by your answer. You must appear spontaneous. Therefore, restrain your impulse to answer quickly; instead, pause and slowly answer.) Tailor your answers to the company's needs. You should know these needs based on what you have already read in one or all of the previously mentioned guides, and you may also know a lot about the company's needs if it advertised the position. Normally, when advertising a position, companies will specify the skills and training that they want in an employee. In any event, just remember that the company is looking for employees that will help it, not employees that the company will have to help.

MAY I SEE A SAMPLE OF YOUR WORK?

This is not an uncommon question, especially for those in technical fields. Andrew Grove, President of Intel, states that the interviewer is "trying to assess how this person performed in an earlier job *using* his skills and technical knowledge; in short, not just what the candidate knows, but also what he *did* with what he knows" (205–06). Therefore, if you are in a technical field such as computer programming or technical writing, have a sample copy that you can give to the interviewer. Make sure that it is a clean copy and one that you are particularly proud of because it displays your talents and what you can offer the prospective employer.

Also remember that if the interviewer asks for a sample copy, do not just hand it over without comment. Take the opportunity to summarize what you have given and highlight the most important aspects of the work. Speak for the document first; do not let the document speak for itself.

This question, should it occur, would be a golden opportunity for you to assert your presence in the interview, to demonstrate and show what you have to offer the company.

WHY DO YOU THINK YOU ARE QUALIFIED TO WORK FOR THIS COMPANY?

When this question is asked, begin by referring to your resume. (You must know your resume and job application letter thoroughly so that answering questions like this is made easier.) If the interviewer does not have a resume on hand, provide the interviewer with a copy that you have brought for the occasion. Next, specify those items in the resume that you believe demonstrate what you can offer the company. Often, such questions are asked to gauge your "*operational values*, those that would guide [you] on the job" (Grove 206). The interviewer wants to know "how the [job] candidate would perform in [the] company's environment" (Grove 206).

Second, even if the interviewer does not ask for transcripts or letters of recommendation, have them on hand and turn them over to the interviewer. In a sense, the fact that you can offer these items shows that you are prepared for the interview, eager for the job, and confident in your abilities.

WHAT ARE YOUR STRENGTHS?

Interviewers love to ask this question—and the same can be said for the question that follows—because they know such a question makes people nervous. Most people are hesitant with such a question because they do not want to appear arrogant or egotistical.

You can avoid the charge or appearance of egotism by having two or three strengths prepared in your mind before the interview. What you want to avoid is giving the interviewer a list of items that shows your strengths. Lists are soon forgotten; specifics are retained. Therefore, concentrate on those two or three items that you feel make you a good job candidate, and provide supporting details for them.

WHAT ARE YOUR WEAKNESSES?

As with the previous question, this question also demands a bit of preparation. Do not say that you have no weaknesses. This will assuredly make you look arrogant, as well as naive. After all, who has no weaknesses? Instead, what you must do is twofold: First, state what your weakness is, and second, state what are you doing to correct it. Acknowledge your weakness, but at the same time show that you are doing something about it. This latter point is crucial because if you are doing nothing about a known mistake then you are obviously none too motivated.

For example, if the interviewer asks you this question, and you state that your weakness is organizing your time efficiently, then you must immediately add what it is that you are doing to correct the problem. In this situation, you might add that you have purchased and are now using a new computer program by which you are organizing and prioritizing your time.

Finally, some people, when this question is asked, try to provide an answer that is actually nonresponsive. For example, they may answer this question by stating that they are too demanding, or that they are perfectionists, or that they work too hard. These answers are nonresponsive because being demanding, hard-working, or a perfectionist are positive qualities rather than weaknesses. Such responses hurt you. Most interviewers are trained professionals; in fact, for some of them, interviewing may be their primary job assignment. Thus, when you give such an answer you are being disingenuous, and the interviewer will recognize this. Such responses will be a strike against rather than for you in your quest for the job.

WHAT SALARY DO YOU WANT?

This is a dangerous question to handle. You certainly don't want to quote a low salary because the interviewer may think you are desperate; on the other hand, a high salary quote may once again make you look naive or unrealistic.

Find out what the salary range for such a position is. You can use two easy methods to discover this range. First, look through a newspaper or business magazine and see what salaries are being offered for the same or similar positions. Second, speak with friends or colleagues and discover the range.

Thus, when the interviewer asks you the question with respect to salary, simply provide the range that you have determined. Of course, some people will object that the company, if it decides to hire, will naturally offer the low end of the range that you provided to the interviewer. That may be true, but so what? If the offer is made, you do not have to accept it. You can negotiate it. After all, once the offer has been made, the potential employer may have already turned down many other applicants, and thus your bargaining position will be better. And even if you are only the first in a line of people to be offered the position, negotiating salary does not necessarily insult the employer—it's merely the nature of the business environment. The point is that this negotiation does not occur during the interview before you are even offered the job.

WHAT ARE YOUR LONG-TERM GOALS?

Interviewers are interested in seeing how ambitious you are. They may ask this question or something very much like it to see not only your ambition but perhaps your naiveté as well. When asked such a question, some people answer that they want to run the company or start their own business. Both of these are poor answers. If you say that you want to run the company, you may appear overly ambitious or unrealistic, depending on the company hierarchy. If you say that you want to start your own business, then the question arises as to why the company would want to invest its time and money in someone who aspires to leave.

WELL, WE WILL LET YOU KNOW OF OUR DECISION . . .

Although this is not a question, treat it as one. Usually something like this is said by the interviewer to indicate that this is the end of the interview. The interviewer may even provide nonverbal suggestions that the interview is over by leaning forward or standing up or by some other nonverbal expression (Bovee and Thill 396). However, you are the one in charge of the interview. The interview ends when you agree that it is over. Of course, the interviewer has precisely the opposite view (Grove 204).

Therefore, when the interviewer concludes, be prepared. First and foremost, if the interviewer has not asked sufficient questions that would have demonstrated your capabilities, then the end of the interview is the point at which you mention them. You should combine them with a conclusion that begins as follows:

Thank you for your time

I certainly would enjoy working in such an exciting environment

I believe my qualifications meet your needs

Any one of these beginnings will display your enthusiasm for the position. However, do not stop here if you feel that crucial information has been omitted. Use this concluding clause as the prelude to what has been omitted:

Thank you for your time, and I would like to add that I believe that I am qualified for this position because . . .

I certainly would enjoy working in such an exciting environment, especially since I possess skills in . . .

I believe my qualifications meet your needs in the areas of . . .

Be prepared to provide omitted information. Of course, this means that you must be alert throughout the interview, but any of the foregoing beginnings should provide you with an adequate start to point out your strengths and key qualifications.

As a final note, remember to rehearse your interview. Stage "mock interviews with a friend. After each practice session, have your friend critique your performance . . . to identify opportunities for improvement" (Bovee and Thill 390).

The Interview

Most people mistakenly believe that the interview begins when they enter the interviewer's office and shake hands. However, human personnel offices have become quite adept at interviewing people when least expected. For example, some offices may ask the secretary in the waiting room to observe how you interact with the other people who are waiting. You may be watched by a "planted" observer in the waiting room itself. You must believe that the moment you enter the building where the interview is to take place, the interview has already begun. What if you met someone in the elevator who asked you a question that you ignored or answered poorly; further, what if this person remembers you in a later conversation with the interviewer? The safest approach to take is to believe that everyone at the company is an interviewer.

Once you enter that building, you must have prepared yourself already. As noted previously, you should have a good idea of your strengths, weaknesses, qualifications, goals, salary, and conclusion. However, you should also pay attention to appearance, punctuality, and behavior. Also, bring certain materials with you to the interview.

APPEARANCE

How you look will often determine how people treat and think of you. If you make a poor initial appearance, the interview may be superfluous. Because you are a professional in the business world, dress like one.

Initial impressions often linger throughout the interview, so make sure that you look good. Dress conservatively, and employ power colors: black, blue, and red (Bovee and Thill 391). A human resources person once told me that the number one thing she looked at were a person's shoes. I have heard similar comments from other human resources people as well. Therefore, make sure that your shoes sparkle.

PUNCTUALITY

Make sure that you arrive on time. Try to be ten to fifteen minutes early. This displays your eagerness; on the other hand, if you show up a half hour earlier, your eagerness may be misperceived as desperation or anxiety. In any event, don't be late. After all, if you are late to the interview, then what can the employer logically expect from you on the job (Bovee and Thill 392)?

BEHAVIOR

Once you are before the interviewer, pay attention to your body language, your gestures. Psychologists have said time and again that communication is not only verbal: It also derives from our posture, position, and facial features. Bovee and Thill point out that

> [a]s you stage your mock interviews, pay particular attention to your nonverbal behavior. In the United States, you are more likely to be invited back for a second interview or offered a job if you maintain eye contact, smile frequently, sit in an attractive position, and use frequent hand gestures. These nonverbal signals convince the interviewer that you are alert, assertive, dependable, confident, responsible, and energetic. (390)

When you arrive in the interviewer's office, do not sit down until invited to do so. Not only is it bad manners to sit down without an invitation, but it may also be perceived as a nonverbal communication that you are not taking the interview as seriously as you should. Further, once you have sat down, make sure that you sit on the edge of your seat—this displays eagerness. If you are too relaxed in your posture, again, you may be perceived as taking the interview none too seriously.

Accomplish four objectives throughout the interview. First, smile. This will relax both you and the interviewer. Second, maintain eye contact. Do not let your eyes wander about the room; this will be perceived as disinterest. Third, answer clearly, slowly, and straightforwardly. If you do so, your answers will appear spontaneous, even when they aren't. If you speak too quickly, you display nervousness and a lack of confidence in yourself. Fourth, demonstrate with your answers that you have something to offer the company. Remember that your primary task is to sell yourself and your abilities.

Finally, there is a word of warning. Never ask for anything: not gum, cigarettes, a pen. If you do, your interviewer may perceive you as a taker, a mooch—you may be sending a message that you are a person who takes but offers little to the company.

MATERIALS

Do not go to the interview empty-handed. Bring a briefcase or a professional-looking folder. The following lists some of the materials that Bovee and Thill suggest you should bring with you to the interview (asterisks have been added to denote items that may or may not be needed):

1. Pen
2. Notebook
3. Resume Copy
4. Transcripts
5. Letters of recommendation
6. Questions that you want to ask
7. Notes concerning the company's business and position in its market
*8. Work samples
*9. Performance reviews
*10. Reports
*11. Certificates. (391)

THE ACTUAL INTERVIEW

As stated previously, you can anticipate some questions that will be asked, but, of course, you cannot anticipate everything. Nonetheless, you can also anticipate some uncomfortable situations, and you must know how to handle them if you really want that job. A few of the more unpleasant situations and how to parry them are discussed next.

Interviewer's Dislike

Situations will arise in which you know from the very outset of the interview that the interviewer doesn't like you. This can be quite unpleasant, mainly because the questions that the interviewer asks may take on the aura of the interviewer's dislike for you. You must defuse the situation as early into the interview as possible. One way to handle these kinds of situations is to focus on just answering the questions. Naturally, this may be of little avail if the questions themselves illustrate the interviewer's dislike because they are flippant or obtuse. If this occurs, tell the interviewer that you do not understand the question, or ask the interviewer whether the question could be rephrased because you believe that you are not answering the question as fully as you would like. This could easily help defuse the situation because you are both blaming yourself and displaying your vulnerability.

Sexist or Inflammatory Questions

Despite current laws that restrict the kinds of questions that interviewers may ask, this is the real world and people will ask them anyway. You must know how to handle these situations if you want the job. No one is saying that you must sit through propositions or advances—you should not and need not tolerate this kind of behavior. However, what is being discussed here are those kinds of questions that are inflammatory, insensitive, or sexist. Of course, you could leave the interview when such a question arises, but this will not get you the job. After all, even if the interviewer is a sexist pig, the interviewer does not necessarily represent the company as a whole. Once you are hired, that is the time to make an issue of the interviewer's question. And even if you are not hired, you can still make the interviewer's questions an issue by filing a complaint with the company, with your attorney general's office, and by hiring an attorney on your own to redress the wrong that has been done. But what should you do during the interview is the real question.

Let us look at two hypothetical situations that illustrate how these provocative situations can be handled effectively. In the first situation, the interviewer, a man, asks you, a woman, the following question: "Why do you need a job? Your husband has a pretty good one." You could leave the interview and seek legal redress at this moment. But this will not get you the job. Further, if you point out to the interviewer that he is a sexist pig, you will not get the job either, and you will have to seek legal redress anyway. So you have this question before you; what do you do? Your answer should begin with something like the following statement: "I need a career in order to fulfill my dreams and aspirations." You then go on to discuss what you want in the way of a career, but again bearing in mind that you want to demonstrate those attributes and abilities that the company would be interested in. What you have done is ignore the inflammatory question; you have focused on an answer that also does not draw attention to the fact that the interviewer is a sexist pig.

In the second situation, the interviewer asks you the following question: "You've taken quite a few marketing classes for a CIS graduate. I always thought those classes were worthless." Again, what you must do is concentrate on answering the underlying question: "what is the value of these marketing classes?" Focus on the underlying question and explain why these classes had value for you and for this company.

Once hired, speak with the company's personnel director and make it plain that the interviewer's questions were inflammatory, insensitive, and/or sexist. It then becomes the company's responsibility to do something about this sort of behavior. (As a further precaution, make your statement both orally and in writing. This will protect you against retributive action as you will have evidence of your complaint and the interviewer's behavior.)

Postinterview

When the interview has ended, the interview process still goes on. To make sure that you have done everything possible to get that job take three more steps: Remember the interview and write down its key facets; write a follow-up letter to the potential employer; and follow up both of the preceding with one or two telephone calls.

WRITING DOWN YOUR RECOLLECTION

Shortly after the interview, write down your recollection of it:

1. Your interviewer's name and the interviewer's general attitude towards you;
2. Your strengths that came across;
3. Questions that you did not answer well or not at all;
4. Topics of discussion and anything that was presented to you. (Bovee and Thill 397)

Because you will try to maintain contact with the company in the coming days or weeks before a decision concerning your job status is made, note the interviewer's name. Further, remember the interviewer's attitude towards you because you will need a clue as to how to approach the interviewer both in your follow-up letter and in your telephone calls. Also note what you did and did not communicate to the interviewer: You need information that you can later use. But just as importantly, note what went wrong so that in subsequent interviews with other companies you can prepare yourself better. Finally, write down what occurred in order, taking note of what the interviewer was impressed by. This information can be used in subsequent communications with this company and also with other companies for whom you will interview in the future.

WRITING THE FOLLOW-UP LETTER

A few days after the interview, write a follow-up letter. Maintain contact with the company. You must demonstrate that you really want the position for which you interviewed (Guffey 477). Persistence often gets you the job; sometimes this persistence may get you the job instead of the person who was actually more qualified.

The letter that you will write will contain four succinct paragraphs, making the letter short and to the point (Bovee and Thill 398):

1. A statement of thanks for the interview and a restatement of your interest in the job (Bovee and Thill 398)
2. A brief paragraph that focuses on anything that particularly impressed you and that the interviewer would be pleased to hear about
3. A brief paragraph that reemphasizes your strong selling points (Bovee and Thill 398)
4. A concluding sentence that tells the reader that you will call to determine the status of your job application. (Bovee and Thill 398)

Let us write an example for each one of these paragraphs.

Paragraph One

This should be the easiest paragraph to write, reading something like the following:

> **Thank you very much for the interview on July 1. I would very much enjoy working for such an energetic corporation as _____.**

Paragraph Two

You have a number of options in this paragraph. For example, did the interviewer take you on a tour of any of the facilities? Did the interviewer say anything about the company's operations that particularly impressed you? This paragraph could read as follows:

> **I was particularly impressed with your CIS facilities. I found the programs you run were ones that I run myself, but I was even more impressed with the programs that you are developing. I especially noted the new LAN system your staff was working on, and I am enthusiastic about the idea of doing likewise.**

This paragraph does four things that your paragraph must accomplish as well. First, it is enthusiastic about the workplace. Second, it still sells your own capabilities. Third, it demonstrates through specifics that you are quite observant. Fourth, it is complimentary to the prospective employer. The paragraph that you write must also acomplish these four objectives.

Paragraph Three

In paragraph two, you showed your enthusiasm. This paragraph must display your skills. This paragraph could read as follows:

> **I learned a great deal about LAN systems when I worked for GT Enterprises. At GT, I developed software that is compatible with other netware users. What I saw in your workplace was something that I enjoy doing and would look forward to doing every day.**

Note that this paragraph is also enthusiastic about the position, provides a transition from the previous paragraph, and it also specifies what you can offer the company. You must do likewise in your own paragraph.

Paragraph Four

Finally, you need a concluding sentence that is enthusiastic and forecasts future communications with the potential employer. This paragraph could read as follows:

> **Mr.[or Ms. or Mrs.]_____, I appreciate the time you took with my interview, and I will call your secretary next week to find out the status of my job application.**

By addressing the reader in this way, you personalize the letter even more. You also place yourself in the reader's mind because you have stated that you will call sometime in the next week. What you are doing with this letter and with the phone calls subsequent to it is making sure to keep the communication lines open between you and the company, and further, making sure that your name is remembered.

Box 15.1 displays the completed follow-up letter. Note its brevity.

MAKING THE TELEPHONE CALLS

About a week later, call and find out your job status. If you can't speak with the interviewer, leave your name, message, and phone number. This will at least ensure that the company knows of your interest in the job. If you can speak with the inter-

---

BOX 15.1

A Sample Follow-Up Letter

Dear _____:

Thank you very much for the interview on July 1. I would very much enjoy working for such an energetic corporation as _____.

I was particularly impressed with your CIS facilities. I found the programs you run were ones that I run myself, but I was even more impressed with the programs that you are developing. I especially noted the new LAN system your staff was working on, and I am enthusiastic about the idea of doing likewise.

I learned a great deal about LAN systems when I worked for GT Enterprises. At GT, I developed software that is compatible with other netware users. What I saw in your workplace was something that I enjoy doing and would look forward to doing every day.

Mr.(or Ms. or Mrs.)_____ , I appreciate the time you took with my interview, and I will call your secretary next week to find out the status of my job application.

---

viewer or the interviewer returns your call, simply begin by asking about the status of your application. The interviewer could simply say that this has not been determined yet; if this occurs, simply restate your enthusiasm for the position. It would be even better if you could have more of a conversation with the interviewer, but this will be determined by the interviewer's tone. If it is friendly, say something about the job, maybe even ask a question about it. If, on the other hand, the interviewer's tone sounds hurried or harried, just ask about your job status and leave it at that. In either case, the company knows who called, and this persistence may pay big dividends.

Depending upon the deadline, you may also call once more before it occurs. Just be careful. Do not overdo these calls; otherwise, your enthusiastic persona may be mistaken for an annoying one.

Conclusion

As you can see, the interview is only one part of a process. You must think of it as a process if you are to maximize your job opportunities. And remember, you may undergo several interviews before the process is complete (Bovee and Thill 381–82).

Box 15.2 (page 214) provides a preparation sheet for an interview and a list of materials to take with you.

BOX 15.2

Job Interview Preparation Sheet

Prepare yourself for the following questions. Write your answers out first, and constantly review them so that they become a part of your memory and preinterview routine.

Why do you want to work for this company?

Why should this company hire you?

May I see a sample of your work?

Why do you think you are qualified to work for this company?

What are your strengths?

What are your weaknesses?

What salary do you want?

What are your long-term goals?

Well, we will let you know of our decision . . .

Materials: This list describes some of the materials that Bovee and Thill suggest you bring with you to the interview (asterisks have been added to denote items that may or may not be needed):

1. Pen
2. Notebook
3. Resume Copy
4. Transcripts
5. Letters of recommendation
6. Questions that you want to ask
7. Notes concerning the company's business and position in its market
*8. Work samples
*9. Performance reviews
*10. Reports
*11. Certificates (391)

Word Choice
and Punctuation

Many people assume that grammar has little value except to the pedant. They could not be further from the truth. Good grammar is a prerequisite to good communication. Time and money is lost when people make simple errors and confuse their readers. In fact, one could say that shoddy grammar displays shoddy thinking.

Grammatical rules are designed to make communication more effective. The worst thing that you can do when writing any business document is to give the reader pause. The reader should never have to pause and wonder what is trying to be said. When a reader pauses and must think about the contents of your message, the odds are that misinterpretation will occur. And, of course, misinterpretation often leads to disaster.

The purpose of this chapter is to provide you with rules that can be easily followed, rules that will maximize your ability to communicate with an audience. Two grammatical areas will be discussed here: (1) word choice and (2) punctuation.

Word Choice

Words are the primary vehicle of communication: They create images in the reader's mind. Therefore, be careful in choosing your words.

DENOTATION AND CONNOTATION

All words have denotations and connotations. Simply put, denotation is the literal meaning of the word, while connotation is the implied meaning of the word. Connotations can be positive, negative, or neutral. A connotation is positive when it implies a good attribute, negative when it implies a bad, and neutral when it implies neither good nor bad. For example the word *man* connotes neither a good nor a bad attribute; it is said to be neutral. However, if someone said, "he is a dog," the word *dog* denotes man, but it implies a bad attribute: one who is unfaithful.

Let us look at another example. The word *cooperation* denotes working together, and its connotation implies a positive attribute. On the other hand, *collaboration* also denotes working together, but its connotation can imply both a positive attribute, as with *cooperation*, and a negative attribute, as in *cooperating with the enemy*. It all depends on the context in which the word is used. In writing, avoid negative connotations.

215

Examine the following sentence:

A cabal of lawyers devised the new corporate plan.

Here, the word *cabal* denotes a group, but it connotes secrecy, intrigue, conspiracy, and illegality. While the writer of the above sentence may have meant nothing more than that a group of lawyers made a new plan, there is much more implied. The reader of such a sentence could easily misinterpret the message being sent. As a writer, you cannot leave words open to interpretations other than those you intend.

VAGUENESS

Because words represent images and ideas, be specific. To use an axiom from composition pedagogy, *show* readers, do not *tell* them. For example, do not write, "The Empire State Building is very large." Here you are allowing the reader to decide what *very large* means. Instead, why not simply give the number of stories that make up the Empire State Building? Surely, the reader can visualize 100 stories easier than *very large*. In fact, avoid words such as *very* that do not create a specific image in the reader's mind. You cannot depend on the reader to understand what you only imply. Stick to concrete images, facts, and specifics, and you will find that your writing will become easier to comprehend, and less likely to be misunderstood.

EUPHEMISMS

A euphemism is a word or words used to express something unpleasant in a nicer way. For instance, you wouldn't walk up to someone and say, "I heard that your aunt died"; instead, you might use the expression *passed away* as a milder way to say the same thing.

Many euphemisms are simply methods by which we state unpleasant things; as such, there is nothing wrong with using them. However, euphemisms can also be deceptive, and they are sometimes used to deliberately mislead or hide unpleasant truths. During the Vietnam War, the news media broadcast the fact that a village had been *pacified*; spy agencies sometimes referred to the *termination* of an employee; a captured spy was often *debriefed*; and today, corporations are *rightsizing*. The problem with each one of these euphemisms is that they mislead, and they are intended to mislead. A village is *pacified* because a B-52 strike has wiped it out; an employee is *terminated* rather than *killed*; a spy is *debriefed* rather than *tortured*; and corporations are *rightsizing* rather than *firing* or *laying off* employees. Each one of these examples illustrates how euphemisms can be misused to hide unpleasant truths. As such, they are little more than lies intended to deceive the hearer.

Should the occasion arise when you feel that a euphemism may be appropriate, you should ask yourself why you are using it. Is your use intended to hide something, or are you using the euphemism to spare someone's feelings? If your use is the former, then you should not use a euphemism; if it is the latter, then a euphemism may be appropriate. (To see a fuller discussion of the misuse of language, including the misuse of euphemisms, read George Orwell's essay, "Politics and the English Language.")

SEXISM

In today's world, women make up a significant portion of the work force. Thus, you must be careful when addressing your audience; you cannot assume that it is predominately male. If you still labor under this assumption, and it comes through in your writing, you will find that you will be alienating and antagonizing a significant portion of your audience. The days when one could address a letter to a corporation or company or agency with *dear sir* are over.

To some, this leads to problems. For example, one may be writing a memo detailing the company health plan, and one of the sentences states, "An employee must fill out all the required paperwork." In the very next sentence the problem of sexist usage arises. Should the writer constantly refer to *the employee*, or choose *s/he*, or choose between *he* or *she*? This is certainly a dilemma for the writer who does not want to appear sexist, but the solution is easy: Simply use the plural. If the writer would have written "employees must fill out all the required paperwork," no problem with respect to sexist usage would have occurred. The writer could then have referred once again to *employees*, but the writer would also have had the choice of the pronoun *they. The use of the plural eliminates the worry of sexist usage.*

Punctuation

Punctuation—like word choice, sentence structure, and paragraph organization—aids the reader in comprehending what it is that you are trying to express. Your punctuation must be exact, for if it is not, the reader may misunderstand your information, and the potential for catastrophe increases.

Punctuation follows rules that grammarians and the general public continually develop over time. Rules of punctuation therefore change over time, but they do so quite slowly. Use the rules current at the time that you are writing.

This section of the appendix discusses five types of punctuation:

Comma

Semicolon

Colon

Dash

Apostrophe

COMMA

Commas have a variety of uses, but they can be categorized according to their functions. Commas are here divided into two categories: (1) separating series of words and phrases and (2) separating clauses. If you follow the rules posited within these two categories, you should have few if any comma errors.

Separating Series of Words and Phrases

One of the most common uses of the comma is to separate words and phrases. (A phrase is simply a set of words that has a meaning.) Nouns, noun phrases, and adjectives that modify a single noun are set off with commas. Or, stated even more generally, if you have a series of items that are all of the same form, then set them off by commas:

He wore a coat, a shirt, and new shoes.

Here, the three noun phrases *a coat, a shirt*, and *new shoes* are set off with commas because they are a series of three. Note that there is a comma before *and*. Many people omit the comma before *and* because they believe that the *and* used with a comma is redundant. But what if I had said, "I have different colored shoes for different occasions: dark brown, tan and black"? How many different colored shoes do I have? Two or three? You really don't know. I could have dark brown, tan, and black shoes; or, I could have dark brown shoes as well as one pair that is tan and black. The omission of the comma makes all the difference. In the sentence above, I possess two different colored pairs of shoes; a comma before the *and* would indicate that I own three. (Of course, if the items are clearly distinct ("I have shoes, shirt and tie") no comma is necessary because no ambiguity can result.)

Introductory and Parenthetical Words and Phrases   Introductory and parenthetical words and phrases such as introductory prepositional phrases should be set off with commas:

In the beginning, there was a void.

The same rule applies to introductory adverbs:

However, I do not agree with the decision.

When adverbs or adverbial prepositional phrases occur in the sentence, they are considered parenthetical and they too should be set off by commas:

I, however, do not agree with the decision.
There was, in the beginning, a void.

However, when the adverbial prepositional phrase occurs at the end of the sentence, it is not set off with commas:

There was a void in the beginning.

But adverbs that function parenthetically retain the comma no matter their position in the sentence:

I do not agree with the decision, however.

Appositives   An appositive is a noun or nominal structure that renames another noun or nominal. Appositives also require commas:

Bob, my best friend, lives next door.

Bob and *my best friend* are one and the same thing; *my best friend* renames *Bob* and is therefore set off with commas. (An appositive can also be a clause; if so, it too is set off by commas.)

Direct Address   Direct address, like parenthetical expressions, should be set off with commas. The term *direct address* is self-defining: Direct address means that you are addressing someone or some group. When this occurs, no matter where it occurs in the sentence, commas are used:

John, why don't you go home?
I am a poor man, ladies and gentlemen.
Ladies and gentlemen, I am a poor man.
I, ladies and gentlemen, am a poor man.
I am, ladies and gentlemen, a poor man.

Participial Phrases   Participial phrases are often set off with commas. A participle is a word that functions both as a verb and as an adjective. Participles end in either *-en* (*-ed*) or *-ing*. The *-en* ending, which can also be *-ed*, identifies the past participle; the *-ing* ending identifies the present participle. When employed as a phrase, the phrase modifies a particular noun in the sentence. When the participial phrase begins the sentence, the phrase is set off with commas:

Having gone to college, I remain uneducated.

Having gone to college is the participial phrase; it modifies *I.*

The participial phrase should also be set off with commas when it ends the sentence:

I remain uneducated, having gone to college.

Clauses

A clause is a structure that contains a subject and a predicate. It may be independent (it can stand on its own terms as a sentence), or it may be dependent (it requires another clause to complete it, and it cannot stand on its own as a sentence). Clauses require punctuation to separate and distinguish them for the reader. A comma may sometimes be the appropriate form of punctuation, depending on the use to which the clause is put.

Dependent Clauses   A dependent clause that begins the sentence should be set off with a comma:

When the moon rose, the werewolf howled.

When the moon rose is a dependent clause even though it does contain a subject, *moon*, and predicate, *rose*, because it cannot stand alone as a sentence; it requires the independent clause *the werewolf howled* to complete its meaning.

Nonrestrictive Clauses   Nonrestrictive clauses should be set off with commas. A nonrestrictive clause is a clause that is unnecessary to the essential meaning of the sentence:

Joe, who is my friend, committed murder.

The relative clause *who is my friend* is not essential to the primary meaning of the sentence: In other words, it is not essential to understanding the fact that Joe committed murder. (A relative clause is a clause that employs a relative pronoun with a clear antecedent as its subject.)

By contrast, a restrictive clause has no commas because it is necessary to the meaning of the sentence:

He who seeks justice cannot be bought.

Here, the relative clause *who seeks justice* is essential to the meaning of the sentence: He cannot be bought <u>because</u> he seeks justice. Both parts of the sentence, main clause and relative clause, are here essential, and thus commas should not be used.

Independent Clauses   Independent clauses that are joined with a coordinating conjunction should have a comma preceding the conjunction:

John went to work, and he soon finished the job.

Contrasting Clauses or Phrases   Contrasting clauses or phrases should use a comma to emphasize the contrast being made:

John was happy, not sad.

Quotations

Quotations are often introduced by a clause or phrase; when this occurs, a comma precedes the quotation:

John said, "I feel happy today."

Numbers, Addresses, Dates, and Degrees

Numbers, addresses, dates, and degrees require the use of commas so that the reader can more easily read the information.

Numbers that exceed one thousand use a comma at every third digit:

8,700 bananas

8,700,000 bananas

Addresses that are used in sentences employ commas to set off the street, city, and state:

We sent the refund to Robert Cason, 6200 Belton Street, El Paso, TX 79935.

Dates that are used in sentences are set off with commas:

We went fishing on November 23, 1994.

However, you can avoid the use of the comma entirely by writing this sentence as follows:

We went fishing on 23 November 1994.

Degrees are set off with commas:

Robert Cason, PhD, JD, wrote this book.

SEMICOLON

Semicolons are punctuation marks that coordinate clauses closely related in idea. You can employ semicolons in three ways:

1. To link independent clauses that are closely related in idea
2. To join clauses that follow a colon
3. To connect lengthy clauses in the same sentence

Linking Independent Clauses

One of the most common uses of the semicolon is to link two independent clauses that are closely related in idea. Rather than separating them with a period, which would indicate two distinct and separate ideas to the reader, you can join them with a semicolon, thus indicating that they are two parts of one idea, as in the following sentence from Sophocles:

> **Dreadful is the mysterious power of fate; there is no deliverance from it by wealth or by war, by walled city or dark, seabeaten ships.**

In this sentence, the first clause mentions *the mysterious power of fate*. The second clause provides an illustration, or perhaps explanation, with respect to why fate possesses a mysterious power. Illustration and explanation are common uses for the semicolon.

Both clauses, however, must be independent.

Joining Clauses Following a Colon

A colon is often employed to introduce a series of words, phrases, or clauses. When the clauses are lengthy, or if they are independent, they should be separated with semicolons. The same sentence from Sophocles could be rewritten as follows:

> **The mysterious power of fate is dreadful: You cannot avoid it with wealth; you cannot escape from it through war; you cannot hide from it behind a walled city; nor can you flee from it in dark, seabeaten ships.**

Connecting Lengthy Clauses

Sometimes you will write a long sentence with lengthy clauses with each clause containing its own internal punctuation. In this case, do not simply connect the clauses with commas because the number of internal punctuation marks will confuse the reader. In his *Modern American Usage: A Guide*, Wilson Follett gives the following example to illustrate the need for semicolons when too much internal punctuation occurs:

> **By this means they became every day more licentious, and the Campus Martius was a perpetual scene of tumult and sedition; armed slaves were introduced among these rascally citizens, so that the whole government fell into anarchy; and the greatest happiness which the Romans could look for was the despotic power of the Caesars. (420)**

Here, commas could be used in place of semicolons, but confusion would probably result.

COLON

You can use a colon in two ways. A colon may

1. introduce a series of words, phrases, or clauses, or
2. explain that which preceded the colon.

In either case, an independent clause must precede the use of a colon.

Introduction

You can use colons to introduce a series of words:

United States coins are minted in three locations: Denver, Philadelphia, and San Francisco.

You can use colons to introduce phrases:

He was a man of many moods: some highly exemplary, others totally ugly.

You can use colons to introduce clauses:

It was a landscape of barrenness: No trees filled one's gaze, and even the sky resembled the dull grayness of the land.

Explanation

You can also use colons to introduce a phrase or clause that explains that which preceded the colon:

The moon shone over the jungle: Its rays illuminated a tangle of black vines and silent, moving forms.

DASH

A dash is probably the most misused form of punctuation. People often employ the dash when parentheses are more effective, or they use it when a comma, semicolon, or colon is more appropriate. In fact, a dash should be used for two reasons:

1. To interrupt the sentence with additional or subsidiary information, or
2. To introduce a sentence appositive

Interruption

Sometimes you may find yourself writing a sentence that you must interrupt to provide additional information. However, the dash, unlike the parenthesis, indicates a strong pause, as Follett says, due to "hesitation, suspense, sudden conviction of ignorance, fear, or what not" (424):

Let me frame the issue—to paraphrase Chief Justice Marshall—and I will win every argument.

Thus, the dash goes beyond the parenthesis, which is used primarily for example or brief explanation.

Sentence Appositive

A sentence appositive is a word or phrase that renames all that the sentence has stated. In other words, it summarizes an entire sentence, and it is usually preceded with a dash:

> **The criminal jumped up and shouted his outrage at the jury—a display of insincere emotion.**

APOSTROPHE

An apostrophe is a grammatical device that you should use in two instances:

> To indicate the omission of letters
>
> To state possession

Omission

The omission of letters occurs when you use contractions:

> **Don't**
>
> **Haven't**
>
> **I'd**

Feel free to employ contractions in your writing; they add an air of closeness with the reader. If you consistently avoid contractions, your writing will appear too formal, too stiff, too alienating.

Possession

The apostrophe can also be used to indicate possession. The possession can be singular:

> 1. **Bob's book**
> 2. **Bob and Joe's game**
> 3. **Pericles' oration**

The rules for the above examples can be formulated as follows:

1. When the possessor is singular, an apostrophe precedes the *s* in order to indicate possession.
2. When the subject is compound, the last item indicates possession with an apostrophe *s*. (Of course, you could even add an apostrophe *s* to *Bob*.)
3. When the single possessor's name ends in an *s*, just add an apostrophe.

The possession can also be plural:

> 1. **Neighbors' houses**
> 2. **Children's toys**

The rules for the above examples can be formulated as follows:

1. When the possessor is plural, add an apostrophe after the *s*.
2. When the possessor has a plural form without having added an *s*, then add an apostrophe before the *s*.

Indefinite pronouns require an apostrophe before the *s*:

One's house

Somebody's book

Everyone's habit

Possessive pronouns do not employ an apostrophe:

Yours

Ours

Hers

The pronoun *it* presents particular problems for readers with respect to apostrophes, but the rules are simple:

1. Use *it's* to indicate *it is*
2. Use *its* to indicate possession

There is no *its'*.

Box A.1 condenses the rules of punctuation.

BOX A.1

Punctuation

The rules of punctuation detailed in the foregoing pages are presented here in condensed form for your convenience.

COMMAS

Commas should be employed to do the following:

1. Separate words and phrases
2. Introduce a series of words, phrases, or clauses
3. Make parenthetical remarks through words or phrases
4. Create an appositive
5. Directly address readers
6. Begin a sentence with a dependent clause
7. Set off participial phrases
8. Set off nonrestrictive clauses
9. Connect independent clauses joined with a coordinating conjunction
10. Mark off contrasting clauses or phrases
11. Introduce quotations
12. Set off numbers, addresses, dates, and degrees

SEMICOLONS

Semicolons should be employed when faced with any of three writing circumstances:

1. To link independent clauses that are closely related in idea
2. To join clauses that follow a colon
3. To connect lengthy clauses in the same sentence

COLONS

You can use a colon to introduce the following:

1. A series of words
2. A series of phrases
3. A series of clauses
4. Phrases or clauses that explain what preceded the colon

You must, however, make sure that an independent clause precedes the use of a colon.

DASHES

Dashes are strong marks of punctuation that can be used

1. to interrupt the sentence with additional or subsidiary information, and
2. to introduce a sentence appositive

APOSTROPHES

Apostrophes can be used to indicate the omission of letters.

Apostrophes can be used to indicate singular possession:

1. When the possessor is singular, an apostrophe precedes the *s* in order to indicate possession.
2. When the subject is compound, the last item indicates possession with an apostrophe *s*.
3. When the single possessor's name ends in an *s*, just add an apostrophe.

Apostrophes can be used to indicate plural possession:

1. When the possessor is plural, add an apostrophe after the *s*.
2. When the possessor has a plural form without having added an *s*, then add an apostrophe before the *s*.

Indefinite pronouns require an apostrophe before the *s*.

Possessive pronouns do not employ an apostrophe.

Exercises

A.1: Correct the word choice in the sentences:

1. We have a real junta in charge of this corporation.
2. Jane, that cute chick, will be at the meeting.
3. You have failed to provide the necessary materials.
4. We conspired in order to devise a more effective marketing strategy.
5. We are a productive department, but our manager dogs us all day long.

A.2: Are the following words euphemisms? Are they intended to hide the truth? If not, in what context are these words appropriate?

1. Terminating
2. Downsizing
3. Rightsizing
4. Sanitation engineer
5. Sales associate
6. Limited earnings

A.3: Rewrite the following sentences to avoid vagueness.

1. He lacked candor.
2. The inventory sheet has a few items missing.
3. I can't make the meeting on Monday.
4. Windows 95 has some problems that require fixing.
5. The enormous room was filled with people.

A.4: Eliminate the sexism in the following sentences.

1. Each employee is responsible for the materials assigned to him.
2. All employees may bring their wives to the company dinner.
3. We must retrain a manager if he cannot communicate effectively.
4. Every salesperson must keep his time sheet current.
5. The secretary in every department should initial all of her typed documents.
6. Each employee should carefully review his pension plan.
7. A professor should give his students adequate time to complete each and every test.
8. The manager of each of our pizza establishments should control his employees' behavior.
9. Employees' wives are invited to this year's open house.

A.5: Punctuate the following sentences with commas (when necessary). If you used commas, explain why you did so.

1. He who sues my client is my friend.
2. You made a big mistake Bob.
3. Compared to last year's dire projections this year's sales are astoundingly good.

4. He said "Seek and you shall find."

5. You create a bad impression when you arrive late for a meeting.

6. Sally who works for Walmart is an excellent salesperson.

7. He was disillusioned having believed so much in the honesty of others.

8. The ties in my closet are red white and blue.

9. Having achieved fame and fortune through his hard work he now feels he deserves a vacation.

10. In 1984 Ross received his B.B.A. in accounting.

11. When you arrive late to a meeting you make a bad impression.

12. Bob the man with the beard made a fine presentation.

13. In my experience however you can both have your cake and you can eat it.

14. Achieving wealth is the goal of many people.

15. They are my friends not yours.

16. He is an old white-haired gentleman.

17. He was a man to be reckoned with instilling fear in all of his competitors.

A.6: Punctuate the following sentences with commas, colons, semicolons, and dashes. Explain your punctuation.

1. They were distraught when the stock market went down they were ecstatic when it re-bounded.

2. You must follow three steps when writing a proper thesis statement for an abstract give the author's name and article's title provide a power verb and paraphrase the author's thesis statement.

3. I have five due dates for my progress report Jan. 15 Feb. 19 March 16 and April 4.

4. You should not stand in front of the stove you might get burned.

5. He had wealth fame power glory everything but happiness.

Sentence Structure and Paragraphing

Sentences are the structures by which you shape the ideas or images that the words create. Sentences hold forth an infinite possibility for the arrangement of your ideas, but if you want clarity and precision to come through your writing, then heed the guidelines given here.

Sentence Structure

A sentence is composed of a subject and a predicate; otherwise, there is no sentence. When a sentence lacks a predicate, it is called a fragment, and it is considered ungrammatical. The subject of a sentence is that which does the action; the predicate is that which contains the action and says something about the subject:

The manager fired the cashier.
subject   predicate

The manager did the firing; hence the manager is the subject. *Firing* is the action, and it is what the manager did; hence *firing* and all that follows it is the predicate.

Sentences can be of any length, so long as they contain a subject and a predicate. However, in business writing, avoid sentences that are unnecessarily complex or lengthy. Remember that the longer and more complicated the sentence, the more demanding the sentence is on the reader's attention. This is really a matter of judgment, but if you can condense a sentence, then do so. Your reader will thank you for it.

This does not mean that you should write short, choppy sentences. Instead, vary the length of your sentences. If all sentences are identical, chances are that you will bore the reader.

POWER VERBS

The effectiveness and strength of any sentence lies in its choice of verb. Forms of the verb *to be* (*am, is, are, was, were, being, been*) are called weak verbs. These verbs are weak because they do not really express a precise action as verbs are supposed to do. Forms of *be* normally introduce subject complements (words that describe or rename the subject), but they do not describe an action. The heart of any sentence lies in what action the subject is taking. If you can easily avoid a form of *be*, then do so, for it will undoubtedly strengthen your sentence. Note how the following two sentences differ through the use of two different verbs:

1. The sentence is strong because the writer avoids a form of *be*.
2. Avoiding a form of *be* strengthens the sentence.

Although both sentences mean the same thing, note that sentence 1 contains a form of *be*. As such, the verb, *is*, does little more than introduce the subject complement, *strong*, which, in turn, describes the subject, *sentence*. By contrast, sentence 2 uses the verb *strengthens*. Here, *strengthens* precedes the direct object, *sentence*; but even more importantly, *strengthens* is the action that the subject "avoiding a form of *be*" is doing. Because the subject is doing an action, the verb *strengthens* is preferable to *is*. *Strengthens* expresses power; *is* does not.

Of course, variety heightens the power of your sentences. Therefore, cut down on using forms of *be*, but do not completely eliminate them. Besides, sometimes it is impossible or just too difficult to write a sentence without using a form of *be*.

PASSIVE VERSUS ACTIVE VOICE

English contains two voices that the writer may employ when constructing a sentence: active and passive. The two are readily distinguishable. In the active sentence, the subject comes first, and then it is followed by the verb:

The dog ate the bone.
subject verb

The passive sentence reverses the order of the active: The subject comes after the verb, or the subject may even be omitted. If the subject is stated, it is often preceded by a preposition such as *by*. The passive construction also employs a form of *be* used in conjunction with the past participle form of the verb. In the passive construction, the above sentence would appear as follows:

The bone *was eaten* **by** *the dog.*
be+past participle   subject

Note that the same sentence could look as follows:

The bone was eaten.

It is still grammatical, but the subject has been omitted.

The easiest way to recognize the passive construction (without having to bother about the form of *be* plus the past participle form of the verb) is to ask yourself who or what is doing the verbal action. If the who or what precedes the verb, then the sentence is active; if the who or what comes after the verb or is not stated, then the sentence is passive. Examine the following sentences and identify them as either active or passive:

1. **The manager fired the secretary.**
2. **The factory workers were given a pay raise.**
3. **Chinese immigrants have been flocking to the U.S.**

4. The I.R.S. serves as a government agency.

5. He is considered a great poet by many critics.

To determine whether the above sentences are active or passive, you should have asked yourself the following questions:

1. Who did the firing? The manager. Therefore, the sentence is active.
2. Who gave the pay raise? We don't know. Therefore, the sentence is passive.
3. Who did the flocking? Chinese immigrants. Therefore, the sentence is active.
4. Who did the serving? The I.R.S. Therefore, the sentence is active.
5. Who did the considering? The critics. *The critics* is the subject but it comes after the verb; therefore, the sentence is passive.

As you can see from these five examples the passive voice requires more words than the active. Furthermore, the writer may forget to add the subject in the passive construction and thus confuse the reader. And even when the subject is stated, the reader may still be confused because the writer has delayed the subject unnecessarily. For all these reasons, the passive is not a construction that you want to use too often.

In fact, there are only two occasions when the passive may be appropriate. First, you may use the passive to emphasize a particular point. For example, if you write a paragraph containing all active sentences except the last sentence, you may use the passive because you want to emphasize the last item. In other words, you have led up to it, and you want it to stand out—a proper use of the passive. Second, you may use the passive to downplay bad news. For example, as a credit manager, you might write to one of your clients:

You have not paid your monthly bill.

Not only does the pronoun *you* here personalize the bad news, but the sentence blames the client rather brutally. But the same sentence could be rewritten as follows:

The monthly bill has not been paid.

Here, there is no personal blame at all. In fact, if you read the sentence, the blame lies with the monthly payment, not with the client. It is as if it is the monthly payment's fault that it has not been paid.

Other than on these two occasions, avoid the passive. It really does not add clarity or precision to your writing.

AGREEMENT

Faulty agreement is a common problem that often leads to confusion. By agreement, grammarians mean that the verb agrees with its subject in number. Thus, the sentence *they was here* is ungrammatical because the plural pronoun *they* requires the plural verb *were*, not *was*. This kind of agreement problem is easily identifiable, but other agreement problems are less obvious. Look at the following sentence:

A bird or birds (is, are) a holdover from the age of dinosaurs.

Which is it: is or are? The grammatical rule states that the verb agrees with the subject that comes after the conjunction *or*. Thus, the correct verb to use here is *are*.

Compound subjects can also lead to agreement problems:

The employees, the managers, and the president (agree, agrees) that a restructuring plan is necessary.

The grammatical rule is that compound subjects require plural verbs. Thus, the correct verb in the above sentence is *agree*.

Collective nouns are words that signify many but can be treated as one. Words such as *family, committee*, and *group* each contain many members, but when it comes to agreement, they are treated singularly:

The *group* has many members.

But, when a part of the group is referred to, the verb agrees with the part:

The *members* of the group were furious.

Indefinite pronouns can also be a problem. Indefinite pronouns such as *anyone, everyone, somebody*, or *someone* are all treated as singular subjects.

Everyone *is* happy.

Other pronouns can also create agreement errors. One of the reasons for the problem lies in the idea of case. A holdover from the influence of European languages on English, *case* refers to the grammatical role that the pronoun fills in the sentence. If the pronoun serves as the subject of the clause or sentence, or if it is the subject complement, it must be in the subjective case. If the pronoun serves as the object of the verb in the clause or sentence, or if it is the object of a preposition, it must be in the objective case. And if the pronoun identifies possession, it must be in the possessive case. Table B.1 provides some pronoun examples illustrating case: The question of agreement may thus be one of case:

1. **I gave the package to (he, him).**
2. **He is the one (who, whom) stole the package.**
3. **To (who, whom) am I speaking?**
4. **I gave (him, he) the package.**

The answer to number one is *him*. *Him* is the object of a preposition and thus must be in the objective case. The answer to number two is *who*. *Who* is the subject in its own clause and thus must be in the subjective case. The answer to number three is *whom*. *Whom* is the object of the preposition *to* and thus must be in the objective case. The answer to number four is *him* because *him* is the indirect object, and thus must be in the objective case.

TABLE B.1 Case

Pronoun	Subjective	Objective	Possessive
I	I	Me	My, mine
We	We	Us	Our
He	He	Him	His
Who	Who	Whom	Whose

The question to ask yourself with respect to this kind of pronoun problem is what is the grammatical role of the pronoun in its sentence or clause. Once you know that, then you know which pronoun to employ.

TRANSITIONS

Sentences as well as paragraphs must logically hang and flow together. Each sentence must be logically connected to the one that preceded it; the beginning of each paragraph must be logically connected to the last sentence of the paragraph which preceded it. If the sentences are not logically connected, then you force the reader to make the transition for you—an act of poor writing. Or even worse, you may lose or confuse the reader.

In writing, you have four types of transitions to choose from:

Repetition

Synonym

Idea

Transitional expression

Repetition repeats a key word to connect sentences:

Bob went to the store. Bob wanted to buy a hat.

Here, the transition is the word *Bob*. Obviously, overuse of this type of transition can dull the reader's interest.

Synonyms, words that differ in form but mean the same thing, can also connect sentences:

Bob went to the store. He wanted to buy a hat.

Bob and *he* are synonymous; the two words connect the sentences.

Ideas can connect sentences implicitly. In other words, the reader knows that you are discussing the same thing in both sentences, but there is no direct linkage as with repetition or synonym:

Bob went to the store to buy a hat. Black or blue would be the best color.

The first sentence mentions a hat; the second states which color for a hat would be best. The reader knows without specifically being told that sentence two refers to the hat. The two are connected in idea; they both refer to the same thing. But unlike the first two mentioned forms of transition, transition by idea is implied rather than made explicit.

Transitional expressions connect sentences explicitly. Transitional expressions are phrases or words used solely to get the reader from one sentence or paragraph to the next. (Box B.1 provides a list of transitional expressions categorized by their purpose.) Transitional expressions, however, should not be overused. Think of them as the transitions of last resort. Transitional expressions tend to stick out on the page, and if you overuse them the reader may become focused on which transitional expression will come next, rather than on the content of the message. The overuse of transitional expression is a lazy form of writing; limit their use whenever possible.

Having said all this, you may now wonder which form of transition is the most effective and reliable. But there is no one form that will solve all your transition problems.

Transitional Expressions

Transitional expressions can be divided into classes according to the kind of relationship you are trying to establish between sentences. Here is a list of common transitional words and phrases by classes.

Example
occasionally, usually, often, frequently, especially, specifically, principally, mainly, namely, significantly, indeed, for example, for instance, first of all, for one thing, most important, to illustrate, in particular, in general

Addition
and, also, furthermore, first, second, third, next, other, besides, too, likewise, moreover, last, again, finally, in addition, in the first (second, third) place, what is more, as well, at last, next to

Comparison
similarly, likewise, like, as, at the same time, in the same way, in like manner

Contrast
but, however, yet, or, nevertheless, still, nonetheless, conversely, nor, rather, whereas, though, on the one hand, on the other hand, on the contrary, by contrast, in contrast, even though, at the same time

Concession
doubtless, surely, certainly, naturally, granted that, although this may be true, no doubt, I concede, I admit

Repetition
again, as has been pointed out, to repeat, in other words, as I have said above, once again

Result
then, therefore, thus, hence, so, consequently, as a result, all in all

Conclusion
finally, then, thus, hence, therefore, so, in conclusion, to sum up, to summarize, to conclude, in short

Time
before, earlier, formerly, afterward, later, subsequently, presently, soon, shortly, meanwhile, simultaneously, now, then, after a while, at last, at that time, in the meantime, in the past, until now

Place
here, there, elsewhere, above, below, behind, beyond, nearby, adjacent to, farther on, in the background, opposite to, to the right

Source: Parks, A. Franklin, James A. Levernier, and Ida Masters Howell. *Structuring Paragraphs: A Guide to Effective Writing*. 2nd ed. New York: St. Martin's, 1986. 118–19.

If you want to avoid boring your reader, vary your transitions to keep the reader's attention and interest. Do not rely on only one form of transition, but use all four types of transition in your writing. Synonym and repetition are the easiest to use, and they could be seen as your primary modes of transition. Idea is also a fine form of transition, but it is often difficult to use and somewhat dangerous as well: that which is implied must nonetheless be clear to the reader. When all else fails, a transitional expression can be used.

CONDITIONAL VERBS

Sentences may be vague because of the verb that you choose. As mentioned previously, you want to employ power verbs, but these verbs should not imply a conditional state. For example, many businesspeople will employ one of the following sentences in a letter or memo:

> We *hope* **to continue serving you in the future.**
>
> We will *try* **to correct the problem.**
>
> We will *attempt* **to meet with you next week.**
>
> We *seem* **to have misunderstood one another.**

Each one of the underlined verbs above creates a conditional state. In other words, the reader does not know whether something is or is not: *hope* does not suggest that service will continue in the future, only that it might; *try* does not mean that the problem will be corrected, only that an effort will be made to correct it; *attempt* does not mean that the meeting will take place, only that an effort will be made to set the date for next week; *seem* does not mean that we did misunderstand one another, only that this is one possibility.

From the reader's perspective, all of these verbs are inexact. They are vague and illusory because the reader cannot fix a precise meaning to them. As a writer of business documents that demand precision and specificity, avoid what can be termed conditional verbs. They will only confuse the reader; the reader may even be angered or frustrated because no clear answer has been forthcoming.

REDUNDANCY

Redundancy means to say the same thing twice. One would think that any writer would avoid this obvious mistake, but such is not the case. Many writers create redundancies because they think they sound good. For example, politicians sometimes say, "The year of 1976." But is not 1976 a year? Why say the same thing twice? The only answer to this question lies in the fact that more words are often mistaken for increased intelligence. Avoid redundancies.

VERBIAGE

Cutting down excess words is one of your primary tasks as a business writer. Avoid those stock phrases that can be reduced to one word:

> **Due to the fact that = because**
>
> **Have been informed that = know**

Writers also often create unnecessary verbiage when they change a verb into a noun:

Achieve completion = complete

Render assistance = assist

Gained acceptance = accepted

The power of any sentence lies in its verb; therefore, when you change verbs into nouns you are diminishing the effectiveness of your sentences.

ELUSIVE REFERENTS

To achieve clarity in your writing, be sure that all words have clear referents. If what the pronoun refers to is unclear, then the reader becomes lost. Three words are apt to lead to this problem of the elusive referent.

First, the word *there* often causes vague, wordy phrasing. *There* is either an adverb or an expletive. As an adverb, *there* refers to place and direction; the reader usually has little difficulty grasping this meaning. But when it is used as an expletive, the reader may have problems determining meaning.

An expletive is a word that means nothing; we use it to glue sentences together. For example, in the sentence *there are two ways to do the assignment, there* means nothing. It is not an adverb, nor can it be anything other than an expletive. *There* is used in the sentence so that the subject slot appears to be filled—a common use of *there* as an expletive. The problem here is that because *there* means nothing, it may be best to avoid it, and the appropriate subject slot can be filled with a more exact noun phrase: *two ways to accomplish the assignment.*

Second, the pronoun *it* can be elusive if a clear referent is not stated. If the sentence preceding the *it* mentioned three items, then how is the reader to determine which one *it* refers to? The same can be said with respect to all pronouns: Make sure that the pronoun has a clear antecedent (that which the pronoun refers to or renames).

Third, the word *this* can also confuse the reader if the reader does not know what *this* refers to. *This* can lead to the same problem as *it*: multiple antecedent possibilities. An easy way to solve this problem is to place a noun immediately after *this*; in this way, the referent is clearly and precisely understood.

PARALLELISM

Parallelism means that when you write a list or a series of words, phrases, or clauses, they must all be in the same grammatical form. Thus, the following list is inexact because it fails in

1. achieving parallelism,
2. to reduce wordiness, and
3. eliminates verbiage.

Note that the first word of each item begins with a different kind of verb: (1) participle, (2) infinitive, and (3) verb. To achieve parallelism, each word must be of the same kind. The following list is grammatically correct because it

1. achieves parallelism,

2. reduces wordiness, and

3. eliminates verbiage

Likewise, phrases and clauses must also be parallel in structure:

When we write, we must achieve parallel structures, reducing the wordiness, and trying to eliminate verbiage.

This sentence contains the same problems as illustrated in our list: the problem lies in three clauses that are not parallel. To achieve parallelism, the sentence must be rewritten:

When we write, we must achieve parallel structures, reduce wordiness, and eliminate verbiage.

In addition to ensuring that your words, phrases, and clauses are in the same grammatical form, strive to make the words, phrases, and clauses of relatively equal length. Note in the previous example, that after the *we must*, the clauses contain three words, two words, and two words. These clauses are relatively equal in length. If structures are parallel in form and in length, readers will comprehend more swiftly.

NUMBERS AND ABBREVIATIONS

Observe two rules when using numbers. First, write out numbers that are less than one hundred; otherwise, give the numbers themselves. (The exception to this occurs in the use of legal, scientific, or some business documents: in these instances, both write out the numbers as well as give them, for you may suffer legal repercussions if you do not do so.) Second, avoid beginning a sentence with a number. Either move the number to a later part of the sentence or type it out for the reader.

When using an abbreviation, make sure that the reader understands the abbreviation. If you are unsure whether the reader understands the abbreviation, then give the abbreviation; and, in parentheses immediately following the abbreviation, write out what the abbreviation stands for. You need do this only the first time that you use the abbreviation; once you have done it, you need not do it again.

REFERRING TO THE READER

Writers are often unsure when it comes to addressing their reader. Some simple rules can resolve this apprehension or uncertainty.

When the information that you are providing to readers is negative, do not use the pronoun *you*. If you provide negative information and you use *you*, readers will feel that you are blaming them. Therefore, in this case, avoid the pronoun *you*. Instead, in negative, persuasive, or problem-solving situations, use the pronoun *we*. This pronoun will make readers feel as if both you and they are in this thing together. You will then have created a situation of mutual cooperation and trust, rather than one of blame.

When the information that you are providing is positive or neutral, then by all means use the pronoun *you*. Readers enjoy good news, and if you use the pronoun *you*, it is as if you are personalizing the positive information for that reader.

Paragraphing

Paragraphs are blocks of information founded upon one idea: the topic sentence. The entire paragraph explains and validates the general premise that the topic sentence asserts. But this is not enough to create a fine paragraph. A good paragraph consists of much more than a topic sentence. It must also provide the reader with an appropriate length, an effective organization, and a good concluding sentence.

TOPIC SENTENCES

The first sentence of any paragraph in a business document must be the topic sentence. Place this sentence first because this is what a business reader will expect and because such placement facilitates skimming. You cannot assume that readers will read every single word. In the fast-paced business world, they just don't have time for this. Instead, readers will skim documents and read those paragraphs relevant to them. Thus, if your topic sentence is not placed first, you are slowing readers down and causing loss of time.

The topic sentence asserts something about a particular subject. The assertion itself is a general one because the rest of the paragraph will validate it. The topic sentence can also forecast the structure of the paragraph, either by implying the structure or by explicitly stating it:

Stretch targets came to the forefront of management strategies in the 1990s.

In this example, the subject is *stretch targets*, the assertion is that these targets are primary management strategies, and the date implies that the paragraph will employ a chronological organization. (The various types of paragraph organization will be discussed subsequently.)

If the topic sentence does not forecast the structure of the paragraph, then the second sentence of the paragraph must do so:

Top CEOs use stretch targets to get the most from their managers. CEOs employ stretch targets in seven ways.

Here, the second sentence tells the reader that the paragraph will use signposting as the organizational principle for the paragraph.

Every sentence in a paragraph must explain or validate the topic sentence: by example, analogy, statistics, history, or citation to an authority on the topic. If a sentence in the paragraph does not explain or validate the topic sentence, then it is irrelevant or tangential to the paragraph's point. Such a sentence should be eliminated, placed elsewhere in the document, or revised to conform with the topic sentence.

LENGTH

Before turning to the organization of the paragraph, a few words concerning paragraph length are in order.

Although there is no length requirement for a paragraph other than it must fully explain and validate the topic sentence, avoid lengthy paragraphs. The reason for this avoidance is simple: Lengthy paragraphs intimidate readers. This is especially true for paragraphs that begin business documents. If the first paragraph is lengthy, you take the chance of frightening readers away. So why do it? Any paragraph can be broken apart or reduced in length, so do it and make your readers happy.

On the other hand, do not make the mistake of assuming that paragraphs must be newspaper-length. This is not the case. Just as overly long paragraphs should be avoided, so should excessively short ones—except in two instances. First, a paragraph may be excessively short (one or two sentences) if it is used for transition. This is a particularly appropriate use when the business document is lengthy and you require an emphatic transition from one section of the document to another. Second, a paragraph may be short when it is used for emphasis. For example, you might write a series of paragraphs leading up to a significant point. You could emphasize that point by placing it in a separate and short paragraph.

Furthermore, when writing a paragraph, do not make every paragraph the same length. If you do, readers may get bored, or they may even lose their place in the text because every paragraph looks the same.

Finally, do not assume that every paragraph must follow one pattern of organization. Although one pattern of paragraph organization may be predominant, a paragraph is structured according to the data available. Some data will fit one pattern of organization better than another. You are to decide what pattern is the simplest to comprehend from the reader's perspective.

ORGANIZATION

Paragraphs must be organized in a logical manner. You have already seen that the topic sentence must follow a particular pattern, and so should the paragraph. You have numerous options for organizing a paragraph, but which option you choose will often be determined by the kind of data that the paragraph will incorporate. Of course, you are seldom limited to one choice with respect to paragraph organization, and thus some of the most typical patterns for organizing a paragraph will be explained:

> Chronological
>
> Spatial
>
> Emphatic (signposting)
>
> Comparison and contrast
>
> Cause and effect

Chronological

Organize the chronological paragraph around the idea of time or sequence. In other words, the paragraph moves from one point in time to the next point in time. (Do not mix up the order or skip about in various times; this will confuse the reader.)

The topic sentence for a chronological paragraph could appear as follows:

Stretch targets came to the forefront of management strategies in the 1990s.

The next sentence would make explicit the chronological order:

Beginning in 1992, . . .

The paragraph would then proceed year by year explaining how stretch targets came to the forefront of management strategies.

But chronology need not depend on a clear division of time by days, months, or years. You can also establish chronology by using such words as *then, now, after*, and *next*. (For a more substantial list of these more general terms of transition, see the heading *Time* in box B.1.)

Following is an example of a chronological paragraph:

> **The leasing system, called Rentrak, works like this: Studios charge Rentrak $6 per tape, and Rentrak, in turn, charges the retailer $8. Then, each time a tape is rented, the retailer keeps 45% of the rental fee, the studio gets 45% and Rentrak keeps the other 10%. By the end of 1989 Berger had signed up about 1,000 outlets—including stores outside his chain. Revenues that year topped $11 million, with most of the money coming from the $5,000 fee retailers paid to hook into Berger's Rentrak system. (Gubernick 82)**

Spatial

Organize the spatial paragraph around the idea of space. Provide your reader with a focal point that will hold the paragraph together because everything you write proceeds from it or refers to it. This kind of paragraph often answers questions that begin with a *how* or a *why*.

The topic sentence for a spatial paragraph appears as follows:

> **To create a new directory in your computer, you must enter the File Manager.**

In this topic sentence, *the File Manager* is the focal point because the writer will orient the reader by proceeding from it and by constantly referring to it. After the topic sentence, the paragraph could continue as follows:

> **You can open File Manager by using your mouse and double-clicking the icon which looks like a file cabinet. After double-clicking, you now have a series of program names before you. Skim the programs until you find the program in which you want to create the directory. Move your mouse to it and highlight it by clicking twice. You have now entered that program and the computer has displayed the current directories. Look at the headings above the list of programs and locate "File." Click the file with your mouse and a menu is displayed. Towards the bottom of the menu, you should find the heading that says "Create Directory." Click it with your mouse. The computer now asks you to write the name of the directory that you want to create. Do so and either click the "Ok" symbol with your mouse, or hit the enter button. Your new directory should now appear in File Manager.**

This paragraph contains a logical pattern as each step moves from the one that preceded it. Further, the paragraph begins and ends with *File Manager*, which provides the paragraph with a neat appearance of completion and closure.

Note also that the paragraph uses transitions of place as well as time. Both may be necessary in a spatial paragraph, although time is usually subordinated to place. (For a list of these terms of transition, see the headings *Place* and *Time* in box B.1.)

Following is a spatial paragraph that describes how to calculate MVA:

> **To calculate MVA, Stern Stewart adds up all the capital a company has collected from equity and debt offerings, bank loans, and retained earnings over its life. The firm**

makes further adjustments, capitalizing R & D spending, for example, as an investment in future earnings. Stern Stewart then examines the market's verdict on how well the company has employed its capital by checking the value of the company's stock and debt. The difference between total market value (the amount investors can take out) and invested capital (the money they put in) is MVA. If MVA is greater than zero, the company has created wealth for its shareholders. But if MVA is negative—as it is for such celebrated enterprises as Ford and Apple Computer—the company has committed business's inexcusable sin of destroying investor's capital. (Tully 143)

Emphatic (Signposting)

You organize the emphatic paragraph around the idea of importance. This kind of paragraph will organize its elements by moving from least to most important or by moving from most to least. The order is up to you. You must decide whether you want to lead up to the most important point or whether you want to begin with it. In most business documents, the preferred method is to give the most important item first because that is the item that will be of primary importance to the reader. Such placement will also facilitate skimming on the reader's part.

Although emphatic paragraphs need not be signposted, signposting is a good idea nevertheless. Signposting provides the reader with an easy-to-follow organization, and it also makes it easier for you to write the paragraph.

The topic sentence for an emphatic paragraph appears as follows:

Top CEOs use stretch targets to get the most from their managers. CEOs employ stretch targets in seven ways.

You would then go on and explain those seven ways. Each number would serve as the indication of transition.

Following is a paragraph that uses signposting:

That means you may not come to grief if you install Windows 95 today. But your chances of avoiding problems will be even better if you wait six months while the ten million guys who absolutely have to have it now test it for you. If you can't wait, do three things before you install your new operating system. First, check in with the publishers of the programs you use regularly. You may need a patched version of your current software, or you may want to buy a Windows 95 release. Second, back up your hard disk. If you don't have a tape backup, this is a good time to buy one. Finally, make sure you have enough space on your hard disk; Windows 95 stakes out 40 to 60 megabytes of real estate. (Himowitz 196)

Signposting can even be used in conjunction with a list:

Stephen Covey's Seven Habits of Highly Effective People, briefly, are these:

(1) **Be positive.** *Take the initiative and be responsible.*

(2) **Begin with the end in mind.** *Start any endeavor—a meeting, a day at the office, your adult life—with a mental image of an income conforming to values you cherish.*

(3) **Put first things first.** *Discipline yourself to subordinate feelings, impulses, and moods to your values.*

(4) **Think win/win.** *Just as it sounds.*

(5) **Seek first to understand, then to be understood.** *Listen with the intent to empathize, not with the intent to reply.*

REMINDER STATEMENT

The reminder statement is, to some extent, self-defining. In the opening sentence, you remind the reader why you are writing the memo and provide a generalized statement as to the memo's topic.

FORECASTING STATEMENT

The forecasting statement tells the reader what the memo discusses, the topics involved in the discussion, and the topics' order of appearance in the memo. Write the forecasting statement after you have decided on what headings the memo will contain. The forecasting statement would then simply include the headings.

The reminder statement and the forecasting statement can often be combined into one sentence.

HEADINGS

Headings must be appropriate to the audience as well as effective in transmitting information. You have three choices available to you with headings:

Questions

Phrases

Statements

Headings should be boldfaced and placed on the left margin. The first letter of each important word is capitalized, as is the first letter of the first word (Locker 129).

GOODWILL ENDING

The ending to a memo has no heading. Simply skip a few spaces and begin writing. It should do one of the following:

Add details with respect to people in the corporation.

Add details that demonstrate you are focusing on your corporation specifically.

Add details that speak to the audience's needs or aspirations.

Ask the reader to do something.

Invite the reader to do something.

Choose the ending that will be most appreciated by your audience. What you really want to avoid is an ending that is generic and depersonalized. You want to involve your audience from the memo's beginning to its end.

ADEQUATE SPACING

Single-space paragraphs and double-space between them (Guffey 513). Provide enough spacing around visuals and lists so that the document appears well balanced and accessible, not crowded and intimidating.

PAGE NUMBERS

If your memo is longer than one page, you may paginate in either one of two ways. First, you could center the following information along the top:

Reader's Name   Page Number   Date

Second, you could place the following information in a block in the upper left-hand portion of each subsequent page:

> Addressee
>
> Page #
>
> Date

Choose either one of the above methods of pagination and use it consistently throughout the memo (Bovee and Thill 633; Guffey 515).

Box C.1 provides a schematic that contains the elements of an effective memo.

EXAMPLES OF INEFFECTIVE AND EFFECTIVE MEMOS

To demonstrate how a document should be designed and formatted for complete effectiveness, you will be shown, step by step, how the memo illustrated in box C.2 can be revised.

BOX C.1

A Schematic for an Effective Memo

Date:
To:
From:
Re:

Reminder statement + Forecasting statement

First Heading

Topic sentence
Signpost and list when appropriate and effective

Second Heading

Topic sentence
Signpost and list when appropriate and effective

Goodwill Ending

BOX C.2

A Poorly Designed Memo

Date: 16 Nov. 1994
To: All Managers
From: G. Peterson
Re: New Form

All managers are to use our new form 10B when receiving deliveries. 10B forms are designed to make our accounting easier. They will also make sure that we will receive and pay for goods promptly.

Form 10B

Make sure that you sign the form! Failure to sign will delay payment. Form 10B is different from our previous form. You must now make sure to attach a complete inventory of your delivery and mark the box on line two. Write your name on line one, and the vendor's name on line three. On line seven, where it says date paid, put down the date when the goods were delivered. If anything is missing from the order, make sure that you so designate on line six. If you do not write it down, then we are paying for goods never received! On line five designate any damaged items. The vendor should sign on line four. Keep the gold copy for yourself and give the white one to the vendor. Make sure to send the pink copy to accounting.

Thanks for attending to this matter. We hope that this will lead to cost and time savings.

This memo is poorly written and open to criticism on eleven fronts:

1. Why is the memo addressed to *all* managers?
2. Does G. Peterson have a title?
3. Why is the subject line so general and uninformative?
4. Why is the first word of the memo italicized?
5. Where is the reminder statement?
6. Where is the forecasting statement?
7. Why do the headings tell the reader nothing?
8. Why does the information beneath the heading lack a topic sentence, signposting, and listing?
9. Why is one sentence underlined?
10. Why is the ending both conditional and depersonalized?
11. Why is spacing so lacking?

Let us now take up each one of these criticisms and suggest revisions.

1. Why is the memo addressed to *all* managers?

Why not just managers? The writer is making here a distinction without a difference. If some managers were exempt from the details of the memo, then that distinction should be specified. But here, the word *all* is unnecessary. **Revision:** Omit *all*.

2. Does G. Peterson have a title?

If you, the writer of the memo, possess a title, give it immediately after your name. This will help the intended audience know the level of importance it should attach to the memo. **Revision:** Add *Vice-President of Operations*.

3. Why is the subject line so general and uninformative?

The subject line does not tell the reader what the memo is about. What new form is the memo discussing? The writer could easily be discussing health insurance or business practice—who can tell? **Revision:** Change to *Form 10B to be Used for Deliveries*.

4. Why is the first word of the memo italicized?

Italics are used to emphasize information. But what is being emphasized? No new or important information is conveyed here. **Revision:** Omit *All*.

5. Where is the reminder statement?

A reminder statement should begin the memo. The reminder statement should state the purpose of the memo and provide a general statement with respect to its contents. **Revision:** Add *As of 17 Nov., managers will use the new form 10B when receiving deliveries. This new form will ensure accurate accounting: Vendors will be paid promptly, and we will pay promptly.*

6. Where is the forecasting statement?

The forecasting statement should detail by heading the contents of the memo. This memo lacks such a sentence. **Revision:** Add *The following memo details how you should use the new form and the efficiencies that will result.*

7. Why do the headings tell the reader nothing?

Headings are designed to inform readers through the specific information that they provide. This heading does neither of these things. **Revision:** Add the following headings: *How to Use Form 10B* and *How Form 10B Leads to Efficiency*.

8. Why does the information beneath the heading lack a topic sentence, signposting, and listing?

The information given beneath the heading is a mass of confusion. It is totally disorganized. To organize it, note that two different items are discussed: how to use the form 10B and the reasons for using it. **Revision:** Each item can be placed under one of the two headings here established, each heading requiring a topic sentence; furthermore, a list should be used under the first heading, and signposting should be used under the second heading.

9. Why is one sentence underlined?

The sentence is underlined primarily because it is lost amid the confusion of the paragraph. **Revision:** If placed beneath the second heading, no such underlining would be required.

10. Why is the ending both conditional and depersonalized?

In such a memo, you have five possible endings to choose from:

1. Add details with respect to people in the corporation
2. Add details that demonstrate you are focusing on your corporation specifically
3. Add details that speak to the audience's needs or aspirations
4. Ask the reader to do something
5. Invite the reader to do something

Revision: An ending for each of the listed possibilities would look as follows:

1. **As Vice-President of Operations, I want to thank the managers in advance for their cooperation.**
2. **With this new form, our company's projected savings for the next quarter will be $40,000.**
3. **With Form 10B, we will gain savings that can now be used to send you to the regional meeting in February.**
4. **Please look over Form 10B and let me know by next Wednesday if you have any suggested changes.**
5. **On Dec. 15, Mr. Rodney Sims, President of Operations, will hold a meeting at 10 A.M. at the downtown Marriott to discuss the company's last quarter financials. Feel free to attend and bring your suggestions with you.**

You must decide which ending is the most appropriate. You must know your audience. For example, if perks excite the managers, then use number 3; if attending a meeting of top execs excites them, then use number 5; and so on. No one knows or should know your audience better than you, so make the appropriate choice.

11. Why is spacing so lacking?

The document is far too crowded. Too much information is squished together. Further, the margins are not justified, giving the memo an unprofessional look. **Revision:** Add spacing between headings and justify the margins.

Box C.3 (page 252) provides the revised memo.

Letters

The primary difference between a memo and a letter lies not in its format, but in its audience. The letter is a far more formal business document. It is to be used for clients and those who are higher up in the corporate hierarchy. (However, a memo may do even for higher-ups if the message being sent is primarily informative.)

Many businesses have their own letterhead, but if yours doesn't, then follow the guidelines given in the following subheadings. A letter should contain (1) your address, (2) the date, (3) the addressee, (4) the greeting, (5) the subject line, and (6) the close, with the writer's name, title, and organization. Optional items in the letter can include (1) initials of writer and typist, (2) enclosures, (3) copies, and (4) headings. Align all items on the left margin. In addition, pay care to adequate spacing and pagination.

BOX C.3

The Revised Memo

Date: 16 Nov. 1994
To: Managers
From: G. Peterson, Vice-President of Operations
Re: Form 10B to be Used for Deliveries

As of 17 Nov., managers will use the new Form 10B when receiving deliveries. This new form will ensure accurate accounting: Vendors will be paid promptly, and we will pay promptly. The following memo details how you should use the new form and the efficiencies that will result.

How to Use Form 10B

You can use Form 10B quite easily. You need only make sure to enter the correct information on the following lines:

1. Write your name
2. Check the box to acknowledge receipt
3. Enter the vendor's name
4. Have the vendor sign
5. Itemize all damaged goods
6. Itemize missing goods
7. Enter the date of delivery

In addition, you must sign the form at the bottom and attach the inventory-order sheet. When this is done, retain the gold copy for yourself, give the white one to the vendor, and send the pink one to accounting.

How Form 10B Leads to Efficiency

Form 10B leads to efficiencies both for us and for our vendors. First, this form ensures that we get what we paid for. Second, it makes accounting easier since we will have a paper trail for the goods. Third, our vendors will receive prompter payments. Fourth, disputes with respect to deliveries will be lessened because we will have a record of deliveries.

With Form 10B, we will gain savings that can now be used to send you to the regional meeting in February.

ADDRESS

Unless you are using letterhead, place your address in the upper left-hand corner.

DATE

Place the date a few spaces below your address on the left margin (Guffey 511).

ADDRESSEE

Skip a line or two and give the name and address of the company or person to whom the letter is being written (Guffey 511).

GREETING

Begin with *Dear*, add the person's title (e.g., *Mr. Ms., Mrs., Dr.*), name, and follow with a colon (Guffey 511, 513).

SUBJECT LINE

If you need one, place your subject line two lines beneath your greeting. (Some companies place the subject line two lines above the greeting. Adopt the style that your company uses.) Use the word **Subject** and **Re,** boldfaced, followed by a colon, and then the precise subject line (Guffey 513).

Subject lines are generally used in letters written to other businesses and letters written within the company. Company policy may vary on this. Adopt the style that your company uses (Guffey 513).

CLOSE

Skip two or three lines beneath the end of your letter, and type the ending (*Sincerely Yours, Respectfully Yours*, or *Cordially*) and place it flush with the left margin (Guffey 513). Sign your name in ink beneath the ending. Skip one line beneath your written signature and type your name, title, and company name. You may divide these items into two or three lines to achieve a neat appearance (Guffey 514).

INITIALS OF WRITER AND TYPIST

If you wish, or if your company does so, two lines after your name, title, and company name, type the writer's initials in capital letters. Then, the typist can type his or her lowercased initials (Guffey 515).

ENCLOSURES

If you attach documents to the letter, then you must let the reader know this. Two lines after the initials of the writer and typist, you can write out the word Enclosure or Attachment, or you can use the abbreviations *Enc.* or *Att.* You can even state what is enclosed (Guffey 515):

*Enc.: **Resume***

COPIES

If you have sent copies of the same letter to other people, then, towards the bottom of the page, you may type *cc*: for carbon copy, *pc* for photocopy, or *c*: for any copy (Guffey 515). After the colon, briefly indicate who received the copy, and give the recipients' titles:

cc: Jonathan Smith, CEO
Donald Evant, Account Executive

HEADINGS

Headings are optional in a letter. If the letter contains complex information, you may want to use headings; if the information is straightforward, omit them (Guffey 122).

If you choose to use headings, boldface and align them on the left margin. The first letter of each important word, including the first letter of the first word, is capitalized (Locker 129).

SPACING

Single-space paragraphs and double-space between them (Guffey 513). Make sure that you provide enough spacing around any visuals and lists so that the document appears well balanced and accessible, not crowded and intimidating. Depending on your audience, use justified or unjustified margins.

PAGINATION

If your letter is longer than one page, you may paginate in either one of two ways. First, you could center the following information along the top:

Reader's Name   Page Number   Date

Second, you could place the following information in a block in the upper left-hand portion of each subsequent page:

Addressee

Page #

Date

Choose either one of the above methods of pagination and use it consistently throughout the letter (Bovee and Thill 633; Guffey 515).

Composition Guidelines

When you have determined and analyzed your audience, and keeping your audience always before you, you can begin the writing process. *And you must remember that writing is a process.* No one sits down and begins to write without some degree of preliminary thinking and organizing.

The writing process comprises nine steps:

1. Gathering the data
2. Categorizing the data
3. Outlining the data
4. Writing the rough draft
5. Evaluating the writing
6. Receiving criticism
7. Revising the rough draft
8. Editing the rough draft
9. Proofreading

Gathering the Data

The first step in writing is to ensure that you have all the necessary and available data. At this point, do not worry about organizing it, merely go about obtaining it. You will obtain data by one or all of the following:

Someone else will have presented you with it.

You will have researched the matter.

You will have brainstormed.

It is not uncommon in business for you to receive a task from someone else. Often, the data will be provided to you, and you are asked to put it in a presentable form. You may also be given a task that requires you to do some research. In addition, you may be given a task that requires a bit of creativity on your own part. In this situation, brainstorm. To brainstorm, sit down and think of all the relevant data that applies to the situation. Just write it down and do not worry about how it will be organized. The process of gathering data often involves all of these possibilities, and seldom can you rely on only one to help you in gathering the information.

Categorizing the Data

After having gathered the data, categorize it. In other words, give the data a form, a shape.

You begin this process of shaping the data by looking at it and deciding in what categories the available data can be placed. Think of general categories not specific ones. In this way, you will begin to separate the data into large categories. Once you have determined the categories and placed the relevant data beneath each one, arrange your categories as you think they will appear in the business document.

Outlining the Data

You can now begin the further refinement of your large categories. Think of these large categories as the major headings in your business document. You have already placed the relevant data beneath the appropriate heading; now you must order it. Is each item of the data an important element itself, and thus a separate paragraph or subheading, or can pieces of the data be grouped around one idea, thus creating a subheading or separate paragraph? To illustrate, let us look at two examples. In the first, let us say that you have the following on a sheet of paper:

> *Background*
> **History of Company**
> **1908—founded**
> **1938—invented formula**
> **1957—merged with DCI**
> **1978—acquired by MTE**
> **1992—went public**

In the above, your major category is *Background*. What are you to do with the elements that follow? *History of Company* should be a subheading with the dates providing the relevant data for that subheading.

In the second example, let's say that you have the following on a sheet of paper:

> *Background*
> **History of Company**
> **1908—founded**
> **1978—merged with DCI**
> **Financial growth**

Here, your major category remains *Background*, and you have the subheading *History of Company* with the dates providing the relevant data for the subheading. But what about the last item? It, too, appears relevant to the subheading *History of Company*, but at the same time it deals less with history and more with financial data. Therefore, a separate heading is in order.

In any event, after you have thus further categorized and subdivided, ask yourself how should the items beneath each heading be arranged: in time, in importance, in space, cause, effect? Ask the same questions with your subheadings or paragraphs.

Once this is done, make an outline. Your headings will be displayed beside roman numerals; your items (subheadings or paragraphs) beneath these headings will be displayed beside capital letters; your data relevant to the subheadings or paragraphs will be displayed beside numbers:

I.
  A.
  B.
II.
  A
    1.
    2.
  B.
    1.
    2.
III.
  A.
    1.
    2.
  B.
    1.
    2.
  C.
    1.
    2.
    3.

Now fill out the outline. Often, you will find that more ideas and data will occur to you as you shape the data. Just place the new ideas or data in the outline's framework. Outlines provide order for your writing, and if you get into the habit of using them, even if they are quite rough or incomplete, they will ease your task.

Writing the Rough Draft

Once you have an outline, you are ready to write a rough draft. Write the entire document based on your outline. Write it through one time without worrying excessively about transitions and topic sentences.

Evaluating the Writing

Once you have written through the document one time, go back over it. Are the topic sentences adequate and correctly placed? Are the headings in the right order? Are the subheadings or paragraphs in the right order? Are the elements that make up the subheadings or paragraphs in the correct order? Does the document follow the appropriate format? Is everything grammatical? These questions should be resolved at this stage of the composing process.

Receiving Criticism

You now require someone else to look over the document and give you criticism. You may not always have the time for this stage of the composing process, and it may not be necessary if the business document is short or routine, but if it is lengthy, complex, or important, then criticism by someone else is advisable. Because you have lived with the document for some time by this stage of the process, you may not even catch simple things like misspellings, much less errors in content or organization. You need someone else's opinion.

Revising the Rough Draft

With the criticism that you have received, you are now ready to revise your business document. Of course, the decision with respect to revision is yours, and no one else's. Just because someone didn't like something or would change something does not mean that you revise blindly. You must determine if the criticisms received are valid and appropriate to your document. If they are, revise accordingly; if they are not, then ignore them.

Editing the Rough Draft

Your final task is to edit your document. This means that you go through the document sentence by sentence, ensuring that all are tied together with appropriate means of transition.

Proofreading

Lastly, give the document to someone else to proofread. Tell the person to read the document for spelling, punctuation, and sentence structure. Again, the reason for this lies in the fact that you will seldom catch your own mistakes at this stage of the writing process. Mistakes that are found can and should then be corrected.

Your document can now be sent to its audience.

Works Cited

The American Heritage Dictionary. 2nd ed. Boston: Houghton Mifflin, 1991.

Auletta, Ken. "TV's New Gold Rush." *New Yorker* 13 Dec. 1993: 81–88.

Birchard, Bill. "Making It Count." *CFO* 11.10 (1995): 43–51.

Black, Henry Campbell. *Black's Law Dictionary.* 5th ed. St. Paul, MN: West, 1979.

Boone, Louis, E., and David L. Kurtz. *Contemporary Business Communication.* Englewood Cliffs, NJ: Prentice Hall, 1994.

Bovee, Courtland L., and John Thill. *Business Communication Today.* 4th ed. New York: McGraw-Hill, 1995.

Bremner, Brian, and William Glasgall. "Another Billion Dollars Falls Through the Cracks." *Business Week* 9 Oct. 1995: 60.

"Bringing Back That Great, Fresh Image Has Simply Never Been Simpler." [Canon Advertisement]. *Business Week* 23 Oct. 1995: 37.

Bruce, Harry J., Russel K. Hirst, and Michael L. Keene. *A Short Guide to Business Writing.* Englewood Cliffs, NJ: Prentice Hall, 1995.

Brusaw, Charles T., Gerald J. Alred, and Walter E. Oliu. *The Business Writer's Handbook.* 3rd ed. New York: St. Martin's, 1987.

Bylinsky, Gene. "The Digital Factory." *Fortune* 14 Nov. 1994: 92–110.

Byrne, Thomas C. "Paradise Lost." *Individual Investor* July 1995: 72–74.

Concise User's Guide: Microsoft MS-DOS 6. Microsoft, 1993.

"The Cost of Fast Growth." *Inc.* Nov. 1995: 92.

Curtis, Carol E. "Japan at a Discount." *Individual Investor* July 1995: 78–80.

Darling, Charles B. "VINES Makes the Grade." *Datamation* 1 Sept. 1995: 74–77.

Einhorn, Bruce, and Dexter Roberts. "China's Other Exchange Reaches for the Spotlight." *Business Week* 25 Sept. 1995: 106.

Eisenstodt, Gale. "Breaking Up." *Forbes* 24 May 1993: 88–89.

Eng, Paul M., and Susan Chandler. "Prodigy: A 5-Year-Old Underachiever." *Business Week* 30 Oct. 1995: 150.

Estess, Patricia Schiff. "Family Values." *Entrepreneur* Oct. 1995: 78–80.

Evanson, David R. "It's Who You Know." *Entrepreneur* Oct. 1995: 48–51.

Follett, Wilson. *Modern American Usage: A Guide*. Ed. Jacques Barzun. New York: Hill and Wang, 1966.

Gibaldi, Joseph. *MLA Handbook for Writers of Research Papers*. 4th ed. New York: Modern Language Association of America, 1995.

Grove, Andrew S. *High Output Management*. New York: Random House, 1983.

Gubernick, Lisa. "If at First You Don't Succeed." *Forbes* 5 Dec. 1994: 80–82.

Guffey, Mary Ellen. *Business Communication: Process and Product*. Belmont, CA: Wadsworth, 1994.

Hadhazy, Allan E. "Will Overvaluation Overwhelm Stocks?" *Mutual Funds* March 1995: 17–19.

Heim, Judy. "The Great E-Mail Shoot-Out." *PC World* Feb 1996: 183–93.

Himowitz, Michael J. "Windows 95: Do You Need the Most Overhyped Product of the Decade?" *Fortune* 18 Sept. 1995: 191–96.

Hoover, Gary, Alta Campbell, and Patrick J. Spain, eds. *Hoover's Handbook of American Business*. Austin, TX: Reference, 1995.

Job Seeker's Guide to Private and Public Companies. Vol. 4. Detroit: Gale Research, 1992, 4 vols.

Khalaf, Roula. "Le *tire*, c'est moi." *Forbes* 1 Aug. 1994: 48–49.

Kirkpatrick, David. "Why Microsoft Can't Stop Lotus Notes." *Fortune* 12 Dec. 1994: 141–57.

Kupfer, Andrew. "AT & T's $12 Billion Cellular Dream." *Fortune* 12 Dec. 1994: 100–12.

Lane, Randall. "I Want Gross." *Forbes* 26 Oct. 1994: 104–08.

Lannon, John M. *Technical Writing*. 6th ed. New York: Harper Collins, 1993.

Leander, Ellen. "Masters of the Move." *CFO* Oct. 1995: 55–62.

Levine, Joshua. "Gutenberg's Revenge." *Forbes* 9 May 1994: 166–67.

Locker, Kitty O. *Business and Administrative Communication*. 3rd ed. Boston: Irwin, 1995.

Loomis, Carol J. "Untangling the Derivatives Mess." *Fortune* 20 March 1995: 50–68.

Mascolini, Marcia. "Another Look at Teaching the External Negative Message." *The Bulletin of the Association for Business Communication* 57.2 (1994): 45–47.

McWilliams, Gary. "Pulling Oil From Davy Jones' Locker." *Business Week* 30 Oct. 1995: 74–76.

"Measuring Team Success." *Inc.* Nov. 1995: 94.

Metzner, Douglas E. "All in the Family." *Mutual Funds* March 1995: 27–29.

—. "Time for Ginnie Maes?" *Mutual Funds* March 1995: 23–24.

Millman, Joel. "Pipeliners." *Forbes* 12 Sept. 1994: 218–20.

Moore, Geoffrey A. "How to Profit from Turbulent Change." *Success* Dec. 1995: 51–58.

Moore, Lisa J. "An Argument for Starting Small." *U.S. News and World Report* 26 Oct. 1992: 85–88.

Nelton, Sharon. "Minority Business: The New Wave." *Nation's Business* Oct. 1995: 18–27.

O'Boyle, Thomas. "Working Together." *The Wall Street Journal* 5 June 1992: A1+.

Ochsner, Neal. "In Search of the Perfect Portfolio." *Inc.* Nov. 1995: 26–35.

Owens, Sondra D., and Michael K. Ozanian. "Peer Preview: How the 500 Most Valuable Companies in the U.S. Should Perform Next Year." *Financial World* 5 Dec. 1995: 56–69.

Parks, A. Franklin, James A. Levernier, and Ida Masters Howell. *Structuring Paragraphs: A Guide to Effective Writing*. 2nd ed. New York: St. Martin's, 1986.

"Poems." [Platinum Technology advertisement]. *Business Week* 9 Oct. 1995: 121.

Port, Otis, and Michael J. Parks. "The Great Silicon Rush of '95." *Business Week* 2 Oct. 1995: 134–36.

Rathbone, Andy. *Windows 3.1 for Dummies*. San Mateo, CA: IDG Books, 1994.

The Rhetoric of Aristotle. Trans. Lane Cooper. Upper Saddle River, NJ: Prentice Hall, 1960.

Saporito, Bill. "The Eclipse of Mars." *Fortune* 28 Nov. 1994: 82–92.

Schwartz, Gil. "E-ffective Mail." *PC Computing* Oct. 1994: 49.

Simons, John, and David Fischer. "High-Tech Karma." *U.S. News & World Report* 21 Aug. 1995: 45–47.

Simpson, David. "Windows 95 Is No Desktop Management System." *Datamation* 1 Sept. 1995: 49–51.

Smith, Timothy K. "What's So Effective About Stephen Covey?" *Fortune* 12 Dec. 1994: 116–26.

Stewart, Thomas A. "How to Lead a Revolution." *Fortune* 28 Nov. 1994: 48–60.

Thornton, Emily. "Japan's Struggle to Restructure." *Fortune* 28 June 1993: 84–88.

Tully, Shawn. "America's Best Wealth Creators." *Fortune* 28 Nov. 1994: 143–62.

Vestner, Charles. "Freedom First." *Individual Investor* July 1995: 68–69.

Weiss, Gary. "Soros: Anatomy of a Comeback." *Business Week* 25 Sept. 1995: 100–04.

Wildstrom, Stephen H. "Can Software Help Memory?" *Business Week* 9 Oct. 1995: 22.

Index